Improvisation Games for Classical Musicians

Improvisation Games

for

Classical Musicians

A Collection of Musical Games
with Suggestions for Use

For Performers, Instrumental Teachers, Music Students,
Music Therapists, Bands, Orchestras, Choirs, Chamber Music Ensembles,
Conductors, Composers, Pianists, Percussionists, and Everybody Else
(even Jazz Players!)

Jeffrey Agrell

GIA Publications, Inc.
Chicago

G-7173
Improvisations Games for Classical Musicians
Jeffrey Agrell

Copyright © 2008 GIA Publications, Inc.
7404 S. Mason Ave., Chicago, IL 60638
www.giamusic.com
Book layout: Robert Sacha and Paul Burrucker
Dust jacket design: Martha Chlipala
Printed in the United States of America

ISBN: 978-1-57999-682-6

Table of Contents

Table of Contents

Q: How do you improvise?

A: What's Stopping you?

—Stephen Nachmanovitch

Foreword

Imagine a world where you could only use other people's pre-existing printed words when speaking to someone else. If you could only use the ideas of other people to communicate instead of your own thoughts, feelings and attitudes, your personal and cultural language would be dead, lacking means of creative expression. Unfortunately, too many musicians live only in this kind of world, taught to speak and read exclusively the ideas of others (composers). Very few musicians are encouraged to speak for themselves.

Jeffrey Agrell spent more than a quarter-century playing the pre-existing ideas of others in a professional orchestra. However, from his creative experiences in performing theatrical improv, playing jazz guitar, writing, and composing he was well acquainted with the power and potential of music as a living language. Jeff also knew that classical performances and improvisation were not conflicting perspectives on music, but rather complementary approaches to the same end: Comprehensive musicianship for performers and more meaningful experiences for audiences. His numerous published compositions and his improvisation performances and recordings embody this philosophy. Jeff left his career as a professional orchestral performer to discover himself as a living musician and educator on a full-time basis. His subsequent work in teaching improvisation at the University of Iowa has been an inspiration to those of us who know him.

Jeff is a master of helping others recognize their creative potential through improvisation. His games are expressed in a very informative and interesting way, so that performing them (or even just reading them) is both fun and enlightening. He guides you through the process of personal musical creativity with ease, humor, and compassion. The improvisation games come in a wide range of styles, topics, and number of players so they can be used in virtually any situation: as part of a semester course, for one player or twenty, for experts or amateurs, in school or at home. Although the games are not designed to teach jazz improvisation, even jazz players will find much inspirational and informative material here. In short, there is something here for everyone. Jeffrey Agrell's collection offers an unparalleled opportunity for nearly everyone to be a creator of music, not just a consumer (watch out, iPod!).

Improvisation was once a part of every (classical) musician's training. I invite you to use this book as a key to unlock this lost art, and to become part of a widespread revitalization of musical practice and tradition for both performers and audiences. With the help of this book, I think that you will discover that improvisation is an essential element in comprehensive music education. If you are not already teaching or performing improvisations, I hope you will consider doing so after reading and using the games from this book. In any case, I know you will enjoy the limitless possibilities presented here. A new world waits.

Let the games begin!

Charles Rochester Young
University of Wisconsin-Steven Point

Preface

I didn't improvise on the French horn for forty-one years. I have improvised on guitar in folk and jazz styles since I was fifteen, and I did quite a bit of theater improv during my college years. I have always had a strong creative itch, but I scratched it by playing guitar (and other instruments) and writing and composing. I played jazz on guitar—but it just didn't seem possible on the horn. I played in a symphony orchestra for a quarter of a century and never played anything but the ink. Then I began a second career at The University of Iowa as a professor of horn. While my main activities remained the same (play and teach solos, etudes, and orchestral excerpts), for some reason I wanted to try something different. I had been playing horn exactly the same way for so many years; it was time for something new. I had always been interested in improvisation, so it seemed to be the way I should go. However, I didn't want to pursue jazz on the horn.

Don't get me wrong. I love jazz. I think every minute spent playing or learning jazz is a minute well spent. But I didn't want to invest the time necessary in learning the jazz tradition on an instrument that was normally outside of its realm. Although there are some brilliant jazz horn players around, it just wasn't for me. What does that leave? How do you improvise on classical horn?

I felt a bit like Columbus—I wanted to head off over the horizon, but all the maps stopped there, indicating only dragons and doom to those who continued. I was terrified, but my desire to try was just strong enough that I did not give up. I needed a guide, who turned up in the form of the amazing improvising pianist Evan Mazunik (a junior piano major at the time). I asked Evan if he would be willing to accompany me on my voyage, and he didn't hesitate. We worked and played together several times a week. We were both composers, so we began constructing pieces that had both written parts and windows for improvisation. The music we created is difficult to categorize, partly because it was so varied. It included hints of jazz, world music, and more than a whiff of different classical influences. It was something borrowed and something new.

After a while we began to give concerts and then workshops in improvisation for classical musicians. We recorded a CD of our compositions and improvisations called *Repercussions*. A grand opportunity presented itself in our second year together in the form of teaching an "Introduction to Improvisation" class, with Evan as the teaching assistant (although he was clearly the greater expert of the two of us at the time). We mixed a bit of jazz study in with the non-jazz elements, but it didn't quite work. It was too much jazz for those not interested in jazz, and not enough for those who only wanted to do jazz. In subsequent years that problem was solved by having two sections: my course (non-jazz), and another course of the same name that concentrates on jazz.

The course varies a bit every year as I learn from previous classes and try out new ideas and approaches. I suspect that it will always be so, since I will always learn from past successes and failures, and new ideas will arise, either from reflection or from learning what others do. I hope that readers of the book will be generous with their feedback on their experiences with using the book and discovering new games.

The results have been very gratifying, judging from student reactions to the course. The course seems to supply something that has been missing from the students' music education from the beginning: a chance to experiment, explore, and use their imaginations to create their own music, and to understand music— at last—"from the inside out." Improvisation is a frightening concept for classical players at first, but before long it becomes an empowering and intoxicating activity. It is my hope that students go out into the world and use the games given here in whatever area their destiny takes them—performing, education, music therapy, or making music for themselves at home. These 500-plus games took shape with their help, and this collection would not have come to be without them. With its publication, both old and new students will finally have a handy collection of all the material (and then some) that we used in a more informal way during the course. The great variety of the collection should make it useful for almost any musical approach or need.

I am indebted to UI Music School Director Kristin Thelander and to Jazz Professor John Rapson for allowing me to teach this unusual course (along with my usual duties of teaching horn solos, etudes, and excerpts). It has enriched me personally beyond measure, and I hope that the course and this book will repay their faith and trust in me by filling a gap and bringing something of great utility and value to the wider world of music.

Charles Young, head of the Theory and Composition department of the University of Wisconsin-Stevens Point has been a continual source of inspiration and ideas throughout the long process of assembling and revising this book. His own courses in theory and composition are models of their kind because of their creative approach to music and pedagogy, and my gratitude and appreciation of his advice and encouragement are quite beyond measure.

Most of all, I would like to dedicate this book to Evan Mazunik, who has mentored me from the beginning and supported me every step of the way.

Postscript: Although Evan now lives and works in New York as a professional musician, we continue to give concerts and workshops nationally and internationally for all kinds of traditionally trained musicians. See www.creativehorn.com for additional information.

I would also like to thank the other teaching assistants who have helped me with the improv course for their invaluable assistance over the past couple years: Matt Hellenbrand and Mike Wall, both horn players who know how to improvise.

I hope that this volume will serve to continue the work of the many other amazing musicians, teachers, and thinkers who have done so much in bringing the art of improvisation to classical musicians, including such bright lights as Christopher Azzara, Carl Bergstrom-Nielsen, Harold Best, William Cahn, David Darling, Eric Edberg, Edwin E. Gordon, William Harris, Keith Hill, Julie Lyonn Lieberman, Edward S. Lisk, Stephen Nachmanovitch, Pauline Oliveros, Rod Paton, David Rosenboom, Ed Sarath, LaDonna Smith, Walter Thompson, and Sarah Weaver, to name just a few.

My fondest wish is that this book introduces a wide variety of musicians to the joys of creating music. I hope that professional and amateur musicians alike discover new musical worlds through this book, as well as music educators and students of every age, conductors, composers, music therapists—and even jazz players, who, although this book does not use the jazz style, just might benefit from this book as much as or more than classical musicians, since they have always had the attitude and ability to learn from all sources.

I can't wait to see what everyone comes up with, and I can't wait to see what composers do when they have the opportunity to write for musicians who are able to add their own imagination and intelligence to the creation of a piece. It might save a lot of ink while breathing new life into contemporary music at the same time. The walls between performance and composition, theory and practice, and literate and aural tradition will fade as a new kind of musician who can create personal contemporary music "on the fly" arises. Audiences will discover a new and exciting experience—being present at the creation of a work (and, possibly even taking part in it, as is often the case now in Sound-painting concerts). We are not giving up any of our rich classical tradition, but we are adding a type of living, breathing music to the museum of great works.

Try improvising and see what happens. How does it feel to speak this new language? How does it feel to have the power to create so easily? Send me a postcard now and then with a word about your latest discoveries (just a short one—then get back to creating!).

Jeffrey Agrell
Iowa City

Chapter 1

Introduction: Why Improvise?

Why don't classical musicians improvise? Why do jazz players get to have all the fun? And how do they develop such fabulous technique and aural skills?

It is often frightening for traditionally trained players to even contemplate having to invent music in the moment. After all, from day one long ago the player's musical education very likely never included any training, encouragement, or even mention of improvisation. Many players entering college conservatories have high resistance to and some very good reasons why they don't even want to consider improvisation. Eric Edberg, the improvising cello professor from DePauw University who is writing a book entitled *Improvisation and the Classical Musician*, sums up some of the usual reasons:

- *We just don't have time to learn how: with 400 years of repertoire to learn, even the time to eat and sleep can seem an irritating distraction.*

- *Performance standards are so impossibly high, at least in part because of the expectations created by studio recordings, that classical performers spend a huge amount of time and energy practicing technique and repeating passages to make them reliable.*

- *The concept of intellectual property/ownership of musical works is now highly developed, and so it feels like a moral crime to even consider the spontaneous alteration of even some aspects of a composed piece. And most improvised music is a spontaneous variation on, or elaboration of, already existing music.*[1]

The students who take my course, "Improvisation for Classical Musicians," are the brave ones who dare to take a course that flies in the face of their training—and they enter the room on day one mostly terrified. After all, this is not a course in answers; it is a course in questions, in looking for solutions that are not already neatly defined. This course asks them to do something that the educational system never has: to use their imagination and intelligence to take risks, to explore, to experiment, to discover, to create, to generate ideas. Traditional musical training stresses (good word) the pursuit of perfection, i.e., consistently accurate playing above all else. Improvisation values imagination and asks students to see unplanned results (also known as mistakes) as opportunities to discover new approaches that might have never occurred to them otherwise. This new attitude can be very difficult for the traditionally trained musician to integrate or understand. The biggest hurdle in the beginning is learning to see the process of music making differently rather than any technical requirements of improvisation.

First and foremost, we work on changing this attitude. A lesson in the history of improvisation in music is the first step, and much of it comes as a surprise, such as the realization that the great icons of classical music (whose every note we now venerate)—Bach, Händel, Mozart, Beethoven, Chopin, Brahms, Lizst, and others—were all widely known as *improvisers* in their day. It is worthwhile to look

---

1   Eric Edberg, http://classicalimprov.blogspot.com/2006_03_01_archive.html (accessed March 28, 2006).

back to the beginnings of humankind's music making and see (and/or imagine) how it all developed. Music was learned aurally and skills were passed on by way of demonstration from teacher to student for thousands of years. Then, in the Middle Ages, music began to be notated—thus began the "literate" tradition. Music notation enabled pieces to be exactly recorded and more complex arrangements to be constructed. A new skill—reading notes—was now expected of musicians, but improvisation was still an important part of a musician's education and job for hundreds of years. But the coming of the huge Romantic orchestra and the written method book was the death knell of improvisation for classical musicians.

Since the beginning of the twentieth century, musicians have become so accustomed to playing their instruments using only prescribed notation that any other way has become difficult to imagine. Most classical musicians today are not only unable to improvise; they are unaware that music was ever taught any other way.

Imagine if basketball were played the way we perform music today. The greatest games of basketball would be recorded and aspiring players would be required to learn a certain player's every move throughout the game by reading a description of each move from a written chart. Students would eventually learn to do the many moves sequentially and skillfully, and, along with other players, would be able to reproduce these great games for an audience. Everything about the games would be already known—the outcome, every move of every player. The measure of success would be the flawless reproduction of every movement—after all, the original "perfect" game would be available on DVD for all to compare. If a player dropped a ball when he wasn't supposed to, or threw a pass a bit too far—it would be seen as a failure. Nothing unplanned or unknown would be allowed to happen. No invention in the moment. No individual expression of ideas. No risking a series of less-than-perfect moves for the sake of imaginative play.

What is lost in a system like this? Should we only allow the greatest games of sports to be replayed? Should musical masterpieces be the only game in town?

It may come as a surprise that the Western system of music making that focuses exclusively on written notation is an anomaly. The past few centuries of Western European art music stand in contrast to nearly all music making on Earth and throughout history with respect to the inclusion of improvisation and aural tradition. Most of the music making in the world takes place without notation. In the West, however, instrumental music is transmitted almost solely via written musical notation.

Consider how children learn to speak. Do they learn their native tongue through books? Are they restricted in speaking only to reciting the orations of others? In school bands and orchestras, students rarely have a chance to create their own compositions, either writing or aural (i.e., improvisations). Are we losing students because this system neglects aural transmission? Are we losing the most creative, those who want to make their own music? What kinds of experiences best prepare our students for a life in music in the world today?

Contemporary music education tends to ossify tradition, split and isolate disciplines (performance, composition, theory, etc.), to define standard practice and to discourage those who are innovative and experimental. The exclusion of musical creation from performance and separation of performance from composition has led to a decline in audiences and a lack of interest from the general public, as well as widespread doubt about the need for music education at all.

Students commonly learn a great deal of music theory without making any connection to practice (only pianists learn theory through their instruments). They learn to play their instruments with an emphasis on accuracy and conformity and rarely use the instrument to explore music making or their inner selves. Most not only fail to find their individual voices, but remain unaware that such a thing exists.

An underlying tenet of the current system is that the accumulation of knowledge is a prerequisite to real understanding of music. Why is it that a garage band can create its own music but the average conservatory graduate is incapable of creating music even for his/her own instrument, and has likely never played a note that did not originate from a dead composer's pen?

To infuse life into the system as well as our own playing, to acquire comprehensive musicianship once again, we need to have the skills, the knowledge, and the attitudes that come from being able to improvise. The aim of this book is to provide experience in the aural approach to learning music as a complement to the "literate" approach that comprises the majority of traditional musical training.

> The chief reason to learn improvisation is simply that our musical personalities are incomplete and underdeveloped if we are unable to express ourselves in a spontaneous fashion. The ability to improvise is central to our musicianship; without it, musicians are simply not "compleat."
>
> —Gerre Hancock[2]

---

[2]   Gerre Hancock, Improvising: How to Master the Art (New York: Oxford University Press, 1994).

Chapter 2
Who Should Use This Book?

With some five hundred games of every kind in this collection, the answer is almost everybody. Following are some specific reasons for various types of musicians. Have a look also at Chapter 3, *Suggestions for Use*, which provides sample lists of specific games for each kind of potential improviser.

• Performers

- This method gives classical players the opportunity to enjoy at last the benefits of improvisation without having to learn jazz tradition or jazz style and repertoire. Now players whose instruments are not commonly used in jazz or who are not interested in pursuing jazz style can learn to create music spontaneously. Every kind of instrumentalist (as well as vocalist) can use this book.

- This method builds improvisation ability by using the technique and knowledge that traditionally trained players already have. The universal terror and ignorance most classical musicians have of improvisation disappears with the use of these games.

- The games presented here give performers the flexibility to be ready for any musical situation, and the power to renew tired old practice routines by using the same material in fresh contexts.

- With the modern emphasis on absolute perfection in performance, traditional solo concert performance is often very stressful. Training in improvisation provides a welcome balance to this. Now communication, expression, and imagination are the highest values rather than just the perfect negotiation of a succession of pitches.

- Complete musicianship is a combination and integration of literate and aural studies. Traditional academic organization keeps performing, composition, theory, and history separate and isolated. Improvisation integrates them in a healthy balance, much as it was before the Romantic era.

- The musician of today needs to be prepared not just for the music of a century (and more) ago; she needs to learn improvisation as a vital supplement to contemporary music skills and understanding, and as a necessary part of comprehensive musicianship preparation.

- The musician of today needs to be a producer as well as a consumer of music to have the most favorable chance to succeed in the difficult climate faced by the arts. Learning improvisation is the quickest way to learn to create music, and this collection finally brings this skill beyond the realm of jazz to traditionally trained musicians.

• Music Educators

– The National Association of Schools of Music (NASM) and Music Educators National Conference (MENC) require training in improvisation at every level. Teachers now finally have an option other than jazz, both for themselves as well as their students.

– The games described here build on classical training, so teachers can use what they already know, and can experience this kind of non-idiomatic improvisation along with their students even if they have never had the opportunity to improvise before.

– This book provides the basis around which a one- or two-semester course in improvisation may be constructed.

– Using this method, improvisation classes now may be led by applied teachers and theory/composition teachers.

– Jazz teachers now have an alternate way to teach those students whose instruments, needs, and interests are not suited for jazz.

– General music teachers and music appreciation teachers will find ways here to involve students actively in music and have them experience music firsthand rather than "at a distance," using traditional texts and methods that are more "about music" than doing music.

– The games are adaptable for use at many levels, from elementary school through conservatory. Users of this volume are encouraged to adapt any of the games at any time and to develop their own.

• Music Students

– In traditional training, the only instrumentalists who get to experience music theory "through their instruments" are pianists. With the kind of improvisation methods presented in this book, all instruments can do the same. In traditional music education, theory often seems to be a foreign and abstruse academic system (with little or no connection to the instrument or its music) that is endured in the classroom for a short time and then forgotten. Improvisers quickly learn that every bit of theory training helps the success of improvisations; theory is experienced firsthand and valued as a necessary key to deep musical understanding.

– Improvising means knowing music "from the inside out" and, besides being enjoyable in itself, improvisation practice and training can raise technique to higher levels because more of the knowledge is "in the player" rather than just on the page.

• Bands, Orchestras, and Choirs

– Are your students exhausted and bored from preparing for yet one more concert or competition? Supplement routine rehearsals and keep interest high by adding exercises from this collection. Band, orchestra, and choir directors will discover new ways to involve students creatively, keep them alert and highly motivated by using improv games where they have a chance to "think in music" and create, rather than to just "recite" music made for them by others. Learning to create easily and naturally through improvisation leads to students creating their own compositions, arrangements, and chamber groups, all of which are hits with parents, administrators, and the community.

• Chamber Music Ensembles

– Chamber music is a valuable part of a musical education. Improvised chamber music balances and completes this education in ways that written music does not.

– Established chamber music groups will enjoy the challenge of improvisation games, which may easily lead to new concert pieces that will add sparkle to the traditional repertoire and delight a wide range of audiences. The sky's the limit for a chamber ensemble that improvises and produces, rather than just consumes, repertoire.

– Improvised chamber music allows the formation of new groups for which there is little or no repertoire. If a clarinet player has good friends who play marimba and bassoon, they no longer need to wait eons for composers to create pieces for that prescribed instrumentation; they can begin performing together right away.

• Music Therapists

– As Kenneth Bruscia says, "Improvisation is the very essence of [music] therapy."[3] Training in improvisation provides the daily skills and the attitude needed by the music therapist, which is not provided in a particularly suitable way with jazz improvisation (usually the only option available in school, if any). This method supplies a wide variety of non-jazz approaches to improvisation, which is essential for every music therapist.

• Pianists

– Your choices have always been to play alone or to accompany someone else's music. Now you can enjoy a new kind of solo and chamber music playing that will revitalize your practice, performance, and teaching. Pianists can use almost every game in the book.

• Percussionists

– Percussionists don't always get parts in Western music that reflect the full potential of their instruments, but the good news is that percussionists have more variety than anyone, and they usually are well-acquainted with improvisation. This collection attempts to make percussionists out of everyone (percussion can be added to almost every game here). Bona fide percussionists can have the fun of finally using every kind of instrument in their arsenal and being a sought-after member of any size group engaged in playing these games.

---

[3]   Kenneth Bruscia, *Improvisational Models of Music Therapy* (Springfield: C.C. Thomas, 1987).

• Theory and Composition Teachers

– Add the element of improvisation, and the study of theory and composition changes from being dry and distant to vital and immediate. Students who improvise are motivated to learn all they can about all kinds of theory and composition.

• Jazz Players

– Jazz players have always had a tremendous advantage over their classical colleagues in that they are also improvisers and composers, and thus are more mentally and musically equipped to learn from any source and integrate the results into their playing and compositions. Although this collection of improvisation games is not jazz-oriented, because of their background, abilities, and attitude there is probably (and ironically) no one who will learn more and benefit more quickly from this collection than jazz players, who may feast on the rich cornucopia of possibilities, ideas, and techniques presented here.

• Everybody Else

– It is great to play in a community band, orchestra or chamber music ensemble, but these groups are not always around or conveniently available. Add to the joy of music by making your own. This formerly terrifying and mystifying concept is made plain, simple, and downright fun through the many musical games presented in this collection. Learn quick and easy ways to improvise on your instrument—or improvise during your daily life even if you don't play an instrument (all you need is your hands, feet, and voice and the desire to make your own music). Don't miss out on the fun!

Chapter **3**
Suggestions for Use

One of the great joys of being an improviser is that I can play with practically any musician in the world. It is like being fluent in dozens of languages.

—Matthew Barley[4]

1. Semester Course: Introduction to Improvisation for Classical Musicians

The NASM and MENC require improvisation study; this book finally makes possible an alternative to jazz as the only approach to improvisation. The games in this collection can be used to build a semester course in improvisation for classical musicians. It is an ideal way to introduce students who have had no improvisation training but who would like to learn the basics. How the class is structured is up to the instructor (who may or may not be learning improvisation along with the students. There is a first time for everything). We have done the class a bit differently every year at Iowa as we gain experience and try new ideas. Planning a schedule is a good idea, but the instructor should be ready to alter the plan at any time according to the needs of the class.

Keep in mind also that the games that worked marvelously one year may fall flat the next with a new group and a new assortment of instruments, and vice-versa. Each class has its own personality, attitude, and abilities; but the broad spectrum of games in this collection (plus the opportunity to invent new ones) leaves the instructor in a good position to plan a balanced and varied schedule. In any case, the following are some ideas that an instructor might consider when planning:

- Class size. The higher the enrollment, the less each player gets to participate. The absolute ideal might be eight or twelve, but sixteen works well, especially if you have access to several rooms for dividing occasionally into smaller groups (see the next item).

- It is ideal to have several rooms available. Our course has access to four, which works well with an enrollment of sixteen (four quartets, two octets). The first two weeks of the semester we do only whole-class games. After that we alternate between quartets, octets, and the whole group. The most important unit, however, is the duet, allowing for maximum participation and feedback. Some of the whole-class, quartet, or octet games are "serial duets," with those not playing providing a very valuable resource: the audience (also a source of feedback). Students are informed that they must spend a good bit of their at-home practice time working in teams of two to get maximum benefit from their practice.

---

4   http://www.matthewbarley.com

- The instructor and the TA play with the students in the small group sessions, moving from group to group. For example, in quartets, each group will have the instructor or TA with them for half the period.

- Record student performances often. Students are advised to bring recording devices (iPods, e.g., can be fitted with inexpensive microphones) to record themselves during class and are advised to record themselves at home. Play recordings in class and discuss what worked and what didn't.

- Small groups are pre-assigned. There are four sessions during the semester, and each session has groups with different mixes of players. Each group has a Leader who is assigned from the quartet on a rotating basis. The Leader is responsible for organizing and leading the games, and perhaps selecting some of the games. Later in the semester, Leaders can be expected to invent games as well.

- Games can be assigned for each of the small group sessions, either specifically or generally. A general assignment might be that the group must play one game in each of the following categories during the hour: Rhythm, Melody, Harmony (or Bass Line), Free Choice, and a free piece (no discussion, just play, listen and make a piece). Making specific game assignments ensures that everyone experiences the same game. A combination of the two is possible, with the instructor assigning several games, letting the Leader pick one game of free choice.

- Groups of any size should follow an improvisation with a short discussion of what worked and what didn't and what could have been done to improve the piece. It is not particularly useful to talk about likes or dislikes. It is more useful to ask if the group achieved 50/50 unity/variety, or "told a story" in creating a piece that had a beginning, middle, and an end. An audience's reaction should also be considered—if you can't make a piece interesting enough to keep their attention, something needs to change.

- Students are required to keep log books of their home practice to keep them accountable in their practice time.

- Along with this collection of games, the required text for the course is *Free Play* by Stephen Nachmanovitch. Several articles are also required reading. Although most class time is reserved for improvising, discussions on the reading material are held occasionally. Brief one-two essay question quizzes are checks on article reading comprehension.

- Several improvisation "compositions" are assigned: *Bricolage and Body Percussion* (see Composition Games).

- The students give a public concert of an improvised piece at the end of the semester. Although the thought of this is terrifying at the beginning of the semester, by a month or so before the concert, most students can't wait to get out there and show what they can do.

- Have a duffle bag or two (or three) full of small percussion instruments (things that shake and clank and thunk). Having some skinhead drums (e.g. djembe, dombek, bongos) and slit drums on hand is also a distinct plus. Some kind of percussion can be added to nearly any improvisation, and students are expected to be able to do rudimentary improvisation on simple percussion instruments, piano, and voice as well as their primary instrument. Having some percussion "toys" around also takes care of the problem of having more pianists than pianos, and at the beginning of the semester, it pays to spend a good bit of time on purely rhythmic improvisation. As a matter of fact, classical music students' rhythmic sense almost always needs a good deal of extra reinforcement.

- Students need to pay special attention to aural skills, but not the kind usually learned in theory or music history. They need to learn to hear as *composers*, to be able to hear a snippet of melody (played by themselves or a partner) and aurally identify scale steps, then find the notes and immediately play them back on their instrument. Work on this early and often, but start very simply (see Call-and-Response Games). It is also good if they hear some live examples—you or guests, for instance. CD listening for examples can also be good, but it has a built-in problem: recorded music is usually too "perfect," and sounds the same every time. Most of the recorded examples we use are from improvisers I know or myself.

- Traditional studies have something of a disconnect between technical exercises and playing. Students need to learn the value of working on scales as *music* (i.e., with variations, rhythms, embellishments, articulations, etc.) and learning patterns in all keys as a means of developing a broad vocabulary of melodic possibilities that can be executed effortlessly and automatically on the instrument.

- Soundpainting is a kind of real-time improvisational composition that uses a system of gestures developed over several decades by New York composer, conductor, and performer Walter Thompson. It is a very effective way for classical musicians to learn to improvise. The best way to learn it is from another Sound-painter, but the basics can be acquired from the manual and DVD available at www.soundpainting.com (see Resources for a list of basic gestures). We use Soundpainting (and Soundpainting-derived games) nearly every day with the whole group, and we always have a Soundpainting piece in the final concert.

First third of the semester:
- Warm-up games
- Drum Circles (see Resources for recommended books)
- Call-and-Response games (many types)
- Soundpainting (see www.soundpainting.com)
- Hand Drills (acquiring some facility and fluency in tapping rhythms, being able to beat both consistent and steady duple as well as triple patterns, and add accents)
- Body percussion (clapping, slapping, stomping, mouth noises, etc.)
- Be able to produce (extreme) contrasts in music.
- Perform students' *Bricolage* and *Body Percussion* pieces.
- Begin work on technique (patterns, scales, arpeggios, etc.) in all keys and in other scale types
- Duets with the instructor and with each other
- Listen to recordings of students

Middle third (continuing most of the above while adding these):
- Matching games (match, imitate, echo what you hear)
- Play familiar tunes by heart; change modes, add embellishments and variations.
- Play over drone (unpulsed, pulsed)
- Ostinati. Be able to build, hold, and change an ostinato figure

- Improvise over simple harmonies (one chord; two chords; three chords)
- Play from nontraditional scores
- Play simple form games
- Acquire a vocabulary of extended techniques and integrate it frequently into improvisations
- Work on various accompaniment roles
- More duet playing, plus trios and quartets

Last third:
- Work on motivic development techniques
- Play more and more "free" pieces
- Play more student-created games
- Depictions
- Longer pieces—five-, ten-, twenty-, or thirty-minute pieces—even up to forty-five minutes!
- Play quotes
- Play back longer segments of just-heard music
- Play vignettes
- Combine games to form longer pieces
- Work on the discipline to *not* play, especially in larger ensembles to keep from continually having a thick texture
- Final public concert of improvised pieces

> *Note:* All suggestions here are just that: players are free to investigate other games beyond those listed in their particular categories or try things in a different order. These are just ideas to get you started.

2. Instrumental Teachers

Free form expression/improvisation is based upon scale knowledge. ...Within a short period of time your students will naturally experience success when playing free form melodies and find the need for scale knowledge to expand their improvisational possibilities.

—Edward S. Lisk[5]

Instrumental teachers of any level can easily add improvisation to lesson time as a way to deepen and broaden technical, aural, and musical skills. Games can be played as duets in lessons or assigned as homework. The following are but a few possible suggestions for games that could be used in instrument lessons:

- Warm-Up Games
  Warm-Up Long Tones 56/71   Warm-Up Interval Piece 72
  Feel the Beats 71   Brass Warm-Up 73

---

5   *The Creative Director: Intangibles of Musical Performance* (Ft. Lauderdale: Meredith Music Publications, 1996).

Chapter 3: **Suggestions for Use**

- Melody Games
  - Rainbow Scales 54/113
  - Daily Arkady 114
  - Two by Two 116
  - Quotes Only 118
  - Twisted Quotes 118
  - Medley 119/219
  - Drone 57/112
  - Hold/Move 120
  - Interior Decoration 122
  - Canon 1, 2, 3 122
  - Row, Row, Row… 122
  - Bumblebee 126
  - Mock Audition 123
  - Tension/Release 58/125
- Accent Games
  - Accents I, II, III, IV 65/106
- Rhythm Games
  - Hand It Over I 78
  - Rhythm Symphony 80
  - You Crack Me Up 81
  - Team Groove 81
  - Offbeat Metronome 53/82
  - AMAPFALAP 84
  - Ostinato 57/89
  - Odd Meter Drone Ostinato 90
  - Odd Ostinato 97
  - Groove + Long Line 90
  - What's In a Name 57/93
  - Swing It 54/86
  - Rhythm By the Book 99
- Accompaniment Games
  - Foreground/Background 218
  - Initiator/Responder 218
  - Familiar Tune Accompaniment 218
  - Triad Accompaniment 219
  - Morphs 219
- Aural Games
  - Replay 159
  - Play It Again Sam 55/160
  - Play It Again, Sam, Again 160
  - Sing It, Sam 161
  - Play the Shape 162
  - Familiar Tune 53/139/164
  - Call-and-Response games (various) 166-170
- Bass Line Games
  - Oom Pah March 59/155
  - Plain Descender 156
  - Walking Bass 156
- Miscellaneous Games
  - Concerto! (takes three+ players) 249
  - Simon Says 250
  - Opposites 253
  - Trading Fours 255
  - Free Play Game #1 and #2 60/258
- Timbre Games
  - Unfamiliar Tune 196
- Technique Games
  - Que Será Será 214
  - Thirds—A Charm 214
- Style Games
  - Matching 183/223
  - Reflecting 184/223
  - Build a Band 227
  - March Madness 227

13

3. Professional Musicians

You're really good at what you do: interpreting music literature from the printed page. You've practiced an uncountable number of hours and it paid off: you have a job (or a steady series of jobs) that pays the bills and enables you to do nothing but music. You have a warm-up routine and a practice routine, and you're a great sight-reader. How could life be better than this? In your heart of hearts, there is a tiny voice that murmurs the answer. If you have been working in the profession for some years, you can even make out what the voice is saying if you really listen: *In spite of all the riches of classical music, the routine of practice and performance...ah...after a long time...gets...old.* The repertoire was so exciting the first time through it all. Then it came around again, and maybe that zing and sizzle wasn't quite what it was the first time. Now, well...going to work is, well, going to work. You go and do the job and do it well (again) and go home. You don't talk much about the music during the intermission anymore. You talk about the kids; about the cats; about the canoe trip you're planning; about your collection of pre-Columbian art. Music used to be like being in love, that dizzy, dancing way you feel, as the song says. Now it's a comfortable old shoe, an old spouse that you love and quarrel with, but you don't really have those moments you used to have, when you couldn't think of anything else, didn't want to do anything else but live, eat, breathe, think about it, talk about it, analyze it, and love/hate it.

But now you're holding this book. That stale, pale feeling is about to disappear. The thought of creating your own music may be a bit scary. It will take some gumption and go against a certain amount of your grain. But since you're here, you're also brave enough (or at least curious enough) to sample the world of improvisation. Good for you. What awaits you here? More than can be said in a sentence, but for starters you'll find new ways to play those old daily warm-ups and scales and arpeggios. You'll discover that you can even do them with other musicians. You'll get the same nutrients, but you'll be performing them as *music*, not sterile drills, more like chamber music than exercises. You'll wonder why you haven't been playing like this all along. You'll marvel at the fact that you can do the same things you always did, but now it's more fun (and you may even get suspicious because of it. Music is serious, isn't it? It isn't supposed to be fun. Is it? Well, we do *play* our instruments, even though it never seemed like play. Until now.) You vow to continue to dip into this tome and harvest ideas to renew your old routine and feel something passionate about making (really *making*) music again. The feeling of getting to play something you created (as opposed to only playing music by someone far away and likely dead) is intoxicating. And now it's easier to sit in your day job in the orchestra (having warmed up on whole tone scales with odd meter accents). You feel alive again, balanced, healthy, flexible, ready for anything; you are once more young and in love! And you didn't have to learn jazz to do it (although now, jazz looks a lot less formidable that it once did...).

Below are some games you might consider as you begin your new adventure:

- Warm-Up Games
    - Warm-Up Interval Piece
- Rhythm Games

AMAPFALAP	Try to Shake 'Em
What's in a Name?	Odd Ostinato
Move It	Transformation
Swing It	Rhythm by the Book

- Melody Games

Rainbow Scales	Tonal/Atonal
Daily Arkady	Canon 1, 2, 3
Nostalgia	Old and New
Quotes Only	Old and Argh!
Twisted Quotes	Anything Goes
Medley	Great Minds…
Far Out	Whole (Tone) Transformation

- Harmony Games

Familiar Tune	Reverse Crunch
Change of Mode	One Chord—Major
Double Crunch	One Chord—Minor

- Style Games

Where Are We Going With This?	March Madness
Fanfare	Here Comes the Bride
Serenade	Variation City

- Technique Games
    - Que Será Será
- Miscellaneous Games

Concerto!	Simon Says

- Form Games

Developing AB's	Sonata
Rondo	Etude

- Aural Games

Nostalgia	Call-and-Response (any type)

- Timbre Games

Unfamiliar Tune	Something Borrowed

- Accent Games
    - Scale Accents

4. Music Students

Whether your teacher takes inspiration from this book or not, your studies and routine will be more complete and interesting if you incorporate some of the ideas and approaches presented through the games of this book into your playing. Start with the ideas presented in the section Technical Training for Improvisation. Explore all sorts of different games. Feel free to tweak any of the games to suit your studies and take inspiration from them to create new games. You might even consider starting an improvised chamber music ensemble with like-minded players. One very important thing to do right away is to find an improvisation partner: the duet is the basic unit of improvisation. Your playing partner can be anyone—they do not have to play the same instrument. Befriend any creative percussionists or pianists you know, and then meet regularly. Working with a partner will energize, inspire, and challenge both of you, and allow you to reach heights and areas that are unattainable alone. If/when a partner is not yet available or handy, use a metronome (for rhythm games) or computer program such as GarageBand or Band-In-A-Box to fill the bill in the meantime.

Record as many of your sessions as you can. Keep a notebook to write down ideas for new games and compositions that come to you during or after your sessions. Adopt and adapt the idea of the Daily Arkady (see Melody Games); revise and energize the warm-ups and technical workout sections of your daily practice with improv ideas. Below are some ideas to work on alone and with a partner to get you started:

- Games for one player:
    Warm-Up Games
        Warm-Up Interval Piece 72

    Rhythm Games
        World=Percussion 53/77   AMAPFALAP 84
        Hand Drills and Skills 77   Rhythm Walking 87
        The Long and the Short of It 80 Swing It 54/96
        Offbeat Metronome 53/82   Rhythm By the Book 99

    Melody Games
        Glacier Music 112   Mixed Messages (piano) 119
        Rainbow Scales 54/113   Intervals 127
        Daily Arkady 114

    Harmony Games
        Chord Melody 150   Rhythm Scale 156
        Rhythm Chord 151   Chromatic Challenge 152

    Aural Games
        Play It Again, Sam 55/160   Sing It, Sam 161
        Play It Again, Sam, Again 160   Familiar Tune 55/139/164
        Play It Again, Sam, One More Time 161

    Miscellaneous Games
        House Music 245   Duet for One 56/256
        Shower Music 56/246   Swing it – 96

    Technique Games   Pace yourself – 129
        Que Será Será 214   Quick Variations – 259

- Games for two players:
    Warm-Up Games
        Warm-Up Long Tones   Feel the Beats 71
        56/71

Rhythm Games
 Hand It Over I and II   Mixed Meters III: or 3/4 vs. 6/8
 Rhythm Symphony   Against the Grain
 Team Groove   Try to Shake 'Em
 Don't Duet   Ping Pong
 Ostinato   Rhythm By the Book
 Odd Meter Drone Ostinato   Anticipation Angst
 Odd Ostinato
Melody Games
 Leaps Aloud   Interior Decoration
 Quotes Only   Row, Row, Row…
 Medley   Bumblebee
 Drone   Old and New
 Hold/Move   Great Minds
 As You Were Saying
Harmony Games
 Double Your Pleasure
Bass Line Games
 Bach Bass
Accompaniment Games
 Foreground/Background   Triad Accompaniment
 Initiator/Responder   Morphs
 Familiar Tune Accompaniment
Aural Games
 Play the Shape   Lightning Arrangements
 Familiar Tune   Call-and-Response games (various)
 Improv on the Chords
Bass Line Games
 Oom Pah March   Walking Bass
 The Low Down
Depiction Games
 Adjective/Noun   Country Music
 Suggestion Box   Guess the Emotion
Technique Games
 Thirds—A Charm
Style Games
 Matching   March Madness
 Reflecting   Fusion
 Build a Band   Guess the Style
Miscellaneous Games
 Simon Says   Free Play Games #1 and 2
 Opposites

5. General Music Teachers

Your students may or may not play an instrument, but the way to get them to appreciate and understand music is to get them making some music any way you can. Percussion is a great way to get everyone involved! Below are some examples:

- Rhythm Games:

World=Percussion	African Switchback
Hand Drills and Skills	Ostinato
Drum Circles	Call-and-Response—Rhythms!
You Crack Me Up	Foot Music
The Big Machine	Drumalogue/Drumversation
Entrainment	What's in a Name
AMAPFALAP	Try to Shake 'Em
Eight-Count Rhythm Machine	Ping Pong
Rhythm Walking	

- Call-and-Response games can be done at any level (see Aural Games).
- Style Games
    - Holiday Time
- Text Games work well with students who don't play instruments.

Conversations	Name Game
Ensemble Telepathy	As I Was Saying
Dramatic Names	

- Storytelling Games

Grimm Tales	Movie Soundtrack
Hans Christian Andersen	Teddy's Funeral
Various Tales	Dragon Tale
The King's Challenge	

- There are games from all different categories that could work, e.g.,

Emotional Symphony (Depictions)	Dancing Long Tones (Warm-Up Games)
Accent Template (Accent Games)	Hum-Up (Warm-Up Games)
Tapversation (Accent Games)	Dark Music (Warm-Up Games)

6. Band and Orchestra

Adding intervals of improvisation to regular ensemble work transforms lethargic and/or fatigued students into excited and motivated musicians. There are various ways to do this (see Conducting Games), but one of the most effective is the gestural system of improvisation invented over two decades ago by New York conductor, instrumentalist, and composer Walter Thompson.

Soundpainting is an ideal supplement to conventional conducting skills. When your group needs a break from concentrating on difficult material, throw in some Soundpainting gestures and watch them come alive (see Resources for a list of basic gestures). Although there are approximately a thousand gestures in the complete language, any group at any level can begin Soundpainting immediately with just a few gestures. Example: using the syntax: Who—What—Play—Exit, a simple "piece" could be Whole Group-Long Tone-Play-Exit. Slightly more advanced pieces might be: Brass-Long Tone-Play-Volume Up-Volume Down-Exit. Or: Woodwinds and Percussion-Long Tone-Enter Slowly-Volume Up-Pitch Down-Pitch Up-Pitch Up-Volume Down-Percussion Exit-Pitch Down-Woodwinds Exit Slowly-Brass. The early stages of Soundpainting are very approachable for both conductors and players.

Soundpainting is still more widespread in Europe than it is in the U.S. (just as jazz was first fully appreciated abroad); you may have the chance to introduce Soundpainting into a concert and perform something highly original and attention getting. See www.soundpainting.com, which offers more information as well as an instructional DVD and manual.

Working with smaller groups—with or without sheet music—can hone ensemble skills (intonation, rhythm, etc.) better than is possible with the large group. For use with sectionals or chamber ensembles, following are a few possible examples for use:

- Aural Games
  - Familiar Tune   Lightning Arrangements
  - Try to Remember   Call-and-Response
- Conducting Games
  - Play What You See   Conducting a Chorale
  - Shapeline   Freeform Conducting
  - Point to Point   Crossover
  - Cell Point to Point
- Rhythm Games
  - Rhythm Symphony   Synch or Swim
  - Offbeat Metronome   Eight-Count Rhythm Machine
  - AMAPFALAP   Ping Pong
- Melody Games
  - Conducting a Chorale
- Style Games
  - Build a Band   Matching
  - March Madness
- Bass Line Games
  - Oom Pah March

7. Choirs and Singers

Choirs can use almost all of the games that instrumentalists do, but there are some games in the book specifically for voice, including:

- Text Games
  - Conversations   Hallway Recitative
  - Dramatic Names
- Rhythm Games
  - Baby Grand Opera   Rhythm Machine
- Warm-Up Games
  - Hum-Up   Hearing Voices

- Miscellaneous Games
    - Shower Music
    - Scatversations
    - Ritual
    - Cave Celebrations
    - Rhubarb Rhubarb
    - The Incredible Mouth Band
- Timbre Games
    - Howl at the Moon
    - Yes, We Sing Bananas
    - Scat!
    - Mouth to Mouth
    - Mouthing Off
    - Giggle Machine
- Improv Set-up
    - A Little Something About Mary
    - Beware
    - And Another Thing
    - Cowboys and Cooking
    - Sparse Rhythm Machine
    - Days of Old
- Aural Games
    - Sing It, Sam
    - Call-and-Response—Voice Only
- Harmony Games
    - Pentatonic Chant
- Improvisation Game Techniques
    - Sing Sing

8. Chamber Music Ensembles

Most of the games in this collection can be used by chamber music ensembles of any size or instrumentation. Common instrumentations (string quartet, brass or woodwind quintet) will have a chance to enliven programs and please audiences by adding an improvised piece (including pieces invented on the spot from audience suggestions!). Unusual instrumentations will be rescued from repertoire starvation and can create new genres and new experiences for both themselves and audiences.

Tip: Acquire some simple percussion instruments and add them to the mix in some improvised pieces. Following are just a few suggestions for creating your own chamber music:

- Warm-Up Games
    - Warm-Up Interval Piece
    - Tension/Resonance
- Rhythm Games
    - Group Ostinato 101, 102, 103
    - Rhythm Symphony
    - Additive Solo
    - Deep in Hocket
    - Circle Ostinato
    - Mixed Meters I, II, III
    - One Note Chamber Music
    - What's In a Name
    - Swing It
- Melody Games
    - Leaps Aloud
    - Quotes Only
    - Medley
    - Intervals
- Harmony Games
    - Familiar Tune
    - The Mismatch Game
    - Sad One Four Five

- Depictions
  - Suggestion Box   Guess the Emotion
  - Once Upon a Time   Guess the Machine
  - Guess the Animal
- Timbre Games
  - Rainbow X-Tech   Halloween
  - Ambient Rainbow Soundscape   Something Borrowed
- Miscellaneous Games
  - Construction Cards   Immortal Improv Sonata #47
  - Vignettes   Free Play Games #1 and #2
- Aural Games
  - Call-and-Response—various
- Style Games
  - Fusion   Here Comes the Bride
  - Fanfare   Join the Party
  - March Madness   Holiday Time
- Improv Set-Ups
  - Circus Divertimento   Elegy
  - Scale Solo
- Storytelling Games
  - Teddy's Funeral   Dragon Tale

9. Music Therapists

Improvisation is very good training for music therapy, which is heavily based on responding to the needs and the music making of clients. Many of the five hundred games here can be used or adapted for music therapy work; a few examples are given below:

- Energy/Mood Games
  - Matching   Play the Face
  - Reflecting   Oh Yeah?
  - Feelings   Nice to See Your Back
- Miscellaneous Games
  - Toy Music   Make 'Em Laugh
  - Ritual
- Aural Games
  - Replay   Call-and-Response (various)
  - Play It Again, Sam
- Depictions
  - Conversation   Oooh Music
  - Emotional Symphony   Yea! Music
  - In the Mood   Guess the Emotion
- Melody Games
  - Echo   Yes, and…

- Text Games
  - Conversations   As I Was Saying
  - Ensemble Telepathy
- Rhythm Games
  - World=Percussion   Entrainment
  - Hand Skills and Drills   AMAPFALAP
  - Drum Circles   Rhythm Walking
  - Team Groove   Circle Ostinato
  - The Big Machine   Groove + Long Line
  - Pulse/No Pulse   Call-and-Response (rhythms)
  - Free/Strict   Foot Music
  - Going Somewhere   Drumalogue/Drumversation
  - Slowdown   Ping Pong

10. Piano (and other keyboards)

The piano can be an orchestra in itself, but the big drawback of the instrument is having to play either too much solo literature, or being "just" the accompaniment to another instrument's music. The improvisation games and approach of the book allow the pianist to join the group as an equal and to use their imagination to harvest the rich musical resources of the instrument. Piano teachers will find a vast assortment of games that are useful or adaptable for piano lessons. The piano can do almost every type of game; there are, however, a number of games that work best for piano. Some examples:

- Aural Games
  - Twisted Unison 119/165   Copy/Counterpoint
  - Copy Cat
- Harmony Games
  - Crunch Time 58/141
- Improv Set-Ups
  - Quick Variations 259   A Little Something About Mary 240
- Melody Games
  - Twisted Quotes 118   Key Quotes
  - Mixed Messages   Black Key Duet
  - Versatility 63/127   Alternation
  - Pace Yourself 129   Bitonal Bits
  - Copy Machine
- Miscellaneous Games
  - Duet for One 56/252
- Rhythm Games
  - Hand Arguments   Baby Grand Opera

11. Percussionists

This collection is an opportunity for percussionists to shine, to pull out all the stops, to be leaders and teachers, and to have the fun of using every percussive instrument available. Percussionists can participate in almost every game in the book, even when it is not otherwise indicated. Mallet players can have an additional role, playing everything that melody instruments can play. Your rhythmic abilities and versatility will make you king in this kind of improvisation. People will stop you in the hallway and ask you to join their group or to help them solve the mysteries of keeping a beat with a shaker. Have a ball! Suggestions are hardly necessary, since you can do it all, but here are a few to get started:

- Rhythm Games

World=Percussion	Eight-Count Rhythm Machine
Hand It Over I and II	Rhythm Walking
Drum Circle	African Switchback
Rhythm Symphony	Groove + Long Line
You Crack Me Up	Move with the Groove
Team Groove	Double Trouble
Going Somewhere	Call-and-Response—Rhythms!
Slowdown	Foot Music
Entrainment	Drumalogue/Drumversation
AMAPFALAP	Against the Grain
Additive Solo	Mixed Meters I, II, III
Synch or Swim	Sensemaya Step
Don't Duet	Rhythm By the Book (mallets—try both parts!)

- Accent Games

Accent Solo	Tapversation
Accent Template	Super Imposition
Accents I, II, II, IV, V	

12. Theory and Composition

> *I use improvisation for many reasons. It can spark rich ideas for composition, for it gives us a more intimate sense of raw materials of sound. It provides an astonishing physical and emotional release, and helps develop the kind of spontaneity that can transform the way we play Bach or Mozart or Bartók. It creates a more direct personal relationship with an instrument that can melt square-shouldered bravado into keen-eared listening.*
>
> —Eloise Ristad[6]

Music theory is unfortunately often considered by many players to be dry-as-dust historical information of little or dubious usefulness to the player in everyday musical life. Composition is considered an arcane discipline practiced and appreciated by only a few. Part of that is due to the unnatural and unnecessary separation of academic disciplines from each other and from performance. The truth is that theory can be both highly interesting and of vital utility, and that composition needs to be experienced to be appreciated. One way to accomplish this is to use this book to direct and encourage players to learn music theory through their instruments. Even a little bit of improvising makes it clear that there is no upper limit on how understanding music theory helps a player create.

---

6   Eloise Ristad, *A Soprano on Her Head: Right-side-up Reflections on Life and Other Performances* (Moab: Real People Press, 1982).

Improvisation leads easily to composition; first learn to generate ideas quickly, then learn to polish them. Encourage students to find ways to experience historical theory on their instruments (it shouldn't be just the pianist who gets to do this) and/or compose pieces and exercises. This approach adapts to the introduction of all kinds of theory, but one thing that will be most helpful to students is learning jazz terminology. (While this is not a course in jazz style, we can use jazz vocabulary and methods to considerable advantage.) The jazz approach describing the scales and chords is of great and immediate use to an improviser in applying theory to practice. See recommended references in Resources. (NB: Theory/composition teachers, if the jazz teacher or an applied teacher hasn't yet launched a course like this [or some variation thereof], why not you?) Some of the following games may be of direct benefit to theory/composition studies (additional games could be invented using these as models):

- Melody Games
  Modal Transformations   Whole Tone Transformation
- Form Games
  ABA—Played   Etude
  Song Form   Through-Composed
  Rondo   Theme and Variations
  Sonata   Blues
- Compositions Games
  Bricolage   Whole Tone
  Body Percussion Chamber Music   Dorian Composition
  Basketball Piece   Dare to Be Bad
  Quantity is King   Write Something You Can Sing
  I Got Rhythm   Variations Game
  ABA—Written   Triad Compositions
  Minor Pentatonic
- Style Games
  Fusion   Guess the Style
- Aural Games
  Steal That Tune
- Harmony Games
  Familiar Tune   The Mismatch Game
  Improv on the Chords   Suggesting Harmony
- Motivic Development Games
  All: Repetition, Mode Change, Ornamentation, Transposition, Sequence, Subtraction, Addition, Augmentation, Diminution, Retrograde, Inversion, Displacement, Combination
- Nontraditional Score Games
  Nontraditional Scores I, II, III
- Improv Set-Ups
  Quick Variations   ABAC
  Atonal Jazz   Sea Chanty
  Lyrical Piece   Salieri's Test

13. Jazz Players

Although much of standard jazz practice involves playing over chord changes, jazz players may be in the position to assimilate and transform for use many of the non-chord-based improv ideas presented here because of their knowledge of scales, chords, and the ability to hear music as a composer; that is, to understand and integrate it into their playing. Listed below are a few of the games that may be of the most interest to jazz players in search of some fresh ideas and approaches for compositions, performance, or pedagogy:

- Soundpainting. Soundpainting was invented by a jazz player, Walter Thompson (woodwinds, percussion, composition) more than twenty years ago in a spontaneous effort to communicate some complex ideas to his group during a performance. The entire language now has approximately 800 gestures and is capable of evoking music of remarkable complexity and depth yet is also immediately accessible to novices. Soundpainting can be very effectively integrated into jazz performance, as has been done by Thompson, Evan Mazunik, and others. See www.soundpainting.com and the list of basic gestures in Resources.

- Nontraditional Score Games

    Playing the Gallery   Collage Music
    Nontraditional Score I, II, III   With a Little Help From Our Friends
    Mixed Notes   Shapeline
    Ad Music

- Rhythm Games

    Rhythm Symphony   Groove + Long Line
    Drum Circle   Move With the Groove
    Do the Rest   Call-and-Response—Rhythms
    You Crack Me Up   What's In a Name
    Team Groove   Mixed Meters I, II, III
    Offbeat Metronome   Move It
    Free/Strict   Swing It
    Entrainment   Try to Shake 'Em
    AMAPFALAP   Odd Ostinato
    Additive Solo   Sensemaya Step
    Don't Duet   Different Drummers
    Circle Ostinato   Rhythm By the Book
    Ostinato   Riff Game
    Odd-Meter Drone Ostinato

- Harmony Games

    Familiar Tune   Crunch Time
    Improv on the Chords   Double Crunch
    The Mismatch Game   Reverse Crunch
    Mode Mix   Add-On Flats and Sharps
    Drifting   Higher and Higher
    Make Over   Suggesting Harmony

- Aural Games
    - Double Telephone
    - Replay
    - Play It Again, Sam, Again
    - Play the Shape
    - Teach That Tune
    - Steal That Tune
    - Familiar Tune
    - Nostalgia
    - Twisted Unison
    - Lightning Arrangements
    - Call-and-Response games (various)
- Bass Line Games
    - The Low Down
    - Plain Descender
    - Heart and Soul
    - Walking Bass
    - Taking a Walk Outside
    - Follow the *Lieder*
- Melody Games
    - Rainbow Scales
    - Daily Arkady
    - Point to Point
    - Three or Five Only
    - Leaps Aloud
    - Circle Duet
    - Quotes Only
    - Twisted Quotes
    - Medley
    - Bumblebee
    - Far Out
    - Row, Row, Row…
    - Modal Transformations
    - Whole Tone Transformation
- Technique Games
    - Que Será Será
    - Thirds—A Charm
- Accompaniment Games
    - Morphs
- Style Games
    - Fusion
    - Variation City
    - Guess the Style
- Miscellaneous Games
    - Shapeline
    - The Incredible Mouth Band
    - Duet for One
    - Opposites
    - Number of Notes
    - Fun House Mirror
    - Go Wild
    - Vignettes
    - Trading Fours
    - Blind Improv
    - Flexible Chamber Music
    - Immortal Improv Sonata #47
    - Free Play Games #1 and 2

14. Everybody Else: Games for the Rest of Us!

Leaving music to musicians is as nonsensical as leaving health to doctors, cooking to chefs, or fitness to professional athletes. The games of this book open the door to everyone who enjoys tapping a foot or clapping in rhythm, humming a catchy tune, singing in the shower, rapping out a rhythm on a steering wheel, or getting together with friends for the fun of it. Even if you have never studied music a day in your life, you can use the ideas of the games here to add music and rhythm to your life right now. Why let musicians have all the fun? Why let your iPod keep you from experiencing music first hand? Get out there and make your own music and enjoy life the way it was meant to be enjoyed: moving, grooving, dancing, singing, rapping out rhythms, creating fun music with friends and family (your kids will love it—even the teenagers, if you can get them started]). Even your dog will love it. Dogs make excellent percussion instruments and enjoy the attention. Below are a few suggestions to get you started; don't hesitate to change anything to better suit your needs; feel free to come up with new games at any time.

Tips:
- Collect small percussion "toys" to use in many of the games (shakers, rattles, claves, hand drums, etc.).
- Develop a wide variety of body and mouth noises to use as percussion.
- Use anything around the house that makes noise: Pot + wooden spoon, bowl + whisk, spoon + tin can, aspirin bottle half-filled with dry rice, stapler, crinkly plastic, aluminum can, power drill, and so on—as percussion.
- Even with minimal (or no) piano skills, you can play or join many games by playing the black keys of the piano.
- Sing or use vocal sounds and effects to join many games as a "melody" instrument.

So put away your MP3 player for a fortnight and see what happens when you jump into the world of music making—literally.
- Miscellaneous Games

House Music	Cave Celebrations
Car Music	Conversations in Motion
Shower Music	Make 'Em Laugh
Desk Music	Play the Room, Really
Stadium Music	Shapeline
Who was that Masked Man?	The Incredible Mouth Band
Toy Music	New Story
Playground Music	Danceline
Ritual	

- Improv Set-Ups

A Little Something About Mary	Circus Divertimento
And Another Thing…	Scale Solo
Cowboys and Cooking	Days of Old
Lullabye for the King	Beware
Long Tone Tune (piano black keys)	Sparse Rhythm Machine
Name That Pentatonic Tune (piano black keys)	Fairy Tale

- Rhythm Games

World=Percussion	Rhythm Walking
Hand Skills and Drills	Groove + Long Line
Drum Circle	Move with the Groove
The Big Machine	Call-and-Response—Rhythms!
Entrainment	One-Note Chamber Music
AMAPFALAP	Foot Music
Synch or Swim	Chant
Eight-Count Rhythm Machine	Ping Pong

- Aural Games
  - Steal That Tune   Call-and-Response—Voice only; Rhythms
- Depictions
  - Emotional Symphony   Ooh Music
  - In the Mood   Yea! Music
- Text Games
  - Conversations   Name Game
  - Ensemble Telepathy   As I Was Saying
  - Dramatic Names   My Day, So Far
- Melody Games
  - Drone
- Nontraditional Score Games
  - Shapeline
- Composition Games
  - Bricolage   Quantity Is King
  - Body Percussion Piece   Write Something You Can Sing

♦ ♦ ♦

Musical development does not require an instrument from the start. Musical development begins with the music within and extends to singing, clapping, banging around in the kitchen, and eventually playing an instrument.

—Christine Stevens, *The Art and Heart of Drum Circles*[7]

♦ ♦ ♦

Improvisation may be an answer to reinvigorating concert audiences. Prior to the twentieth century, most concerts were part literature and part improvisation. This tradition lives on in the popular music culture today. Do they know something we don't?

—Keith Hill[8]

---

[7]   *The Art and Heart of Drum Circles* (Milwaukee: Hal Leonard, 2003)

[8]   "Improvise Intentionally," http://www.musicalratio.com/startimprovising.html (2005).

Chapter 4
Musical Training for Improvisation

In Search of Melody

I don't know about you, but no one ever asked me to create a melody on my horn—ever—at any time during my musical education, although I had to recreate melodies aplenty. But does endlessly reciting a language give you the same understanding of expression and communication as learning to converse in that language? The goal of the kind of contemporary classical improvisation espoused here is to return to that ability once enjoyed by all musicians, that of having a voice and being able to "think" and "speak" music, as well as being able to recite the texts of others.

What are we trying to sound like in contemporary classical improvisation? Whereas classical training is devoted to conformity and consistency, the answer to this question is different for every person, the same way everyone's speaking voice is different. Our musical voice will be an expression of the sum total of our background: all the music we've heard and played (including non-classical music), all the theory we know, the musical styles we enjoy, and our personality and attitudes, both permanent and transient. What we know will be filtered by what we are able to do: our instrumental technique. At first, just as when we learn a new language, we speak simply. Music education has not equipped our ears or fingers to hear or play unprinted notes or given our imaginations opportunity to create melodies. We know what melodies are, but we have no experience and little knowledge in putting them together. At first we are scared because we are used to performing at a high level, and we can't create at the same level we have learned to re-create. It takes courage to begin, to dare, and patience to learn.

We have to learn from scratch how to "speak melody." At first our melodies are aimless, hesitant, and don't make much sense because we can't settle on one topic of discussion—we keep changing the subject. Or we choke quickly on more notes than we can handle while trying to create an impressive and technical melody that affirms our status as trained musicians. When playing with others in this early stage, we may either ignore or not relate to our partner, so that our duet sounds like two unrelated monologues, or we may not be able to summon the technique to cope with playing from imagination rather than ink. We don't yet know how to support, provide backgrounds, or make our partner sound good. At the same time, we also don't know when to be silent, or play sparsely to give the foreground player room to blossom, or to vary the texture (density) for the good of the piece and for the audience.

With time and experience, we learn to speak less, more to the point, and more simply, and to leave room for each player to "breathe." We learn to echo, initiate, match styles, and to have a real dialogue. We learn to add tension and resolution and to vary the colors (timbre, dynamics, etc.). We learn to sustain and develop an idea over a longer period of time and to create form while playing the piece even if no guidelines were given at the outset.

In short, we learn to make music, to express ourselves, to relate to the other players, and to create a satisfying extemporaneous composition for ourselves and for the audience. (While some contemporary composers and performers are not interested in considering the audience, this author is not among them.)

Learning Goals

The contemporary classical improviser needs to acquire some of the following fundamentals:

• Aural Abilities

IMITATION

Babies learn speech by imitating the sounds of their parents. Classical musicians have never been asked to echo sounds that they hear, only to reproduce what they read on paper. The two are very different. Aural reproduction requires the player to "instantly transcribe" the sounds plus instantly translate those sounds to the instrument. While this process is easy and natural for vocalists, it is not necessarily so for instrumentalists (and the difficulty varies with the instrument). Instrumentalists can learn the process stepwise, as in the following suggestions:

> In aural imitation games (such as Call-and-Response), limit the number of pitches (e.g. 1–5) or measures (e.g. one bar of 4/4).
> Start with a moderate tempo.
> Start with simple rhythms and note values; learn to imitate rhythms as well as pitches.
> Start with major scales.

As proficiency in imitation develops, all parameters can be made progressively more challenging: More pitches, longer passages, quicker tempos, decreased response time, more interesting rhythms, other scale types (various minors, pentatonic, modes, whole tone scales, etc.). See Aural Games.

ANALYSIS

Composers hear music differently than everyone else. Their experience in constructing pieces enables them to aurally decode melody, harmony, form, timbre, and rhythm. Players who play only from the ink develop only rudimentary aural abilities, although they may be trained in deconstructing a printed score. Players who improvise are in effect composers (improvisation is just very quick composition) and need this ability of instant analysis to inform their choices of the moment. For improvisers, music theory is not an abstract system separate from performance; it is a necessary practice, and a highly desirable part of improvised performance.

• Generating Ideas

Echoing what you hear is the first step, and coming up with your own ideas is the next, which may be a completely new concept to many musicians. A quick and easy way to begin this process is to play the Call-and-Response game where the Caller changes each time—every player must in turn invent a measure for all to echo back. Another excellent way for classical musicians to get used to creating is Soundpainting (see the discussion in Soundpainting Gestures: The Basics in Resources as well as www.soundpainting.com). Playing basic scale material against a drone (unpulsed or pulsed) is also a good way to ease into the process.

• **Creating Melodies**

After a player learns to generate ideas, the next step is to be able to organize these ideas into motifs and melodies and to develop this material for an extended period. Following are some suggestions for melody creation (see also *Tips for Melody Creation*):

> Simple ideas are easier to remember, imitate, and develop.
> Using fewer ideas aids clarity.
> Copy (imitate, steal, echo) from others and from yourself.
> Begin using limited scale material. You may add more later to enhance
>   development and drama.
> Developing motifs aids unity. See *Motivic Development Techniques*.)

The main theme here is that limitations are essential. They make the music more coherent (a style is a recurring set of restrictions) and make the player's task of deciding what notes to select much easier. If you begin a piece without setting any restrictions, the first order of business for players is to establish some, such as: key, motif, pulse, rhythm, etc.

• **Form: Contrast and Memory**

Every piece benefits from some kind of architecture or form, which helps both players and audience make sense of the piece. In improvisation, we first learn to imitate, then we learn to generate our own ideas. These ideas may at first sound like previous material, but at some point we will want to create contrasting material. This gives rise to form. The simplest form is AB: Do something, and then do something different. The length of these sections may be very short at first. Later, as we develop aural memory, we will be able to remember what we invented in the first section and bring it back, to make the form ABA (or more likely, ABA', where A' is a variation of A). Some various ways to make a contrasting B section include: melodic style, rhythms, dynamics, timbre, instrumentation, note values, tempo, scale type, mode, harmonies, and so on. See *Form Games* for further discussion of the many possible forms that may be used.

• **Roles: Foreground and Background**

A contemporary classical improviser has a different task than the jazz improviser. The jazz player normally waits his turn, plays a solo with rhythm section accompaniment, hands the solo role off to the next player, and may play again at the return of the "head" (a jazz form meaning main melody). The contemporary classical improviser will need to be able to switch quickly in and out of foreground/ background roles (i.e. solo and accompaniment) in the performance of pieces where the "script" is invented in the moment, which requires sensitivity and skill (see The Art of Accompaniment in Improvisation and Accompaniment Games). Players learn to be selfless for the sake of the piece and to make their playing partners look good. Those who insist on hogging the limelight are soon at a loss for playing partners.

• **Drama and Expression**

You have many arrows in your quiver when it comes to enhancing a performance musically and dramatically for an audience (more than the traditional paradigm may suggest). Some ideas:

1. Set up predictable melodic sequences—then tweak or change them. Aim for 50/50 unity/ variety. The audience will be frustrated if it can't predict what is going to happen next 50% of the time, and bored if it can predict what is going to happen more than 50% of the time.

2. For dramatic purposes, use a wide variety of dynamics and timbre (extended techniques). Stay away from the "middle"—mezzo forte dynamics, middle range, moderate tempo, middling note density, similar note values, few silences, and so on. It may feel safe, but can soon seem static and predictable, i.e., boring. Dare to exaggerate. Due to some psychoacoustic phenomenon, that which seems exaggerated on stage may barely register in the cheap seats. Make everyone sit up and notice that something interesting is happening on stage.

3. Harness the power of "wrong" notes. Dissonant notes create tension, which, when resolved to more consonant sounds, add welcome drama. Experiment with tension and release. Pieces that are all consonant or entirely dissonant get old quickly.

4. Tell a story. Both in macro- and microcosm, music needs to have a beginning, middle, and ending.

5. Don't forget that performances can be greatly enhanced by lighting, and that improv groups can sit in places on stage and in the hall that a traditional chamber ensemble might not consider.

6. Remember that improvisation is not limited to the traditional instrumentations for which composers have written. You can work with anyone who can improvise. You could, for example, form a trio of clarinet, marimba, and tuba if you wished, or you could perform a concert with dancers who improvise to your music as you improvise to their dance (the author has done this and highly recommends it).

7. Remember that your instrument is capable of many sounds other than those found in printed music or method books. Go exploring and develop your own extended vocabulary of sounds.

8. Keep in mind all the resources you have besides your instrument: your voice (you can recite text, speak, sing, make percussive mouth noises), your body (body percussion, stamp feet, stand up and/or walk around, wave/move your hands/arms, face in different directions; use gestures or other signals to communicate with other players during performance), other instruments (small percussion instruments, such as a shaker, mini-maracas, finger cymbals, etc. can be learned quickly). Tradition has rendered us blind to unusual ideas. Open your mind and eyes to the many other possibilities as you create your music.

Summary

In the end, learning contemporary classical improvisation opens up new worlds of sensitivity, under-standing, and flexibility. We hear with new ears when we are responsible for generating music: we are constantly looking for new ideas, sounds, styles, and rhythms, anything to enhance and extend our playing. We learn to instantly adapt to whatever is happening in our ensemble, because we are well versed in aural, visual, and gestural contact. We are comfortable performing in a wide variety of styles, in and out of classical genres, because we are continually adding to our musical vocabulary by learning something from every kind of music that we encounter, even those styles that we don't particularly care for. We are able to assume both solo and accompanying roles skillfully and easily. We have gained access to the world's great musical literature through our literate training, while our aural training has given us a voice, a superior ear, a practical understanding of theory, history, and style through the instrument, as well as the opportunity to create and express ourselves through our instruments.

Chapter 5
Technical Training for Improvisation

Introduction

Although it is possible for musicians at any level of technical proficiency to improvise, the path toward mastery of any craft requires learning basic *domain skills* (including the specialized vocabulary of the trade), imitating models, and acquiring experience in the subject over time. Improvisation uses the same technical material (scales, arpeggios, etc.) as classical music, but the technical preparation is different. Academic study, for instance, often requires passing a scale proficiency exam, which means successfully playing the collection of pitches in a given scale, in ascending and descending order. Since an improvisation may go in any direction, the improviser needs to have experience with a much larger array of possibilities to acquire the necessary flexibility, aural skills, and technical depth. Proficiency is ongoing. It is technique for life, not just a narrow set of skills to pass a one-time exam. The good news is that the approach described below makes the material endlessly varied and always engaging, rather than merely a string of boring exercises to be endured. Our goal as musicians is to be flexible, ready for any musical situation that might arise. For improvisers this is doubly true, since the task to be solved may only arise in the instant before. To attain such flexibility we need to develop several different approaches to music, of which the traditional up-and-down "triangle" scale is but one.

Aural Approach: The Eyes Don't Have It

Classical music tends to supply us with a false feeling of control, because we feel grounded by our eyes. The security we think we have when reading music is an illusion because we're constantly afraid of making mistakes.

—Julie Lyonn Lieberman[9]

The traditional "literate" approach to music is largely a *visual* experience. While this enables us to access written music very quickly, it also has some *disadvantages:*

- **Aural.** Although music is obviously an aural phenomenon, we spend most of our playing time with our eyes glued to the paper—and we don't hear as well because of it. As the saying goes, you hear much better in the dark. Vision is a bully among the senses, and needs to be shut down sometimes to let the others blossom.

---

[9] "From Fear to Fun: Teaching What You Don't Know." In *American String Teacher* 52:3 (August, 2002): 42. Taken from *The Creative Band and Orchestra* (Huiksi Music, 2003).

- **Expressive.** It is very difficult to "lose yourself" in the music or feel anything on a personal level when you are wrapped up in the attempt to reproduce pre-composed notes perfectly and accurately.

- **Creative.** The "literate" task is to re-create, not create. Imagination withers when it is not used. A musical diet consisting solely of playing the music of others with no personal creation soon leads to the firm conviction that it is impossible to create music—or even technical exercises—for oneself. It seems that only the distant "experts" have the know-how or ability to create. This improvisation course and the method of technical practice given here are designed to convince players of the worth of creating written and improvised music, to practice thinking in music, and getting in the habit of creating. Freedom from the printed page gives us a chance to think for ourselves.

- **Technical.** Although our vision gives us immediate access to music, in the end it slows us down because we can only play as fast as we can read. To acquire the kind of technical mastery we want, we have to move beyond the printed page. Our goal should be to put the knowledge and know-how in the player rather than on the page. We want to internalize—i.e., automate— the process as much as possible, and this means learning beyond the visual. We want to acquire comprehensive musicianship and to be comfortable in both literate and aural traditions.

- **Intellectual.** Being highly proficient at interpretation of printed notation is absolutely essential. However, the danger of playing only from the ink is leaving the knowledge on the page, not in the player. A "literate-only" approach may leave theory, history, and performance disconnected, but an improviser must be able to combine instrumental technique, imagination, theory (melody construction, form, harmony), and ear training (instant recognition of intervals, chord and scale types, and rhythms). Classical players often memorize (some instruments such as piano and strings memorize more than others to facilitate technique), which is beneficial and raises ability to play a score, but it is still "reading from a score in the mind" and does not require the depth of knowledge that an improviser needs to make instant informed choices from one note to the next.

Shorthand: Chord Symbols and Scale Degrees

One way to wean oneself from dependence on music notation is to use more general symbols, such as scale degree steps and chord symbols. Jazz terminology is very useful for us as players, even though this book does not emphasize jazz style. For example, in jazz chord symbols, we know that $C_{MAJ}7$ means C–E–G–B; C^7 is C–E–G–B♭, and so on. Further study (and experimentation) teaches us what scales work well with each chord type.

For scales and patterns, thinking in scale degrees helps us to better understand and use scales in our improvisations. For example, a melodic pattern could be written as 1–2–3–1 (in C: C–D–E–C). We could then play this "shape" progressively on every scale step ascending and descending. This brief bit of shorthand—four digits—*cues a series of responses* that may be played quickly and easily without written notation and are thus learned much more deeply than with a purely visual approach. This is possible because the knowledge is now *in the player*—every note need not be written out. The player can use this same pattern/shape for every scale type and often for arpeggios as well.

Besides learning patterns diatonically (where the intervals between the notes change at different levels), we can transpose the pattern through every key in the cycle. In Resources seventeen cycles are given. The first cycles to learn would be the circle of fifths (Fifths descending: C–F–B♭–E♭–A♭–D♭–G♭–B–E–A–D–G), and then chromatically, playing the pattern up or down a half step progressively for an octave.

Less Is More

This description of technical training as well as later descriptions of the improv games *will use as little standard music notation as possible.* The primary reasons are to allow players to develop their imagination (for example, when varying the melody, articulation, timbre, and so on) and to get the knowledge off the page and into the player and dramatically reduce the necessity of writing out every note. Writing out all possibilities is in fact an impossibility, but the player has the power to extrapolate from a basic principle. Thus equipped, a player can continue to develop new material aurally for a very long time. Using shorthand methods, a 3X5-inch card (for instance) could contain more than enough material than is possible to play in a semester. This shorthand approach allows us to have many times the content possible compared to other notation methods.

Variation and Repetition

> *You don't have to practice boring exercises, but you have to practice something. If you find the practice boring, you don't run away from it, but don't tolerate it either. Transform it into something that suits you. If you are bored playing a scale, play the same eight tones but change the order. Then change the rhythm. Then change the tone color. Presto, you have just improvised. If you don't think the result is very good, you have the power to change it— now there is both a supply of raw material and some judgment to feed back the process.*
>
> —Stephen Nachmanovitch[10]

Acquiring the technical skills necessary for high-level music making requires much time and patience. Repetition includes both quantity (repeating the scale patterns many times) and quality (playing accurately and without hesitation). The dangers associated with repetition are boredom and mindless playing, both of which can neutralize the advantages of repetition if allowed to persist. The solution is *variation*: using imagination to enliven practice. In this way one becomes deeply familiar with the notes of the scale by varying pitch order, rhythm, dynamics, articulation, tempo, even timbre. We also use *affect* to give life and meaning to our improvisations (see the article by Keith Hill "On Affect"—available online. See Resources).

Working with a Partner

> *One advantage of collaboration is that it's much easier to learn from someone else than from yourself. And inertia, which is often a major block in solitary work, hardly exists at all here: you release each other's energy. Learning becomes many-sided, a refreshing and vitalizing force.*
>
> —Stephen Nachmanovitch[11]

It's easier to go to the gym and work out if you do it with a partner: courage is additive. Partners can help, advise, and challenge each other. Also possible (and very useful and important) is the opportunity to make up games, which transforms the "medicinal" aspect of scale playing into something resembling a yummy dessert, the same way that a sport transforms an otherwise exhausting and boring physical activity into pure fun. Therefore it is indispensable to not only perform with others, but to practice with as many other players as possible. There is room for two in the woodshed!

---

10   Nachmanovitch, *Free Play.*
11   *Ibid.*

Suggestion: pick a partner, set a schedule of regular meeting times, and stick to it!

Getting Rhythm

The best practice partner is often anything that sets a rhythm. Practice often with a rhythmic source. Human players are the most fun, but when they are not available, it is electronics to the rescue! This means a metronome at minimum, but other good sources include electronic keyboards, which often come equipped with auto-accompaniments, many percussion styles, as well as auto-harmonies). Some computer programs also do a good job. For Macintosh computer owners, GarageBand offers the facility to set up back-up tracks very quickly with of all kinds of percussion and other instruments. PG Music's Band-in-a-Box has an interface that only a mother could love, but it provides a great piano, bass, and drum accompaniments for practicing chord progressions. Start collecting a few percussion instruments then set up regular practice sessions with a friend, and when you get tired of playing your regular instrument, you can switch to percussion!

Rule of Relaxation

The final test of when to increase the metronome speed is not consistent, accurate playing; it is consistent, accurate playing with a feeling of relaxation, of effortlessness, of watching it happen. No tension! If you find yourself getting tense, slow down. Speed cannot be forced; you have to let it happen, and that takes much relaxed practice, i.e., quantity with quality.

Improvisation and the Study of Technique

Improvisation is the truest test of whether you really know your scales, and combines all of the other elements as well: repetition, variation, playing without written material, and (usually) playing with a partner. Improvisation is "thinking in music," and goes beyond learning or memorizing a set of notes in a particular order. When you improvise (not necessarily in jazz or any particular style), you are taking a set of scale notes and spontaneously rearranging them to make musical sense, in the same way that you construct sentences in a conversation. The last part of any technical practicing you do should be concluded with an improvisation session in which you put everything you worked on out of your mind, close your eyes, and let 'er rip!

Approaches to Scale Study

This book will supply some general principles of technical scale practice. Every last detail will not be spelled out: The player is expected to extrapolate imaginatively, add variants for interest and development, and take each exercise off the page as soon as possible. The main idea is to get to know scale materials in as many ways as possible. To save space and simplify the presentation, most exercises have been written only in C major. Be patient; it will take time to achieve mastery. Although it takes longer than visual training, it is a much deeper and more effective assimilation and integration of the material. The good news is that—with imagination– it can be an interesting and rewarding process, every step of the way.

There are several main ways to systematically study scale material.

Scales (the up-and-down kind)

There are three main approaches to up-and-down scales: Length, pitch, and type.

- Length
  Since our final goal is to be able to begin on any note of the scale and play a scale of any length either ascending or descending, we practice scales in all lengths instead of just learning two lengths of scales (one or two octaves).

  In the *Basic Scale Drill*, begin on the tonic pitch of a major or minor scale and play scales that increase by one diatonic step with each repetition up to the ninth. Each scale length is looped until it becomes completely second nature, automatic.

- Pitch
  Choose one pitch as a focus for study, C, for instance. Choose a scale length from one to nine pitches. An octave is fine to start. With C as root, review many types of scales (C major, chromatic scale, C natural minor, C harmonic minor, C melodic minor, C dominant 7th, C Dorian, etc.) Advanced players may spend time on new (unfamiliar) scales (diminished, whole tone, pentatonic, etc.).

- Scale type
  Concentrating on one scale type (e.g., major), play through all keys. Play in all scale lengths or choose one or several scale lengths. Start with concentration on the major scale, and then go to the various minor scales. See the list of scale types in Resources.

Patterns

Patterns are usually three or four notes in a "shape", as discussed earlier (e.g., 1–2–3–1, 1–2–3, 1–2–3–4), and are usually inverted descending (1–3–2–1, 3–2–1, 4–3–2–1). New patterns should be learned on a continuous basis. Practice both diatonic and cycle patterns, repeating the pattern sequence on consecutive scale steps and in all keys. While several books of patterns are available, often the best sources are the solos, etudes, and orchestral excerpts that you are currently playing. See *Patterns* in Resources.

Intervals

Intervals could be considered very short two-note scales, arpeggios or patterns. Their difficulty, as in all things, varies from instrument to instrument. For instance, wide intervals are easy on piano but difficult on the horn. In any case, learning intervals enables you to hear and then play back a melody much more easily. Being able to find and to switch intervals quickly also makes it much easier to play atonal music, which is more difficult than it sounds. Spend a good bit of time on interval training, both alone and with a playing partner.

Diatonic vs. Cycle Study

Both types of scale and pattern study are useful for the improviser's development of technique.

Diatonic study is practicing sequential patterns up (or down) the steps of a given scale. For instance, scale steps 1–2–3 are repeated as 2–3–4, then 3–4–5, and so on. As with all technical study described here, it is best to start with short lengths and gradually build up to longer scale lengths. Sequencing causes the intervals between the notes to change. For instance, in 1–2–3–4 (scale degrees), the steps in between are whole, whole, and half, or the beginning of a major scale. Playing the same shape up a step in the next diatonic sequence would be 2–3–4– 5. Here the steps in between are whole, half, whole, the beginning of a minor scale. In major, the sequences of the octave scales are called modes: C to C (major scale): Ionian mode; D to D: Dorian; E to E: Phrygian; F to F: Lydian; G to G (Dominant 7th): Mixolydian; A to A: Aeolian; B to B: Locrian.

Practice diatonically mainly with patterns, e.g., 1–2–3, 1–7–1 (neighboring tone pattern), 1–3 (scale in thirds), and so on.

Cycle study simply means running a pattern, scale, or scale subset through all keys. Unlike with diatonic sequencing, there is no altering of the scale step relations; 1– 2–3 remains 1–2–3. The most commonly used cycles are the Circle of Fifths (C–F–B♭–E♭–A♭–D♭–G♭–B–E–A–D–G) and chromatic (C–D♭–D–E♭–E etc.). Cycles can and should also be rearranged in many other ways—see the *Cycles in* Resources for additional suggestions; you are encouraged to invent your own.

Daily Arkady

This practice is described in Melody Games. Suffice it to say that a Daily Arkady is "free" playing, exploring melody, rhythm, and mood, integrating all the types of scale, arpeggio, and pattern practices listed here, and directed by the imagination. A Daily Arkady is an imaginative way to practice technique musically, and a great way to start your day.

Two Kinds of Practice

There are two kinds of practice: *review* of what you already know well and *woodshedding* (or development) of new material. At first you will spend more time learning new material (at least as you learn this new approach). As you slowly master techniques, more time will be spent reviewing, but you don't necessarily have to review everything at every session. Reviewing a concept at least once over the course of a week or even more is usually sufficient. In any case, you should not spend more than half your practice time on review. Spend the majority of time working on these new ways to play old scales as well as completely new material. How much time? As much as you can. A half hour a day is minimal. An hour or more is better. Shoot for two hours or more at least once a week. Keep changing variables of articulation, tempo, note values, dynamics, and timbre, and so on to keep practice interesting. Practice playing descending patterns as much as ascending ones. Always practice with a rhythm source, and practice with a partner as often as possible.

Important learning tip: Repeat any new material for at least two days after it is first learned—or it will be forgotten!

Integrated Musical/Technical Practice: Familiar Tunes

A good way to integrate both musical and technical training is to play familiar tunes by ear every day. For more details, see the *Familiar Tunes* described in *Aural Games* and *Harmony Games*.

Chapter 6
The Art of Accompaniment in Improvisation

One essential skill for performers of improvised music is the ability to assume and trade off roles of soloist and accompanist. This requires considerable sensitivity, practice, and awareness to raise this skill to the level of intuition, but pays great dividends musically in any kind of group improvisation. It also requires a thorough practical knowledge of scales and arpeggios. It is as important for the accompanist to "learn the craft" of being able to freely invent music as it is for the soloist.

The accompanying voice should support the soloist in dynamics, rhythmic activity, density, tessitura, and timbre, and there are many ways to do this (including playing the opposite!).

Some possible accompanying roles:

- Rest. Don't play. Silence can be highly effective at times.

- Long tones. Leave the energy or activity in the solo voice.

- Ostinato. Take a very short idea and repeat it. Certain styles may use characteristic rhythms, syncopations, etc.

- Fill in at the end of phrases.

- Bass line. Playing a low register scale can outline a harmony.

- Drone. Hold a note and let the soloist play over it.

- Imitation. Such forms and techniques as canon or *fugato* work well, but you can make interesting and effective accompaniment material that echoes the solo voice activity.

- Dialog or conversation. Trade off roles, perhaps for a set number of measures.

- Counterpoint. Move when the soloist rests, hold when the soloist moves.

To summarize: match the style of the other voice, or provide contrast.

Homework: Listen actively to as many musical styles as possible and make notes on ways to accompany different melodies.

Accompaniment Do's

- Follow the soloist's lead in tempo, style, dynamics, articulation, etc. In theatrical improvisation this is know as "Yes, and…"—accepting what is given and supporting and continuing the idea.

- Balance the accompanying voice dynamically with the soloist.

- Establish a clear rhythm or pulse (except for drone). If the soloist is playing a characteristic style (e.g., Afro-Cuban), use rhythms from that style. A well-crafted accompaniment may provide both harmony and rhythm, but rhythm is the most important aspect.

- Use (at least occasionally) motives from the solo voice to build accompaniment patterns.

- Listen carefully to the soloist for cues on what to do; for instance, a visual cue indicating when to hand off the soloist role.

Accompaniment Don'ts

- Don't play too loudly. Let the solo voice come through.

- Don't play too much. Leave open space for the solo voice to come through. If there is more than one instrument accompanying, this is doubly true.

- Don't play in the same register as the soloist. Normally the accompaniment line is lower, but occasionally it will play above the melody.

- Match the style and density of the accompaniment to that of the solo voice in the moment; change as the solo voice changes, and be ready to fill or trade roles if the solo voice takes a break.

- Contrasting your accompanying voice with the solo voice is the other option. For example, if the solo is playing a long line, you might play a rapid succession of quick notes underneath (although probably in a different register and not too loudly).

- Be predictable. The soloist can feel confident about zigging if she knows when you are going to zag.

- Be alert and flexible. Be ready to adapt and adjust to the soloist at a moment's notice.

Alternating Roles

When playing in a duo format, practice first trading roles in longer sections. Over time, learn to switch off in smaller units: eight, four, two measures, even one measure, a motif, or a note or two. Varying the trade-off units keeps listening engaging for both performers and audience.

See also *Accompaniment Games*.

Chapter 7

Introduction to the Games

Where's the Music?

A quick skim of the contents of this book might surprise some, as there is almost no music notation. There are several reasons for this: First of all, the approach here is aural, not "literate"; we have all learned to take written notes as "gospel", not to be changed in any way. We are taught that our only job is to deliver what the composer has to say and forget that *we* might also have something to say, and that expressing ourselves will better help us express the music of others. The aural approach encourages discovery, imagination, self-expression, and extrapolation. It provides complementary training to the highly efficient interpretation of written music notation emphasized in traditional musical training.

Second, the somewhat fuzzy instructions given here (as text) are also much more concise than music notation: they can be varied and tweaked in many ways. Conventional notation severely limits what can be shoe-horned into one volume. The more than five hundred "fuzzy" games here can easily become five thousand or more with a modicum of invention and variation. In detailed written notation we would be lucky to fit fifty games into the book, and these would probably be difficult to read, mere skeletal outlines with little possibility for further development.

Another reason to use text instead of notation is to awaken the classical player to the power and potential available outside of conventional notation. Complexity that is all but impossible to record in notation can be effortlessly created by a practiced improviser. This method gets the knowledge into the player; conventional notation leaves it mostly on the paper. The author's dream is for all musicians to become comfortable in improvisation. This would open up new worlds to composers, who could then let the players create much of the complexity rather than trying to do it with conventional notation, which often results in sterile thickets of nearly undecipherable signs, lines, and symbols. A fuzzy description might ask the player to "play something that swells irregularly, with accents falling just ahead and/or behind the beat, switching to long tones whenever the flute does," which is very difficult to notate, but easy to describe or play.

Consider one more anomaly in the original question: in the German language, what we hear (*die Musik*) and is distinguished from the ink on paper (*die Noten*). English sadly lacks this distinction, and the resulting tendency is to think you have *die Musik* when all you really have is *die Noten*. As the saying goes, it is okay to use a finger to point at the moon, but don't mistake the finger for the moon. By not using any *Noten* here, we avoid the confusion and thus have only *die Musik* on which to concentrate.

Improv Games: Why Not Just Play?

The most challenging—and fun—way to improvise is simply to play, listen, and respond to what happens in the moment, just as in conversation. But free improvisation is not to be confused with "playing anything you want." Improvisation of any kind means recognizing a spontaneous challenge and using every available resource to respond immediately and come up with the best possible solution. Anyone can hit a tennis ball with a racket, but acquiring skills and learning more about the game gives players more choices and an improved ability to execute those choices. Anyone can improvise *right now* using the skills they already have, but practicing the elements of the process will lead to better results and greater satisfaction. The restrictions of the games given here also make the matter of deciding what to play much easier and thus less frightening or stressful. The games in this book are designed to help classical players start improvising and work on various skills. Players use the same skills they learn in lessons and classes, but this time, they must understand them "from the inside out."

An improviser can prepare (see Technical Training for Improvisation) in much the same way that a proficient debater would. Speakers must be well versed in the vocabulary, grammar, elocution of their language, in analytical and creative thinking (to be able to make logical connections, spot patterns, and invent new and unusual combinations), as well as know their subject matter in great detail. Debate or even good conversation (as well as sports or games like chess) is a good example of "free improvisation"—knowing a subject well, thinking while doing, acting, reacting, adjusting, then trying again.

In music every musical "puzzle" has multiple solutions. Puzzle solving is, in effect, what we are doing as we listen, imagine, and respond in the moment. To find a satisfying solution, the musician must have sufficient "domain skills" to be able to:

- know what is going on and have the ability to identify instantly by ear the intervals, chords, rhythms, and other elements of style;

- imagine multiple solutions to the puzzle in the moment and make an educated guess at which one is best, and

- realize this solution in a fraction of a second and produce it on the instrument.

This is known as "thinking in music," and it requires considerable practice. **This kind of practice is missing from standard instrumental education, which instead focuses on visual interpretation of music notation.** The purpose of this method in general and these Improvisation Games in particular is to supply a large and varied number of ways to acquire the skills needed in a focused way.

Why "Games"?

Why call them "games"? Why not "drills," "exercises," or "systematic text-based task-specific collaborative extemporaneous musical solo or ensemble performance studies"?

Choosing to describe the activities listed in this book as games is somewhat risky. Contemporary culture often equates effectiveness with an air of seriousness, which often translates to a desiccated, humorless approach where presumed value correlates with syllable count. Never say "Be clear" when you can say "Eschew obfuscation." By this light, musical games can easily be viewed as frivolous, pointless pastimes that must be distinguished from "real" or "serious" study. There is, however, a very good reason to assume the risk of packaging the content here as games rather than drills, and that is because *it best suits the needs of teaching the subject matter.*

Learning improvisation for classical musicians means approaching music in a completely different way, and this represents quite a challenge for both teacher and student. An improviser must engage in experimentation, exploration, and personal discovery of music, instrument, and self. A classical musician learns about history—historical facts, theory, technical drills, and the exact interpretation of written notation. Traditional "literate" studies focus largely on avoiding mistakes at all costs. In improvisation, "mistakes" are players' opportunities to discover things that they might never have considered otherwise. Imagination, insight, intuition, and inventiveness are valued over the exact repetition of a sequence of notes. It is often difficult for classical players to let go of their fear of mistakes. Thus, **using the term "games" helps us lighten up and lets creativity and imagination flow, instead of blocking it by fear of mistakes.** Let us hear from some experts on this subject:

Music students have been, for generations, terrorized about playing the wrong note, making mistakes or making fools of themselves. But if you begin with nonsense, you're already in the realm of the foolish, so there is no problem making a fool of yourself.

—Stephen Nachmanovitch[12]

Make mistakes a requirement. It takes the fear away from not doing things right and makes it fun. When you declare that mistakes are a good thing, then you can relax into the learning process and go with the flow.

—Rachelle Disbennett-Lee[13]

To avoid situations in which you might make mistakes may be the biggest mistake of all.

—Peter McWilliams[14]

Classical music tends to supply us with a false feeling of control, because we feel grounded by our eyes. The security we think we have when reading music is an illusion because we're constantly afraid of making mistakes

—Julie Lyonn Lieberman[15]

Creativity is inventing, experimenting, growing, taking risks, breaking rules, making mistakes, and having fun.

—Mary Lou Cook[16]

The two approaches—literate and aural—are complementary, not mutually exclusive. They balance each other, develop musicianship skills, and promote health and sanity. To achieve the comprehensive musicianship so vital to a contemporary musician, both approaches need to be cultivated to the highest possible level. (See the Comprehensive Musicianship Chart under Part III: Resources.)

---

12   Nachmanovitch, *Free Play.*
13   http://www.coachlee.com/.
14   Peter McWilliams, *Life 101: Everything We Wish We Had learned in Life in School—but Didn't* (Los Angeles: Prelude Press, 1995).
15   Julie Lyonn Lieberman, *The Creative Band & Orchestra* (Huiksi Music, 2003).
16   Mary Lou Cook, environmentalist and educator.

Practicing Improvisation Using the Games

At every step of the way the player can and should spend some time playing "free," but the majority of the player's practice time, both at home and in class, should be spent acquiring and honing the particular domain skills. At home (alone), this means becoming highly fluent in scales and arpeggios (go far beyond simply running up and down the scales), patterns, new scale types, rhythms, timbres (including extended techniques), and more. In working with one or more partners, this means learning to listen acutely to what others play and being able to either imitate it and match the style (harmony, dynamics, articulation, tempo, rhythms, effects, etc.), support it (play in counterpoint, be silent at times, play a rhythmic accompaniment figure), or contrast it (e.g., play a *cantabile* melody over a jagged ostinato figure). This kind of study is closely analogous to learning a new language well enough to carry on a spontaneous conversation. Traditional studies, by contrast, are analogous to reciting text written by someone else.

Free playing is fun and necessary, but this type of playing is not systematic and playing this way exclusively may leave some holes in the player's education. The games in this book focus on one aspect of the needed domain skills, and, as with vitamins, a variety is needed for the musical health of the player. Small group sessions will concentrate at first on the main areas of rhythm, melody, and harmony, with space left for at least one of the other categories, plus one "free" (unplanned) piece each session.

NB: *All of these games should be considered as starters or suggestions, not Holy Writ.* Players are encouraged to adapt and add variations to the games to fit their particular circumstances, and to invent and discover new games in every category (and even invent new categories!). This collection of improvisation games must be considered a beginning, not an end; it invites players to use their imagination and discover. Keep a pencil handy to record new ideas as they occur. And do send a copy of your inventions to the author!

Chapter 8
Improvisation Game Techniques

This section does not contain games per se, but techniques that can be applied to a wide assortment of games.

Rule Number One of Improvisation: always stay in a comfortable zone. Stay calm, stay in control. Play what you know.

Rule Number Two of Improvisation: Break Rule Number One as often as possible.

Percussion Helps

Almost all games are improved by adding some kind of improvised percussion accompaniment (including body percussion and mouth noises).

Sing Sing

Although most games were constructed with an instrument in mind, players can and should try singing many of the games as well.

Dark Music

For warm-ups—or almost any other game—turn out the lights. Playing in the dark (or near-dark) makes you hear much better.

Hands Up!

The *audience* plays a highly important role for improvisers. The following technique should be used early and often to help developing improvisers.

Have the improvisers play with their eyes closed or with their back to the audience. Audience members must also close their eyes, and are instructed to hold up one hand as soon as they find the improvisation becoming static and uninteresting. If the piece starts to get interesting again, they may lower it. When (for instance) three people are holding up their hands at the same time, the Facilitator stops play. All then discuss what might have been done to keep the piece interesting, and start again afterwards. Suggested by Mike Wall.

Variation One: This time the improvisers face the audience. When they see hands start to go up, they must immediately do something to make the piece more interesting. If the number of hands up continues to increase, at some point the Facilitator stops the piece and all discuss what might have been done differently.

Variation Two: *"Keep 'Em in Their Seats."* Improviser may face the audience or not, but the audience now is instructed to stand up and leave the room if/when the piece fails to hold their interest. They should slow down or stop and then move back toward their seat if the improvisation becomes more interesting.

Room Percussion

Instead of typical percussion instruments, everyone must find ways of creating percussive sounds from whatever is in the room: e.g., slapping palms on floors, desks, staplers, books, walls, etc. Use whatever is available.

Quartet Duets, or "A Little Audience Is a Good Thing"

This technique requires an even number of players. Quartets are probably the optimal group size, but larger groups are also possible. Only half the group plays the chosen game while the other half sits and listens carefully to the performers. The idea is that groups play better (or differently) with an audience and that it is difficult to listen while you're playing; the audience can give valuable feedback afterwards as to what worked and what didn't. (Suggested by Mike Wall.)

Specialized Cells

A group is divided up into cells (smaller groups), and each is assigned a different improv game or improv technique (from this section).

Example: Cell One: long tones only. Cell Two: every melody note must be repeated. Cell Three: only extended techniques. Cell Four: only very low notes.

Memory Technique

This is a technique taken from Soundpainting and can be applied to any game. At any point in the improvisation, a player may make the "Memory!" gesture (point to the temple with the forefinger), meaning "memorize what you are doing at this moment"—for instance, an interesting chord or texture. Then later—but not too much later—call up this Memory by tapping the temple again and giving a Play Now gesture of some sort. The next time a player signals Memory, it erases the old one and identifies a new memory. It is possible to have several Memories at once, labeling each by holding up the appropriate number of fingers of the other hand while pointing to the temple.

Do the Rest

This is a common exercise used in learning jazz solos: against any sort of accompaniment built in eight-bar phrases, the soloist plays six bars and rests for two. The rests give the soloist a chance to recover and prepare for the next eight bars, and also gives the audience's ears a break (it's like conversation: it is more interesting when the speaker takes breaks instead of gabbling on nonstop. The accompaniment player is free to fill the last two bars. Also try using different play/rest counts: play four, rest four, play seven, rest one, etc.

Here is an idea from ace improviser Evan Mazunik: to avoid the common mistake of playing on and on without pause, intentionally introduce three silences into the next improvised solo.

As a general rule, players would do well to remember to rest as much as they play and that the larger the group, the less each player should play.

Go For It!

In the interests of creating an encouraging atmosphere, players should make a point of saying (even shouting) encouragements to soloists *during* the piece. Maintain a good-natured banter throughout.

Different Strokes

When playing any drum (or object serving as a drum), use two different kinds of drumheads or drumsticks, e.g., one hard, one soft, to create two timbres instead of one. Experiment with accents and different sticking patterns.

Change It!

This idea comes from the great theater improvisation teacher, Keith Johnstone. A facilitator or group leader may use a signal (verbal or gestural) to indicate to the group performing that

1. the piece has been static for some time and needs to go on to new material.
2. the piece is aimlessly meandering or has too many ideas swirling about and needs to focus on and develop one strong idea.

Groups that do not react and make the requested change may be stopped by the leader (perhaps by giving a sign to hold a note and then cut off).

Variation: The facilitator may also introduce some dramatic event (like a cymbal crash or a clave beat at a different tempo) to 'tilt' the static proceedings and force the participants to create something new.

Contemporaries report that when he was playing the piano, especially when improvising, he became that other human being they would have liked him to be in his daily life. His expression changed; he seemed to become serene... These must have been the moments (often hours) when he reveled in blissful self-forgetfulness, when he severed his connection with the outside world; here he was the unadorned Mozart, who needed no intermediary in order to communicate – no singers, no instrumentalists or fellow musicians, and no bothersome score, either. Here, and perhaps only here, he achieved true pleasure in his own genius; here he transcended himself, becoming the absolute Mozart.

—Wolfgang Hildesdeimer[17]

---

17   *Wolfgang Amadeus Mozart, Idomeneo: 1781–1981: Essays* (München: Piper, 1981).

Chapter 9
Motivic Development Techniques

Note: Motivic Development Techniques are listed separately from the other Improvisation Games Techniques for the sake of clarity.

One way to capture the attention and interest of the audience is to establish and develop a motif or theme, whether the piece is improvised or composed (a composition is just a polished or edited improvisation). Transforming a motif is an essential skill for the improviser. Ultimately, the various types of motivic development must become so ingrained in a player's mind that they can be used seamlessly and automatically, alone or in combination; but it is good to practice each by itself to acquire mastery. A number of the techniques described here can be found in other games and categories, but they are gathered together here for convenience and emphasis.

> *Rules are the beginning, not the end. No one will notice a rule being broken if there's meaning in it.*
>
> —Charles Rochester Young[18]

> *One useful rule is that two rules are more than enough. The unconscious just needs a little external structure with which to crystallize.*
>
> —Stephen Nachmanovitch[19]

> *Limits are an artist's best friend.*
>
> —Frank Lloyd Wright[20]

> *Improvisation is most effective and creative where a simple idea is repeated, varied, extended and creatively expanded.*
>
> —Tony Wigram[21]

---

[18]   From a personal conversation.

[19]   Nachmanovitch, *Free Play.*

[20]   Quoted in Roger Von Oech, *Expect the Unexpected (or You Won't Find It): a Creativity Tool Based on the Ancient Wisdom of Heraclitus* (San Francisco: Berrett-Koehler, 2002).

[21]   Tony Wigram, *Improvisation: Methods and Techniques for Music Therapy Clinicians, Educators, and Students* (London: J. Kingsley Publishers, 2004).

Repetition

The ability to repeat a strong idea that has just been played is one of the most important motivic devices. To practice, get a partner and trade short motifs; the goal is for each player to play back exactly the motif offered. If Player Two misses a note, Player One must replay the motif until Player Two does it correctly. Both players should start simply (start on middle C in the key of C) with three notes using mostly step-wise motion. As players gain proficiency, the motif inventor can add leaps, more notes, and simple rhythms; other keys may be explored, including minor keys and (ultimately) atonality. All parameters (including tempos) can be increased as facility develops; each player is the "trainer" of the other, and each can help the other attain mastery.

Tip: Record the parameters used in each session (tempo, number of notes, widest leaps, key, etc.).

See also:
- Melodic Games
  Gesture
  Echo
  Replay
  Watching T&V
- Aural Games
  Replay
  Play It Again, Sam
  Sing It, Sam
  What You Hear is What You Get (to do)
  Various Call-and-Response games
- Text Games
  Oh Yes, He's…

Mode Change

Once some facility in repetition is attained, the next step is to change modes of a motif or tune. If major, make it minor, or vice-versa. A good way to practice this is to play (daily!) a familiar tune by ear (see *Familiar Tunes* in Resources) and repeat it, changing the mode. All the above Repetition games are good practice—if the motifs contain the third scale degree.

For more Mode Change games, see:

- Aural Games
  Play It Again, Sam, One More Time
  What You Hear is What You Get (to do)
  Familiar Tune
- Harmony Games
  Change of Mode
  Mode Mix

Ornamentation

A quick and easy way to add interest and vary a repeated motif or melody is to embellish or decorate some of the notes, i.e., add auxiliary tones (upper and lower neighbors, etc). Not every style is suitable for ornamentation, but that is left up to the player. Traditional (baroque) ornaments include trills, appoggiaturas, mordents, turns, and acciaccaturas.

See also *Watching T&V* and *Interior Decoration* in Melody Games.

Transposition

Much home practice for improvisation will consist of playing technical material, patterns, and other exercises in all keys. This makes it easier to go to the next step, which is to transpose a short motif to another key after learning to play it back in he original key.

Sequence

Sequences can combine repetition, change of mode, and transposition. Repeat a motif at successively higher diatonic pitch levels (going up the scale). For example, a three-note major motif consisting of scale steps 1–2–3 (whole steps) in sequence becomes (successively) 2–3–4 (now minor: whole-half), 3–4–5 (now modal: half-whole steps), and so on. Playing sequences adds a very strong element of logic and unity to a piece.

Practice playing sequences with arpeggios and short segments of scales.

Sequence Game: Two players. Each player gives the other player a three-note motif. They then play a duet using the motif as much as possible, in both ascending and descending sequence. Players may make the notes of equal rhythmic value or, for more interest, use unequal note values (e.g. long-long-short, short-long-short, short-long-long, long-short-short, etc.).

Variation: Use longer motives, i.e., four or five notes.

See also *Obstinacy* in Melodic Games.

Subtraction

When repeating a motif, take away a note or two from the original.

See also *Twisted Quotes* in Melody Games.

Addition

When repeating a motif, add a note or notes somewhere.

Augmentation

Rhythmic augmentation develops a motif by increasing the note values. For instance, an eighth note becomes a quarter note (or even a half note); a quarter becomes a half note, and so on.

See also *Watching T&V* in Melody Games.

Intervallic augmentation is also possible by increasing the size of the intervals between the notes in a motif.

Example: A half step becomes a whole step; a whole step becomes a third, and so on.

Diminution

Similarly, rhythmic diminution decreases the note values while intervallic diminution decreases the size of the intervals between the notes.

Retrograde

This works best with fairly short and simple motives. Play them in reverse order. Practicing patterns in both ascending and descending forms helps develop this technique.

Example: C–D–E–G becomes G–E–D–C.

Inversion

Inversion is not an easy technique to do on the fly, but practicing patterns in inverse forms helps, e.g., 1–2–3–1 played in ascending sequence becomes the inverted form 3–1–2–3 in descending.

Displacement

To displace a rhythmic motif, add a rest at the beginning or somewhere in the middle. Octave displacement is another option, which is easier on some instruments than others. Here, one or more of the notes in the motif are played an octave higher or lower than the rest.

Motivic Development Combination Games

When players develop a degree of fluency in two or more of these motivic development techniques, they should try to combine several at once. For example, try replaying (repetition) a short motif backwards (retrograde) with longer (augmentation) and ornamented (ornamentation) note values.

> *A creature that plays is more readily adaptable to changing contexts and conditions.*
> *Play as improvisation sharpens our capacity to deal with a changing world.*
> —Stephen Nachmanovitch[22]

---

[22] Nachmanovitch, *Free Play.*

Chapter 10
Quick-Start Improvisation Game Favorites
(in All Categories)

It may take some time to become acquainted with the considerable array of games, and although multiple indices are available, this section allows the (impatient) player(s) to get started right away by providing a selection of games organized by number of players (one to four, five-plus, and large groups).

Note: Games the designation "plus" (e.g., three-plus players) may also be played by more than that minimum number if desired, depending on how the game is set up. Many games may be performed vocally as well as instrumentally, and most incorporate additional players on percussion whether indicated in the instructions or not.

Games for One Player

World = Percussion [Rhythm Games]

One player. While going about your daily life, turn everyday objects into percussion instruments in any way that you can. Tap a groove on the railing as you go down the stairs. Shuffle your feet in time on gravel or leaves. Beat a tattoo on the book you are carrying. Shake a handbag in time. Snap your fingers or clap your hands. Accompany this beat with humming, mouth noises, a spontaneous rhyming (or not) poem about what you see, smell, or hear, or how you feel. Use anything you have or encounter to create rhythms and sounds. When a lot of people are around, you might consider wearing an iPod [turned off] or holding a cell phone up to your ear so that others make allowances for you being musical on the move.

Offbeat Metronome [Rhythm Games]

One player. When practicing scales or other technical materials, *hear* the metronome click on two and four instead of on one and three. Once you get the hang of it, brag to your friends that you have a special metronome that clicks on the offbeats—and then demonstrate. They may want to know where they can get one, too.

Poet Lariat [Rhythm Games]

One player. Use any poem or famous oration as a source of rhythm for an improvisation. Simply play the rhythmic meter of the poem. Keep pitch choices narrow at first; a pentatonic scale would work well.

Swing It [Rhythm Games]

One player. Take any technical exercise (scale, arpeggio, or other pattern), etude, familiar tune (folk song, camp song, pop tune), classical theme or melody, or invent your own, and swing all the eighth notes. If you don't know what swing is, it don't mean a thing, just go and listen (and sing along) to a lot of big band music from the '30s and '40s until the concept of swing becomes clear.

Variation: Do it all again with a friend.

Transformation [Rhythm Games]

One-plus players. Transform any familiar tune by playing it in another meter (and perhaps style). For example, play *Stars and Stripes Forever* as a waltz, *Yankee Doodle* in 5/8, or *America, the Beautiful* in 7/8.

Scale Accents [Accent Games]

One player. When practicing daily scales and arpeggios, add various accent patterns, e.g., accent every other note, every 3rd note, or every 4th note. For a challenge, accent every 5th note or more. The most interesting patterns are those that do *not* coincide with the meter, such as ternary accents in duple meter or vice-versa.

Additional ideas: Combine odd/even accent groups: e.g. 2+3, 3+2, 3+3+2, 2+2+3, 3+2+2.

                      Irregular accents. Improvise accent groupings as you move up and down the scale, sometimes duple, sometimes triple, sometimes long groupings.

                      Combine accent groupings with various articulations: all *staccato*, all *legato*, combinations of legato and staccato within accent groupings.

                      Double the fun and make it a duet. Share a pulse. Try to play exactly the same accent/articulation patterns as your partner while being independent in choice of accent groupings.

Rainbow Scales [Melody Games]

One player. Play any one-octave scale up and down (only!), but instead of playing it the usual colorless way in straight eighth notes, add all kinds of variation: change the note values, accents, dynamics, articulation, and/or tempo; add rests. In short, make music out of it. Make the scale as musical and interesting as possible.

Variation: Do the same with two players, playing both independently and in relation to each other (e.g., one player may lead as the other imitates, mirrors, or matches style; or both intermittently lead and follow).

Far Out [Melody Games]

One player (or two; you may also add percussion *ad lib.*). Improvise an atonal melody. Emphasize dissonant intervals such major and minor seconds, tritones, and major and minor sevenths. Give the atonal melody coherence by using repetition, sequence, and dynamic phrasing.

Familiar Tune [Harmony Games]

One to four players. This game has so many musical vitamins and minerals that it should be done daily; but the best reason to do it is because it is both challenging and fun. Choose a familiar tune, something that each player knows already *very* well (examples: a children's song, folk song, Christmas carol, etc.) and try to play it by ear. After all players can find the melody easily, one or more players may play the melody while the others play any of the following (all by ear, of course!):

1. Chord roots
2. Harmony part(s)
3. Countermelody
4. Variations on the melody

It is best to add them one at a time. Give everyone a chance to try them all if possible. Then turn everyone loose to play any of the "roles" they like. Do this in an easy key (e.g. C major), and then gradually try it in all keys until they are *all* easy keys.

> *Variation:* Begin again and switch modes, i.e., playing the tune in minor (or in major if the tune was minor). For the daring: add dissonant notes to the harmony.

Play It Again, Sam [Aural Games]

One player. Improvise a bit of music, anything from a short motif (three to four notes) to an entire phrase. Immediately play it back as exactly as possible. If it is too long or complex to remember exactly, shorten and/or simplify. As this facility develops, gradually increase the complexity (key, tonal/atonal, rhythm/meter, etc.) and length.

Fanfare [Technique Games]

One to three players. Pick an arpeggio of any chord type in any key: major, minor, augmented, diminished, etc. Play alone or as a duet (or trio) using notes from the chord (may include the seventh or ninth) in fanfare-style figures (duple, triple, or both).

Dirge [Style Games]

One player. Create the saddest piece possible.

> *Suggestions:* Minor keys, extended techniques, low register, long tones, dynamic contrasts, dissonance, and/or slow tempo. Give the piece a name (as you do all your pieces) and/or dedicate it to a dearly departed one.

> *Variation:* Add a second player to provide accompaniment.

Holiday Time [Style Games]

One-plus players. Invent music that illustrates a holiday.

Example: Create the Fourth of July in music. or play spooky Halloween music (turn out the lights!). Make up music that captures the feeling of Christmastime, or make a musical Valentine. Improvise music that depicts Thanksgiving from either the pilgrims' or turkey's point of view.

Variation: Pick lesser-known holidays to celebrate in music:

> Festival of Sleep Day (January 3)
> National Candied Orange Peel Day (May 4)
> National Accordion Awareness Month (June)
> National Talk Like a Pirate Day (September 19)
> National Cashew Day (November 23);
> See http://library.thinkquest.org/2886/ for more ideas or invent
>   your own holidays:
>   The Day My Car Died (April 7)
>   Musk Ox Appreciation Day (July 31)

Shower Music [Miscellaneous Games]

Typically one player. Your daily shower is your chance to sing your heart out and sound terrific. Feel free to sing the oldies, but use the aural enhancement to create new music as well. Sing about the day, about dirt and soap, about the feeling of hot water and being clean. Sing about a broken heart, about new love, about the sun coming up today. Make it raw, real, and raucous. Do it every day!

Duet for One [Miscellaneous Games]

One player. Piano is highly suggested for this game but it also works on guitar, strings, or mallet percussion. Improvise on the piano while singing exactly the same line in unison. Experiment with leaps, syncopations, repetition of motifs, and other challenges. (Source: Charles Young.)

Games for Two Players

Warm-Up Long Tones [Warm-Up Games]

Two-plus players. While alert and relaxed, play a string of long tones of random lengths and pitches. Use comfortable, varied dynamics, including *crescendi* and *decrescendi*. Leave varying amounts of space between tones; one way is to rest as much as you play (this is essential in larger groups). Try this game freely choosing notes from either major or minor scales, major or minor seventh or ninth arpeggios, diminished arpeggios, or major or minor pentatonic scales. Explore different registers and timbres.

Ostinato [Rhythm Games]

Two-plus players. Player One begins a short ostinato (a short motif continually repeated), then other players enter with complementary ostinati until all are playing.

> *Hint:* Incorporate space in the ostinati to leave room for other parts to come through).

Then go around again and have each player change her ostinato and signal the next player to begin. After the second time around, Player One signals for everyone to finish on a whole note.

> *Note:* The ostinati need only have a common eighth note pulse; a common meter is not necessary.
>
> *Variation:* Players may change their ostinati at will.

What's in a Name? [Rhythm Games]

Two to four players construct a piece based on the rhythms of their names. Use of motivic development techniques (augmentation, diminution, etc.) is encouraged.

Son of Glacier Music [Melody Games]

Two to four players play long pulseless tones in C major. Move up or down to a new note by diatonic scale step (no leaps). Leave a bit of space in between the long notes and listen to the chords created. Decide instinctively whether to ascend, descend or stay the same.

> *Variation 1:* Try in other keys.
>
> *Variation 2:* Try with no set key.
>
> *Variation 3:* Try in the minor mode.
>
> *Variation 4:* Have each player pick a different key independently.
>
> *Variation 5:* Have some other players play ostinati on percussion instruments.
>
> *Variation 6:* Use note values of whole and half notes exclusively.

Drone [Melody Games]

Two-plus players. One or more players play a unison low note as a drone. Each player in turn should experiment playing a slow solo over the drone, noting the effect created by each scale step. Try all the major scales over the drone (e.g., over a C drone, try the major scales of C, D♭, D, E♭, E, etc.), but be very aware of the scale step you are playing.

Pulsed Drone [Melody Games]

Two-plus players. Same as in *Drone*, above. One or more players play steady quarter notes on C (or any given pitch). Player Two solos over this, only this time Player Two can have some fun playing with rhythm, e.g., syncopating against the steady beat.

Variation 1:   Leave out some of the quarter notes, e.g., play quarters only on:

          1, 3

          1, 2, 4

          1, 3, 4

          1, 4

          1, 2, 3

          2, 3, 4

Variation 2:   Give the pulsed drone some kind of catchy/funky/jazzy rhythm.

Third Time's A Charm [Melody Games]

Two players improvise a duet in a major key (preferably one of the most unfamiliar). Players alternate between solo and accompaniment roles.

Special limit: Players introducing a new idea in a solo role are not allowed to develop that idea or to bring in any new ideas until it has been repeated at least three times.

Old and New [Melody Games]

Two to three players. Player One plays any solo from his instrument's literature, looping the selection after one or two phrases. Player Two improvises a second part to make a duet. A third part may be added, but Player Three should limit this part to accompaniment only.

Tension/Release [Melody Games]

Two-plus players. Two or more players improvise a duet in a major key, switching between solo and accompaniment roles as signaled by the solo player. *Soloists must begin and/or end phrases on a "wrong" note,* and then resolve it to a chord tone. Here, "wrong" means tension or a dissonant note. In major, mild dissonance can be obtained using scale steps 2, 4, 6, and 7; in C: D, F, A, B. For sharper dissonance, begin on ♭2, ♯2, ♯4, and ♭6 (in C: D♭, D♯, F♯, A♭).

Crunch Time [Harmony Games]

Two players. One player plays any familiar tune (e.g., "Mary Had a Little Lamb," "Twinkle, Twinkle, Little Star") in any chosen key. Player Two plays simple triads on piano or with mallet percussion to accompany, except that instead of the third of the chord, the accompanist plays a ♭2, 2, 4, ♯4, or ♭6. Use any kind pulsed pattern for the chord or arpeggiation of the triad.

One-Four-Five [Harmony Games]

Two to four players. The I–IV–V⁷ progression is very common in popular and folk music. Set up a bass line and/or rhythm background (e.g., guitar or piano chords) of one measure in 4/4 for the I and IV chords with two measures for the V⁷. Percussion is a welcome addition. Each player solos in turn over the progression, taking care that each "chorus" is different from the last in some way (melody, ornaments, rests, rhythms, dynamics, articulation, etc.). Add different styles (e.g., Latin) *ad libitum*. Soloists make a silent gesture to the next in line to indicate they are done.

Variation 1:	The accompaniment player may change chords at any time, not necessarily following any set number of measures.
Variation 2:	The chord player may change meter (e.g., 4/4 to 3/4) at will.

In both variations the soloist must simply listen and adjust to the change.

Oom Pah March [Bass Line Games]

Two players. One player plays an oom pah rhythm on steps one and five on beats one and three of a measure in cut time. Player Two improvises a march over this accompaniment. Try different kinds of marches: slow, fast, quirky, and/or minor.

Variation 1:	Give the oom pah more interesting rhythms, such as the 3+3+2 clave or other Latin rhythms.
Variation 2:	Have the bass descend on scale steps 1–7–6–5 (in C: C–B–A–G).

Call-and-Response: Basic [Aural Games]

Two-plus players. Player One plays one measure in 4/4; all other players echo Player One exactly in the subsequent measure. Player One should begin very simply and very gradually add more challenging material tonally and rhythmically. If players miss any notes, Player One should repeat the measure, and perhaps make the addition of more difficult material more gradual. Start in C major, and then begin again in another key.

Squiggle Quartet [Nontraditional Score Games]

Two-plus players. Players make quick, rapid squiggles of any sort on pieces of blank paper with pens, pencils, or colored markers. They immediately exchange pieces of paper and play the "piece" without discussion.

X-Tech Ostinati [Timbre Games]

Two to four players. Each player plays an ostinato (with a shared pulse) using an extended technique. Stay with it for a while, then, at some point, change to a new extended technique.

Variation 1:	One player solos over the ostinato.
Variation 2:	Any player may play a long tone between ostinati.
Variation 3:	Add a section of pulseless extended technique playing.
Variation 4:	All players switch rapidly back and forth between as many extended technique sounds and noises as possible.

Guess the Machine [Depiction Games]

Two to four players. Depict a machine (rocket ship, clock, sports car, biplane, typewriter, cell phone, conveyor belt, toaster, espresso machine, tractor, submarine, Mars rover, bicycle, etc.) through music. Listeners must guess what the machine is when the piece is complete.

News Story [Miscellaneous Games]

Two-plus players. Players scan the newspaper for an interesting news story. Capture the mood or message of the article in music.

Location, Location [Miscellaneous Games]

Two players. Player One plays a chord (start with major or minor) at the piano (or guitar, harp, etc.) without revealing to Player Two what key it is in. Player Two, who may only play this game if she does not have perfect pitch, plays a loud, ringing, accented whole tone of her choice. The goal is for Player Two to discern as quickly as possible (instantly is the goal) what scale degree (or altered scale degree) her note is in Player One's random chord and then resolve it by step or half step to the nearest chord tone by diatonic step or by arpeggio to the tonic.

Example:	If Player One's chord is C and Player Two plays an A♭, Player Two hopefully hears that she is playing the ♭6 of the chord and should move down a half step to G, continuing by step or arpeggio to the tonic C. Repeat many times and switch roles after a bit.
Variation:	Player Two may elect to take some time arriving at the tonic, perhaps repeating the first note and its resolution to a chord tone and then continuing the melody in a satisfying manner until final resolution on the tonic.

Free Play Game No. 1 [Miscellaneous Games]

Two players. Improvise a piece one minute long. Have a clear beginning, middle, and end. Player One uses long-short-short rhythms; Player Two uses short-short-long rhythms. Vary the registers. Rest occasionally.

Ideas:	1. Agree on a key.
	2. Don't discuss the key; find a common key as you play.
	3. Don't discuss the key; pick a key independently and stick to it.
	4. Avoid key centers (or visit them only briefly), playing mostly atonally.
	5. Decide on a style or mood ahead of time (march, love song, etc.).
	6. Decide on a style or mood after the piece begins.
	7. Repeat the process with three or four players.
	8. Add other players on percussion, playing mostly ostinati. Percussion is like garlic: it adds a terrific spice to the mix, and there is seldom an upper limit.

Fancy Twinkle [Improv Set-Ups]

Two players. Player One plays "Twinkle Twinkle" in the key most unfamiliar to him, and repeats it many times. Player Two improvises an elaborate countermelody against it.

Variation: *Repeat in a minor key.*

Timing Is Everything [Miscellaneous Games]

Two-plus players. With one person as timer, play a series of short improvisations for a specified number of seconds: e.g. 10", 15", 20", 30", 45". They may have pre-planned titles (e.g. Adjective/ Noun) or be purely unplanned (i.e., figure out the rules as you go). Every piece—however short— should have a beginning, middle, and end.

Games for Three Players

Hold/Move Chamber Music [Melody Games]

Three-plus players may play *Hold/Move*. Each player plays chorale-style melodies consisting mainly of quarter notes plus some passing eighths. This creates a contrapunal texture, which may sound something like a Bach chorale—or not. Experiment using a pre-set major or minor key and then no pre-set key.

Try to Remember... [Aural Games]

Three to six players. All sit in a circle. Player One plays a C. Player Two plays the C, plus any note in the C major scale. Player Three plays both of these notes and adds another note in the C major scale. Continue building the string of notes; if a player can't quite remember the sequence of notes, the last player repeats the line until the new player can remember and play it. At some point the string will be too long for most to remember, but see how far you can get. For groups with really good ears (i.e., those who can remember strings of fifteen to twenty or more notes), go on to repeat this game in other keys and/or other scale types (any kind of minor, dominant seventh, whole tone, blues, diminished, etc.).

Scat! [Timbre Games]

Three-plus players. Using voices only, create a peppy ostinato groove using short scat (nonsense) syllables. Take turns soloing over the groove, singing in long tones.

The King's Challenge [Storytelling Games]

Three players. The King has advertised far and wide that his daughter, the princess (Player One), has never laughed. The person or persons who can make her laugh will get ten million gold ducats and half his kingdom. One small detail: if you fail, you will be hanged. Who (i.e., Players Two and Three) will accept the challenge?

America, the Beautiful [Improv Set-Ups]

Three players. Players One, Two, and Three play "America the Beautiful" in an agreed-upon key without rehearsal. After the first time through, they improvise a new piece based on motives from America.

Variation: Each player selects a key independently.

Askew March [Improv Set-Ups]

Three players. Players One, Two, and Three invent a march in B♭ for a band of people who might have celebrated the big game a bit too much the night before. Extra players may join in on percussion, especially whatever percussion-like objects can be found in the room.

Salieri's Test [Improv Set-Ups]

Three players. Salieri has told the Emperor that your application as court composer should be rejected because you cannot improvise interesting variations given a series of notes. You must prove him wrong. Your notes are C–E–F♯–G–A–B♭. The Emperor grants your request for two backup players of your choice.

ABAC [Improv Set-Ups]

Three players. The form is ABAC and the instrumentation is for voice only. Section A consists of long tones. A signal given by Player One leads to the B section, which is sparse and uses extended techniques only. A signal by Player Two leads back to section A. Player Three signals the shift to section C, which is the coda. There is free choice of style or sounds by all players, but they must relate in some way.

Individual Stories [Improv Set-Ups]

Three players: Player One plays only in major, Player Two only in minor, and Player Three only chromatically. Keys are selected individually. As in all pieces, there should be a beginning, middle, and end. There should also be a switching of solo/accompaniment roles as well as some kind of motivic development. Listen to each other for strong ideas and use them in your improvisation as well.

This New Old Man [Improv Set-Ups]

Three players. Player One plays a very slow version of "This Old Man" in B major. Player Two plays a rhythmic ostinato accompaniment figure that is changed occasionally in small ways. Player Three solos over this, occasionally inflecting scale tones (i.e., adding flats or sharps).

Games for Four Players

Tension/Resonance [Warm-Up Games]

Four-plus players. All eyes are closed. Each player of the group plays the standard tuning note (concert A), choosing the moment to enter individually. Players begin to branch out independently, moving by step or half step to a new note. If the resulting tone feels resonant with the chord of the moment, hold it. If there is tension, change to another note (by step or half step). As the chord changes, the once-resonant note may become a dissonance. Wind players pick a new note after each breath. (Source: Ed Sarath.)

The Big Machine [Rhythm Games]

Four to eight players. Player One repeats a rhythmic noise paired with a movement or gesture using the hands, arms, body, head, etc. Player Two moves close to Player One and does a different noise a nd movement. One by one, the other players also become "machine parts," moving close to each other. When all have joined, the Leader gives a signal and the machine hisses to a stop, with all "parts" slowly collapsing in a heap on the floor.

Echo [Melody Games]

Four-plus players. This works well with a circle of players. Player One plays one note. The player on Player One's right—Player Two—echoes exactly what Player One plays. Continue on around the circle; but if Player Two happens to play something different, this becomes the new note (or interval) to be imitated. This game can be played with different restrictions depending on the level of the players. As players become more adept, the speed of imitation may become quicker. Use the major scale to start; as players become more proficient, try other scale types, e.g., minor, pentatonic, whole tone, diminished, blues, etc.

Variation 1:	Two notes: first a step apart, then expand to larger intervals.
Variation 2:	Three notes, e.g., C–E–G or C–D–E.
Variation 3:	Five notes, e.g., C–D–E–F–G or C–D–E–G–A or C–E♭–F–G–B♭
Variation 4:	Six notes. Start using some easy-to-remember first notes (stepwise or triadic); add more complex interval combinations as proficiency develops.
Variation 5:	More notes. How many can you add?
Variation 6:	Add inflections (e.g., a gliss or slide into the note).
Variation 7:	Change timbre (half-valve, harmonics, etc.).

Versatility [Melody Games]

Four-plus players use, for example, a marimba, voice, piano, and some kind of percussion (*djembe*, bongos, shaker, *claves*, etc.) and improvise a piece. After about a minute, players switch instruments one by one. Continue until everyone has had a chance to play all the instruments. Finish on the instrument on which you began.

Contrast Game [Form Games]

Four-plus players. Player One plays a short phrase. Player Two responds with a phrase that contrasts as much as possible in some way, e.g., note values, dynamics, tempo, texture, register, style, timbre, or meter, and continue the process.

Round Robin [Aural Games]

Four-plus players. The group sits in a circle. Player One plays a three-note motif (or cell). Player Two (to Player One's right) must imitate this exactly, and so on around the circle. The second time around, Player One creates a new four-note motif. Continue until the motif is too long to remember.

Hint: Keep the motifs simple until the aural/technical skills of the group develop; then gradually add complexity, new keys, wider intervals, challenging rhythms, etc. For a highly talented group, edge toward atonality.

Nontraditional Score I [Nontraditional Score Games]

Four-plus players. Each player goes somewhere in the building and makes a score of what she hears using any kind of made-up graphic notation (e.g., squiggles, dots, slashes, geometric figures, etc.). No standard music notation is allowed. Scores should be constructed on a single sheet of paper. Time is measured left to right; ambient noises (e.g., fan whooshing, car door slamming, people talking, neon lights humming, footsteps, bus stopping outside, laughter, etc.) are marked from top to bottom. Return to the room after ten minutes.

Four or five players now "play" each score, independently deciding which line to play and how to play it. The interpretations need *not* have any correspondence to the original noise.

Suggestions: Have different groups of players play the same scores.

Have players play the same piece again, but differently.

Exchange scores and play again.

Variation: Have players write words and/or short phrases on the sheet instead of drawing, or have some players write words and others draw.

Freeform Conducting [Conducting Games]

Four-plus players. Player One conducts in any manner she desires: light-heartedly, heavy-handedly, in three, four, or seventeen, cueing solos or accents, throwing in cut-offs and entrances at will. Players must do their utmost to give the conductor everything/anything she asks for. The conductor may also appoint anyone in the ensemble to come up and take over as the new conductor at any time. Continue until all are exhausted.

Variation: The conductor may also shout additional information ("C major! No, Minor! *Staccatissimo!* Lowest register! Voice only! Everyone hum! Brass be quiet!") along with the gestures.

Feelings [Energy/Mood Games]

Four-plus players. The group brainstorms a list of emotions, moods, emotional or energy states, and the like. The list should have at least a dozen terms; include both positive (love, pity, proud, eager, jolly, bold) and negative (lethargic, regretful, timid, frightened, crazy, hateful, angry, lonely) terms. Don't edit, but write down anything the group comes up with without worrying whether it fits exactly. This list is a resource for the players to choose from, but any player may choose a word not on the list at any time if inspiration hits.

The play: the group is seated in a circle. Player One mentally selects a term and creates music that embodies the emotional term. Player Two listens for a moment, then plays music that either matches or reflects Player One's. They continue for a short time (approximately twenty seconds), then find an ending. Player Two then selects an emotion and plays music embodying the feeling for Player Three. The process is repeated until all have played.

Ad Music [Depiction Games]

Four players. Player 1 has spent some time at home going through various kinds of magazines (Vogue, Field and Stream, The National Inquirer, Entomologist Monthly, Sports Illustrated, National Geographic, etc.) cutting out the most graphically interesting advertisements. Two, three, or four players sit or stand before music stand as Player 1 places an ad before each player as a score. At a signal from Player One, they all begin, each playing her advertisement. During the playing of the piece, Player One may elect to switch ads between players, replace any ad with a new one, or rip an ad in half.

Size Matters [Miscellaneous Games]

Four-plus players. The ensemble begins and ends without any planning; rules are made on the way. The only requirement is length: make this a *long* piece.

Options: 7-8'; 15', 30', 45'[!]. Tell a story! Strive for contrasts! Listen! Imitate! Spend time not playing to vary the texture. Develop motifs! Be dramatic! Consider unity (be the same) and variety (be different). Enjoy the journey. Find a satisfying ending.

Games for Five or More Players

Accents I [Accent Games]

Six-plus players. Half the group (Group One) establishes a solid quarter note beat in 4/4 using a drum, desk, cardboard box, or even the floor, using drumsticks or just hands. The other half of the group (Group

Two) plays eighth notes over the quarter note pulse. When Group Two is solid and comfortable playing the eighths, players may then gradually introduce accents, first with the dominant hand, then later with the non-dominant hand.

Practice accenting the strong beats (one and three), then the weak beats (two and four) with each hand in turn. After Group Two has acquired some experience and control of accenting with each hand, switch roles with Group One.

Accents II [Accent Games]

Six-plus players. Repeat *Accents I*, this time in 6/8 time with two groups of three eighths in a measure. Note that the hand playing the accent changes each [dotted quarter] beat (**L**RL **R**LR). Spend some time on this until it feels completely automatic and natural. Then have the rest of the group (even if it is only one player) lay down a solid pulse of beats while you accent the after beats only (tap all the beats, but accent only the after beats). Over a rock-steady (but not too loud) accompaniment of dotted quarter notes from the other drummers, improvise a solo characterized by a mix of regular and irregular accents. Play all night; trade off at will.

Conducting a Chorale [Conducting Games]

Five-plus players. Player One conducts each note of an improvised chorale, played by four players (this is "Shapeline Conductor" in Soundpainting). Players may add passing tones. Start with a key; then try free choice of key. With practice, the conductor can add dynamics, swells, and so on. This may be done entirely vocally as well.

Floating Duet [Texture Games]

Eight-plus players. This game comes from the Soundpainting gesture "Coming and Going," and is a useful way for large groups to play without getting too dense. Players enter and exit at will, trying to keep approximately two voices going at all times. Players do not have to wait until someone drops out; it is permissible to charge in and "force" one player to drop out. Be bold: when the texture thickens, drop out; when it is too thin, join.

Variations: make a different number of voices the goal: 1, 3, 4, or 5.

Bricolage [Composition Games]

[*Bricolage* is making do with what you have, i.e., composing with found percussion.]

Five players (a leader plus quartet). Each member of the quartet brings from home: shop, kitchen or household objects that can produce some kind of sound. Examples: a power drill, towel, stapler, umbrella, bowl and spoon, rice in Tupperware, crinkly plastic, etc. The leader has previously invented interlocking ostinato rhythms for each player and teaches each one in turn aurally. The Leader, conducting, brings them in one by one. When all are playing, leader points to a soloist, who abandons the ostinato and plays freely and extravagantly against the it. Each player becomes the soloist in turn. The Leader signals a final "hit" to end the piece.

Once Upon a Time [Depiction Games]

Five-plus players: One speaker plus four-plus players and/or conductor (optional). The audience contributes a protagonist, setting, and a problem.

One player makes up a story based on these elements, leaving space for the other players to invent appropriate music to illustrate the text. A conductor may be useful to cue the players and/or select who is to play each excerpt.

Teddy's Funeral [Storytelling Games]

Five players. Player One plays a one-handed ostinato on piano in A minor for the funeral of a teddy bear. The mournful solo reminiscing about poor Teddy is sung by Player Two. Players Three, Four, and Five provide background humming.

Dragon Tale [Storytelling Games]

Five players. Players One and Two alternate telling a fairy story with a beginning, middle, and end (speaking part). The story ends differently than one might expect.

- Player Three is a handsome prince.
- Player Four is the fair maiden.
- Player Five is the ferocious dragon.
- Any player may add necessary sound effects along the way. This is a great chance to try out some extended techniques!

Elegy [Improv Set-Ups]

Seven players. Brass players One and Two play with mutes and make up an interlocking ostinato. Player Three plays an introduction in Af minor for a plaintive song about the death of a beloved goldfish sung by Player Four. Players Five and Six, directed by Player Seven, sing a long tone or drone background.

Games for Large Groups

Universe Symphony [Rhythm Games]

Twelve-plus players—as many as will fit in the room. Charles Ives's magnum opus was his *Universe Symphony*, which survives through a heap of sketches and fragments. Several brave souls have put together (very different) performance versions of it. What we want to borrow for this game is the idea of a huge percussion ensemble that "plays the pulse of the cosmos"; rhythms that cycle over and over throughout the whole movement. Find a recording and listen to it to get an inkling of the possibilities, and then form a large percussion ensemble with at least half of the class or group and create a cycling rhythmic pattern. The rest of the group may play an extended improvisation independently of the percussion that calls up every improvisation/musical technique in the book: long tones, extreme registers, extended techniques, varying densities (including silence), random hits, vocal sounds, and so on. Play for as long as you are able – aim for an hour if possible. The group can decide whether it wants to end with a bang or a whimper.

Emotional Symphony [Depiction Games]

Six to twelve players. Players are assigned different emotions (fear, love, grief, joy, etc.) and must depict them on their instruments. A conductor cues the entrances, and may have the emotions played one at a time or simultaneously. This game may also be done entirely vocally.

Ritual [Miscellaneous Games]

Eight-plus players. Each player creates an ostinato using either mouth noises, body percussion, vocal sounds, any combination of these, or an instrument. Start very softly. The ostinato doesn't have to be continuous; leave some silences. Every so often (but not too often) each player may have an "outburst"—a brief, loud, frantic episode of chaos and noise—and then return to the ritual ostinato. Make the outburst *extreme* in contrast to the group sound, and avoid making an outburst at the same time as another player. Very gradually increase the dynamic level. Take time with this; there is no hurry. Outbursts gradually begin to overlap and become longer. At some point, the noise level will be very loud and the outbursts will become almost continuous. At this point, the Leader signals the group to begin to find some kind of common pulse, synchronizing their sounds. When this is accomplished, the group maintains the synchronized sound as the dynamic level very slowly fades to nothing. When the group reaches silence, everyone freezes for a few moments to let the mood slowly fade away.

Cave Celebrations [Miscellaneous Games]

Eight-plus players. Vocal game for a large group. Player One embodies a cave man who has just returned from a hunt; he boasts of his exploits in a guttural, rhythmic song-chant in a made-up language. One by one the group joins the chant. The volume, energy, and motion gradually increase until a frenzy is reached at top volume. At a signal from Player One, all suddenly go silent. The piece ends with Player One singing a low tone on a scat syllable—all join in and hold for the length of one breath.

Combination No. 1 [Extended Combination Games]

Twelve-plus players. A combination of *Accents*, *Drone*, *Long Tones*, and *Group Point to Point*. The form is ABA'C (coda).

SECTION A:
- **Group One** (six-plus players) plays steady eighth notes at a moderate tempo on a variety of drums or drum-like instruments, which may include found percussion (e.g., noisemakers from the kitchen, shop, bathroom, office) and body percussion. Those with the deepest drums may

beat half notes. After a while, players may decide on a repeating accent pattern. This may be one accented hit every so often (e.g. every ten, six, five, four, three, or two beats. Don't try to accent every beat! Other possibilities: combine 2+3, 3+2, or 2+2+3 accent patterns. These patterns may continue or may be isolated by stretches of steady, unaccented eighths. It is also possible to accent two notes in a row, followed by a stretch of unaccented notes. Finally, any instrument may be silent for a stretch.

- **Group Two** plays a low drone. The group may synchronize (i.e. find each other on a common pitch) or not.
- **Group Three** sings long tones in the middle register. They may have a common key and a conductor who uses hand gestures to indicate relative pitch level (high-middle-low).
- **Group Four** (if there is one) uses any instrument or voice to issue sharp hits or stabs of very short, loud notes that are cued by a conductor (or player acting as one).

SECTION B:
- This section is completely free, except that only one or two groups may play at a time; these groups are indicated by a Leader or conductor. They play as long as the Leader is pointing at them and are silent otherwise.

SECTION A':
- Repeat Section A. At a signal from the Leader or Player One, go to the (brief) Coda.

CODA:
- Everyone plays in their lowest register some kind of trill-esque, bumble-bee sound and progresses quickly to their highest range indicated with a hand gesture by the Leader, increasing in volume until the Leader gives a cut-off.

Combination No. 6 [Extended Combination Games]

A combination of mixed meters, *Accents V, Chant(?), Pointillism, Free* and *Sparse Texture*.
Many players (sixteen-plus). Form: ABA'.

SECTION A:
- **Group One:** Player One plays straight quarter notes at ♩=ca. 72 on any large drum (or drum-like object), accenting every fourth beat. Player Two does the same (a drum is recommended, but the instrument is negotiable), but accents every third beat. Player Three does the same with a smaller drum, accenting every fifth beat. If additional players are available, they accent every second, seventh, eleventh, or thirteenth beat respectively.
- **Group Two:** Player One of Group Two plays steady eighth notes on a smaller percussion instrument, accenting every fourth note. Player Two does the same, but accents every third note. Player Three does the same, accenting every fifth note. As with Group One, more players may be added.
- **Group Three** includes a large group of players who either sing or play instruments capable of holding sustained notes (e.g., no pianos, marimbas, cymbals, guitars, etc.). This group floats freely in D minor Dorian and a soloist chooses which long note in the scale to play, and when; all others must pay attention and follow the leader by changing to the new note as directed. There will be a delay as all find the leader's pitch. This is okay.

- **Group Four** is composed mainly of instruments that play short notes well (piano, marimba, *clave*, guitar, wood block, *kalimba*, etc.). One person is designated as the leader (perhaps at random) and chooses to make brief, intense, but widely spaced flurries of short random hits.

These four groups enter one by one and play for a considerable period.

SECTION B:
- At a signal from the leader of Group Four, the entire group abandons the roles described here and plays freely, the one restriction being that each player must rest for approximately five times as long as she plays. Continue in this way for a while.

SECTION A':
- At some point, the leader of Group Four signals the return of the beginning of the piece. After all have joined and play has gone on for some time, the leader of Group Four gives one more signal to indicate that all players should wind down and stop within the next three minutes, each player choosing when. Players who have stopped should simply sit quietly and listen, eyes closed. When all players have stopped, everyone sits motionless for thirty seconds, then eyes are opened, everyone breathes deeply, smile, stands up, stretches, and go on with life.

Chapter 11
Warm-Up Games

Remember: Almost all games, including Warm-Ups, are improved by adding some kind of improvised percussion accompaniment (including body percussion and mouth noises). Also: although most games were constructed with an instrument in mind, players can and should try many of the games vocally as well.

The first notes I play every day are simple, abstract, improvised warm-ups, not industrious routines full of structure and repetition. What's important is how things feel, not whether I dutifully slog through my daily dozen. Scales and arpeggios, played at a good clip are not warm-ups at all, but feel much more like preliminary performances. Just as athletes warm up their bodies before an event, musicians need a good leisurely getting-reacquainted-with-the-instrument warm-up before attempting any sort of measurable result, such as a scale, arpeggio, or specific exercise.

—William Westney, *The Perfect Wrong Note*

I warm up by playing [i.e. creating] music.

—jazz hornist Arkady Shilkloper[23]

Warm-Up Long Tones

Two-plus players. While alert and relaxed, play a string of long tones, random both in length and pitch choice. Use comfortable but varied dynamics, including *crescendi* and *decrescendi*. Leave varying amounts of space between tones; one way is to rest as much as you play (this is essential in larger groups). Try choosing notes freely from either major or minor scales, major or minor seventh or ninth arpeggios, diminished arpeggios, or major or minor pentatonic scales. Explore different registers and timbres.

Feel the Beats

Two players. This game works best between two adjustable-pitch instruments. Players select a pitch and start in unison. Then one player varies the pitch slightly. Feel the "beats" that arise from the mis-tuning. Vary the pitch and feel the change in the speed of the beats. Experiment with different degrees of out-of-tuneness, occasionally going back to a beatless in-tune unison.

---

23   Personal conversations with the author.

Warm-Up Interval Piece

One to four players. It is always a good idea to *make music* during practice (as opposed to running through routine exercises), even (or especially) during warm-ups. In this specific application of long tone warm-ups, choose two to four intervals and make up a slow piece. This game is very good for one player, but can also be done with two, three, or even four players at once, who may either agree upon the same variation (listed below) or may select independently.

Suggestions: Vary the number of beats (♩=60) of each long tone from two to nine (or more) beats.

Don't forget to put some emotion into your music. Add some heartfelt dynamics, *crescendi* and *decrescendi*, and silences.

You may discontinue a line at any point, rest, and then begin anew some time later. For example, the line may lead to the top of the staff. Hold it out, rest for four beats, then begin again on middle C.

All of the variations below may use whole and/or half steps occasionally as transitions between the main interval(s).

Variation 1: **Atonal One:** major or minor sevenths and tritones.

Variation 2: **Atonal Two:** fourths and tritones.

Variation 3: **Atonal Three:** minor ninth (♭9) and tritone.

Variation 4: **Heroic:** fourths and fifths.

Variation 5: **Dolce:** major thirds.

Variation 6: **Romantic:** major and minor sixths.

Variation 7: **Dark:** minor thirds.

Variation 8: **Custom:** Pick from a combination of intervals, e.g., minor third and major seventh, minor second and perfect fourth, major third and minor seventh.

Variation 9: **Whole Nine Yards:** free choice of any and/or all intervals.

Variation 10: **Diatonic:** free choice of intervals, chosen from an agreed-upon key.

Variation 11: **Wide:** free choice of intervals larger than a minor sixth.

Variation 12: **Narrow:** use only whole or half steps.

Don't forget to leave space now and then, especially if playing in a group (good advice for all improvising!).

You may think you know your intervals, but you might be astonished by the hesitations you experience at first when calculating the proper interval ("Let's see, a major sixth down from D♭ is, um..."). Be patient. Traditional music training does not teach us to know music through the instrument very well. It takes time for "theory" through the instrument to become automatic and easy, but this is the essence of "thinking in music" and improvisation.

Brass Warm-Up

Two to six brass players. Use overtone series only. Like brass should use the same overtone series (i.e., use the same fingering). Each player picks a pair of notes in the overtone series (including the out-of-tune seventh and eleventh harmonics) and slurs back and forth between the two in either duple or triple rhythm at any tempo. Add hairpin dynamics (*crescendo-decrescendo*). At the end of a breath, leave some space, then pick a new pair of notes and start again. See also *Murmuring*, below.

Body Warm-Up

Two-plus players. Put the instrument down and do some slow and deliberate stretches accompanied by deep breathing. This may be done with half the group while the other half does, for example, the *Long Tone* or *Interval* warm-up games above. At some point the two groups switch.

Dancing Long Tones

Two-plus players. Just as in *Body Warm-Up* above, except that players do some kind of dance movements instead of stretching. This game may be a seamless segue from the *Body Warm-Up*. Again, it works well with half the group playing and half the group moving.

Hum-Up

One to twenty players. Add humming or chanting using an oo, ah, or oh to either the *Body Warm-Up* or *Dancing Long Tones*.

Dark Music [Technique]

For warm-ups—or almost any other game—turn out the lights. Playing in the dark (or near-dark) makes you hear much better.

Warm-Up/Connections

Two-plus players. This warm-up exercise works with any size group. All players play together their daily independent warm-up routines. After a few minutes (perhaps at a signal from the facilitator), players begin to listen to each other and very gradually begin to relate their warm-ups to what they hear. After a while all players will be playing roughly the same thing (synchronized notes, pulses, and rhythms).

Variation: Continue from this point and progressively relate less and less until all players are again independent.

Warm Up Your Feelings

Two-plus players. After some preliminary tones to awaken the body and reacquaint it to the instrument (or voice) again, veer thoughts away from technique and toward expression. How do you feel today? Make appropriate noises, sounds, tones. Let it drift toward extremes.

Tension/Resonance

Four-plus players. Also known as *Tension/Release* or *Tension/Resolution*. All eyes are closed. Each player of the group plays the standard tuning note (concert A), and enters individually. Players begin to branch out independently, moving by step or half step to a new note. If the resulting tone resonates with the chord of the moment, hold it. If there is tension, change to another note (by step or half step). As the chord changes, the resonant note may become a tension. Winds: pick a new note after each breath. (Source: Ed Sarath.)

Hearing Voices

Four-plus players. Each member of the group *sings* a long tone using an invented scat syllable (bah, lu, fa, boo, lee, ku, shu, mah, etc.). At some point players begin switching to instruments. After all are playing instruments, players begin switching back to vocal sounds.

Murmuring

Two-plus players. Undulate smoothly and softly back and forth between two notes a whole or half step apart. Every so often, move to a new pitch level (i.e., higher or lower). Feel free to leave space before you leap to the new Murmur.

Variation:	Use a major or minor third.
Idea:	Have half the group do *Murmuring* while the other half plays (for example) the *Warm-Up Interval*.

Red Light, Green Light: or, Yer Out!

Four-plus players. The Leader (or Player One) stands about ten feet from the group, facing away. The group makes any kind of random noises, sounds, or tones as long as Player One is facing away. Player One may turn around quickly at any time. When she does, all must stop playing. If Player One *sees* anyone playing, she may indicate (point and yank thumb) that that player is "out". Repeat until only one player (the winner!) remains.

See also:	*Son of Glacier Music* in Melody Games, *and Text Games* for more games useful in warming up the creative spirit.

• • •

I noticed at some point that I was doing the same warm up every single day. This, I think, isn't necessarily the best way to go. I realized that some days I needed to work my bow, other days I hardly needed any warm-up at all. What's best I decided is to check yourself out, play a few quiet notes, and think, "What do I need today?" Just by asking this question and experimenting will help you discover a better, more personal approach towards warming up and to playing too. The other thing is to try and not get too hooked into needing a lengthy warm-up in order to feel comfortable playing. It becomes more a psychological crutch than an actual physical necessity and there are going to be situations when you need to be ready to play without a lot of time for the "usual" warm-up, so try to vary the amount of time you warm-up too.

—Eric Friedlander[24]

• • •

Doesn't it strike you as odd that we can spend many years teaching an art that is totally inaccessible to our students unless they are staring at dots on a page, playing someone else's musical creation?

—Julie Lyonn Lieberman[25]

---

[24] www.Erikfriedlander.com/makeitcount/hotelroom.htm
[25] *The Creative Band and Orchestra*: 42.

Chapter 12

Rhythm Games

Rhythm is a notoriously weak element in Western music and musical training. Using the games in this chapter exclusively for a while in initial encounters with improvisation is an excellent idea. Many instrumentalists are extremely pitch-oriented and are under the impression that they need to play a flurry of different notes quickly to create an impressive solo. But every player needs to be able to invent an interesting solo with just rhythms using only one pitch. Percussionists do it every day. Be a drum for a while! See also *Accent Games*.

Everyone should be issued a drum at birth. Rhythm is the native language of us all, but needs a chance to flourish, preferably early and often.

—Jeffrey Agrell

World = Percussion

One player. While going about your daily life, turn the world around you into a percussion instrument. Tap a groove on the railing as you go down the stairs. Shuffle your feet in time on gravel or leaves. Beat a tattoo on the book you are carrying. Shake a handbag in time. Snap your fingers or clap your hands. Accompany this beat with humming, mouth noises, a spontaneous rhyming (or not) poem about what you see, smell, or hear, or how you feel. Use anything available or that you encounter to create rhythms and sounds. When a lot of people are around, you might consider wearing an iPod [turned off] or holding a cell phone up to your ear so that others will make allowances for you being musical on the move. People in this culture are not used to witnessing genuine spontaneous music making in public unconnected to the iPod or a misuse of prescription medicine....

See also: *Rhythmic Walking*, *Room Percussion*, and *Foot Music* in Rhythm Games.

House Music, *Car Music*, *Desk Music*, and *Shower Music* in Miscellaneous Games and *Bricolage* in Composition Games.

Hand Drills and Skills

One-plus players. Many improvisations are improved or made richer by the addition of percussion. Every improviser should have some basic manual percussion skills and be able to switch comfortably to a percussion instrument of some sort at any time. Here are some very basic and concise pattern drills for the hands to be repeated over and over. They may also improve rhythmic abilities on the player's main instrument as an extra benefit).

Key: R = Right Hand
             L = Left Hand

Pound these patterns on anything handy (drum, lap, table top, floor, overturned waste basket, etc.). Use a metronome or other rhythm source! Strive to play each pattern automatically (i.e., relaxed, with no conscious effort) at any tempo.

R–L–R–L	Sounds simple, but practice anyway to be able to maintain an absolutely steady beat.
	Variations: Accent every R, every other R, or every fourth R.
L–R–L–R	As above.
R–L–R, **L**–R–L	Triplet pattern. Accent the first of each three (in bold).
L–R–L, **R**–L–R	As above.
R–L–**R**–L–R–**L**–R–L	This is the so-called clave beat, with accents on one, four, and seven of the eight-note pattern.
L–R–L–**R**–L–R–L–R	You've guessed by now that we learn to begin every pattern with either hand.
R–L–**R**–L–R–**L**–R–L	Experiment with different accent groupings so that you can change them at will. Here, accents are on one, three, and six of the eight-note pattern.
R–L–R–R–L–R–L–L	The paradiddle.

These drills can be learned relatively quickly and will equip players to make up basic accompaniments and to improvise solos. Practice them regularly!

More ideas to carry these basics to new levels can be found in some of the exercises that follow.

Hand It Over I

Two to three players. Player One plays a duple pattern (use any of the patterns in *Hand Drills and Skills* above) on the lap, a drum, etc. Player Two plays the triplet pattern against it, sharing a common eighth note pulse with Player One. Player Three may be added as a soloist who freely improvises rhythms.

Variation: Practice scales using this technique using two players.

Hand It Over II

Two to three players. Player One plays her choice of two patterns: long-short-short (LSS), short-short-long (SSL), or short-long-short (SLS) on any percussive "instrument." Player Two joins in using a different long-short pattern. Player Three may join in as a soloist.

Tip: Have each player use a different timbre.

Group Ostinato 101

Four to six players. The group decides on a key or scale, e.g., C major, G Dorian, F whole tone, E♭7, D harmonic minor, etc. Create a one-measure ostinato in 4/4. Each player picks two of the four quarter notes to play.

For example, a player may choose to play on beats one and four. Pitches are chosen from a common key or scale. The player may decide to play the same note on each beat, or change pitches.

A pulse is established by the leader, by Player One, or by other players sitting in on percussion. After a while, players may select new quarter notes (e.g., change to quarters on beats two and four), either at a signal from the leader, Player One, or by independent choice.

Idea:	This exercise and its variations may be used as an accompaniment for solo players.
Variation 1:	At a signal from the leader, Player One, or by independent free choice, each player may play two eighth notes for one or both of the quarters. The eighth notes may be on the same pitch or on two different pitches.
Variation 2:	Accent one of the pitches. Accenting may be regular or irregular.
Variation 3:	Change dynamics as you play. This may be done using gradual *crescendi* and *decrescendi* over a number of bars, or clearly contrasting dynamics from note to note.
Variation 4:	Vary the timbre of some pitches, perhaps using extended techniques.

Group Ostinato 102

Four to six players. Repeat *Group* Ostinato *101* with variations, this time with the option of beginning quarter notes or pairs of eighths on the second eighth note of the measure (the *and* of the beat).

Group Ostinato 103

Four to six players. Repeat *Group* Ostinato *101* or *102* with variations, this time lengthening the ostinato to two measures.

> *It is very easy for the teacher or facilitator to underestimate the degree to which repeating an idea can be musically valuable. This may be because western European music places so much emphasis on developmental procedures throughout its history; but other world musics tend to be more rooted in ostinato patterns, and in improvised music, the ostinato can be regarded as an essential point of departure. Repetition maintains energy flow.*
>
> —Rod Paton[26]

---

[26] *Living Music* (West Sussex County Council, 2000): 24.

Rhythm Symphony

Two to six players. Using *Hand Skills and Drills*, a groove (background accompaniment pattern) is created by one to three players using percussive instruments of any kind (including body percussion, mouth noises, or found percussion). One to three players are added on melodic instruments playing each note pair (including long-short) accompaniments using notes of the C pentatonic scale. Remaining players take turns soloing over these patterns. A facilitator may signal for accompaniment players to switch to a new pattern at various times.

The Long and the Short of It

One-plus players. Vary the alternating patterns from *Hand Skills and Drills* (R–L–R–L, etc.) by using different rhythms, beginning with long-short-short (LSS)— quarter-eighth-eighth perhaps—short-short-long (SSL), and short-long-short (SLS). Clearly accent the beginning of each pattern, and practice until all can be effortlessly integrated into the creation of accompaniments and improvised solos. Remember to include rests!

Variation: Give long and short durations different *timbres* (e.g., low or high sounds).

Drum Circles

Four-plus players. A drum circle is a special kind of social/musical happening that has no peer. In the words of Arthur Hull: *The community drum circle is an open space for people to come together and share the love of drumming, dancing, and singing. It is a celebration of life and community.*[27] I won't discuss drum circles here, but I encourage you to check out books by Christine Stevens, Arthur Hull, Kalani, and others (see Resources) that provide details beyond the scope of this volume. Although drum circles are better experienced in person than through a book, these books can point the way to an activity that *everyone* should do.

Do the Rest

Two-plus players. This is a common exercise in learning jazz solos. A soloist plays six bars and rests for two against any sort of accompaniment built in eight-bar phrases. Rests give the soloist a chance to recover and prepare for the next eight bars, and also give the audience's ears a break (a conversation is more interesting when a speaker takes breaks than when speaking nonstop). The accompaniment player is free to fill the last two bars. Try using different play/rest counts, e.g., play four, rest four, play seven, rest one, etc.

Back and Forth

Repeat any of the *Hand Skills and Drills* on the piano or your primary instrument. Begin with two adjacent notes of a major scale, then any two notes of a triad. When this has been mastered, change pairs of notes at will, but spend some time on each pair.

---

[27]   *Drum Spirit Circle* (White Cliffs Media, 1998).

Tip: Repeat the exercises above, especially *The Long and the Short of It* using the pentatonic major scale (scale steps 1–2–3–5–6, or C–D–E–G–A based on C).

You Crack Me Up

One player. Initiate a rhythm source (metronome, computer program, playing partner) and play in all the "cracks," seldom landing on the beat. (Source: Charles Young.)

Team Groove

Two players, although probably more fun with three or more. Repeat *You Crack Me Up* with a friend, interacting as play.

Afterbeats Only

Two players. Player One plays *staccato* on the beat. Player Two plays *staccato* on the offbeat (the *and* of beats one, two, etc.). It may be helpful to begin with some kind of rhythm source, such as a metronome, to keep absolutely steady time. Players choose a major, minor, or chromatic scale. Move only stepwise from note to note. Tempo is moderate to brisk.

The challenge is for Player Two to be dead-on precise in placement of the afterbeat. When this seems easy, gradually increase the tempo. As faster tempos are mastered, add random leaps to the stepwise motion. If you need further challenges, change the meter to 6/8, 3/4, 5/8, 7/8, etc.

Afterbeats with Gaps

Two players. This is just like *Afterbeats Only*, except the players do not play on every beat (or afterbeat). Pre-select beats to play on, e.g., in 4/4, play only beats one and four, or one, three, and four, etc. Patterns over two measures are also possible, such as playing on beats one, two, and four in measure one and two and four in measure two. As above, Player Two needs to be absolutely precise in placement of the after beats.

Hand Arguments (Piano)

One player, piano only. The left hand plays a simple stepwise melody in quarter notes while the right hand plays either (mostly) syncopations (between the beats) or a three-against-two triple feel against the duple of the left hand. Repeat, reversing the roles of the hands. (Inspired by Azadeh Raoufi.)

Variation: The left hand plays a repeated chord on quarter beats.

Morse Code Piece

One player. Morse code, with its dots and dashes, can be used as the basis for an improvisation. Take any word (short words of one to four letters might be more wieldy, but experiment and decide) and translate it into Morse code (see below). For more information on the concept of converting language into rhythm using Morse code see www.philtulga.com/morse.html and/or http://homepage.ntlworld.com/ dmitrismirnov/MorseMusic.html. The results can be translated into half notes and quarter notes, quarter notes and eighth notes, or both. Notes may be assigned to any pitches.

INTERNATIONAL MORSE CODE

Character	Code	Character	Code	Character	Code
A	· —	J	· — — —	S	· · ·
B	— · · ·	K	— · —	T	—
C	— · — ·	L	· — · ·	U	· · —
D	— · ·	M	— —	V	· · · —
E	·	N	— ·	W	· — —
F	· · — ·	O	— — —	X	— · · —
G	— — ·	P	· — — ·	Y	— · — —
H	· · · ·	Q	— — · —	Z	— — · ·
I	· ·	R	· — ·		

Offbeat Metronome

One player. When practicing scales or other technical materials, *hear* the metronome click on two and four instead of on one and three. Once you get the hang of it, brag to your friends that you have a special metronome that clicks on the off beats, and then demonstrate. They may want to know where they can get one, too.

Shakin' Shakespeare

One player. This one-player game is from Bruce Adolphe's *The Mind's Ear*.[28] The player "reads" any Shakespeare soliloquy (for instance) with his instrument, improvising pitches to go along with the rhythms of the speech.

Poet Lariat

One player. Take *Shakin' Shakespeare* a step further by using any poem or famous oration as a source of rhythm for an improvisation. Simply play the rhythmic meter of the poem. Keep pitch choices narrow at first; a pentatonic scale works well.

The Big Machine

Four to eight players. One player repeats a rhythmic noise paired with a movement or gesture using the hands, arms, body, head, etc. Player Two moves close to Player One and makes a different noise and movement. One by one, the other players also become "machine parts," moving in close to each

---

28   *The Mind's Ear: Exercises for Improving the Musical Imagination for Performers, Listeners, and Composers* (MMB Music, 1991).

other. When all have joined, the leader gives a signal and the machine hisses to a stop, with all "parts" slowly collapsing in a heap on the floor.

Pulse/No Pulse

Two-plus players. Improvise a piece that alternates between a strong rhythmic pulse and no discernable pulse at all. How many different ways can you repeat this game?

> *Variation:*   Improvise a piece with a strong pulse. Transition to a contrasting, no-pulse section, and then go into a new section that has a strong pulse once again, but at a different tempo and in a different style. Continue in this manner.

Free/Strict

Two players. Player One plays a sharp, dry, sparse ostinato figure that clearly delineates a key and a pulse/tempo. Player Two plays a long-tone *cantabile* melody that floats independently over the pulse. Player Two should try to ignore the clear pulse of Player One and strive for a long soaring line with an indiscernible pulse.

> *Idea:*   Try the free melody in the lower voice and the strict ostinato in the upper voice for a change.

• • •

Drums somehow overcome all the things that stop people from making music. We may turn away, but the primal beat just keeps on calling.
—Christine Stevens, quoted in the *Fort Collins Forum*[29]

• • •

Going Somewhere

Two-plus players. Start a piece with a very slow pulse or tempo. Very gradually increase the speed until finally reaching the fastest tempo possible. Find an abrupt end through gesture or other nonverbal communication.

> *Suggestion:*   Experiment with adding dynamics. Maintain the dynamics and increase the tempo, get louder as the tempo increases, or get softer as the tempo increases.

Slowdown

Two-plus players. Start a piece at breakneck speed. Very gradually decrease the tempo until the piece moves at a snail's pace. At some point, all instruments should lock on to a very long held note and fade out.

---

29   www.ubdrumcircles.com/about_philosophy.html

Entrainment

Four-plus players. *Entrainment* is a term used in drum circles: it means the tendency of players to fall into a synchronized beat. In this game, everyone begins—independently, with no set beat or pulse—at the same time on a percussion instrument (including, besides regular percussion, body percussion, found percussion, desks or other furniture, even the floor). Gradually entrainment sets in, and the group unites on a common beat.

AMAPFALAP

One-plus players. The acronym stands for As Much As Possible From As Little As Possible, a game described by W. A. Mathieu in *The Listening Book*.[30]

Over any kind of rhythmic accompaniment (e.g., two or three players playing shakers or drums and/or a minimalist ostinato) or drone, the solo player may improvise using only one note. The soloist must create interest using rhythms, timbre (including extended techniques), and dynamics. Don't forget the power of rests.

Variation 1: The soloist may use two adjacent notes.

Variation 2: Use three tones, either three adjacent notes:

1–2–3
1–2–♭3
1–♭2–♭3
1–♭2–3

or two adjacent notes and a major or minor third on either side of the middle note:

1–2–4
1–3–4
1–♭3–4.

Variation 3: Repeat with two soloists. The soloists should relate in some manner (or not).

Note: It is advisable to do this one vocally at first. Do not add more pitches until you have spent quite a bit of time experimenting with just one note. When you start adding pitches, do not forget to maintain the variety (rhythm, timbre, etc.) just used in the one-note solo. Western music is very pitch-centric and rhythm poor. Enrich yourself by reversing the values and becoming skilled at inventing rhythms, changing timbres, exploring dynamics changes, and extremes.

Variation 4: Add one more player who may only copy bits of what he hears.

---

30 Shambala, 1991: 143.

Additive Solo

Two to four players. The group establishes a steady background of some sort. Player One is the soloist, but must start the solo as in *AMAPFALAP*: one note only! The idea is to make an interesting solo from one note using imaginative rhythms. Player One may then progressively add a second note to the solo, and later a third, fourth, etc. Repeat until all have had a chance at soloing in this manner.

Synch or Swim (Entrainment II)

Four-plus players. All play simultaneously on either a percussion or non-percussion instrument with clearly defined rhythm. The idea is for all players to synchronize to a common pulse with a designated player as quickly as possible (this is the Soundpainting gesture *synchronize*).

Don't Duet (Un-entrainment)

Two players on either a percussion-like instrument or playing percussive idioms on regular instruments) enter one after the other with rhythmic figures at slightly different tempos. The goal is to resist the pull of the entrainment phenomenon (the tendency of players to fall into a synchronized beat) and maintain independence of tempo.

Variation: Begin in synch. One player changes to be slightly ahead or behind the other. See if you can hold it!

Duet–Eventually

Two players. Both play obstinately independently of each other with separate pulses, rhythms, styles, keys, etc. Gradually the players start listening and relating to each other, eventually uniting on the same pulse, key, style, etc. Players could start off facing away from each other, and then gradually turn to face each other as entrainment (the tendency of players to fall into a synchronized beat) sets in.

Eight-Count Rhythm Machine

Four-plus players. For all variations, players stand in a circle and *step back and forth*, left-right in a steady, moderate pulse, which is understood to be quarter notes. Players then vigorously count *out loud* the numbers from one to eight in an eighth-note pulse, repeating (looping) without a break after each series. Notated using the Time Unit Box System (TUBS). The eight counts represent one measure in 4/4. The idea of TUBS used here comes from the wonderful book *A Rhythmic Vocabulary* by Alan Dworsky and Betsy Sansby[31] (run, don't walk to buy a copy!).

Count	1	2	3	4	5	6	7	8
Step	X		X		X		X	

---

31   Alan L. Dworsky and Betsy Sansby, *A Rhythmic Vocabulary* (Mel Bay, 1997).

Variation 1: Players select (independently) any two non-adjacent numbers and clap when these numbers come up as they count (continuously) from one to eight. Be vigorous! When your foot marks one, stomp a spider! When you clap, slap that mosquito! Don't forget to count up to eight out loud!

Example with three players (X = clap):

Count	1	2	3	4	5	6	7	8
Player One		X					X	
Player Two		X		X				
Player Three	X				X			

Variation 2: Repeat variation 1, giving one of the numbers a different timbre (e.g., any body percussion sound except clapping.

(X = clap, O = other sound, [e.g. finger snap, thigh slap, mouth noise, etc.])

Count	1	2	3	4	5	6	7	8
Player One	X					O		
Player Two				X				O
Player Three		X					O	

Variation 3: Use three numbers: two adjacent and one number nonadjacent, clapping only.

Count	1	2	3	4	5	6	7	8
Player One		X	X					X
Player Two	X				X	X		
Player Three			X				X	X

Variation 4: Give the single number a different timbre.

Count	1	2	3	4	5	6	7	8
Player One	O			X	X			
Player Two		X	X				O	
Player Three			O			X	X	

Variation 5: One player solos, using this "rhythm machine" as accompaniment. When finished, the soloist joins the ostinato and the next player solos. Continue until all players have had a chance to solo.

Variation 6: Repeat variation 5 with "rhythm machine" players playing a note on their instruments instead of clapping or other percussion. Players may agree on a key or have free choice.

Variation 7: Repeat using three different timbres.

Variation 8: Repeat the game or any variation, counting up only to seven or five!

Rhythm Walking

One player. The idea for this comes from chapter 14 of *A Rhythmic Vocabulary* by Dworsky and Sansby.[8] The idea is to practice (and enjoy!) rhythm patterns while walking. From now on, don't walk anywhere without practicing your rhythm walking as described below.

For ostinati: Your feet supply the basic pulse. For a slow 4/4 pattern, each step is a quarter note beat: 1–2–3–4. For a quicker pulse, your steps are on one and three.

Count	1	2	3	4
Step	X	X	X	X

In 6/8, step on one and four, but you may have to walk too slowly this way. Also try thinking of your steps as falling on one, three, and five.

Count	1	2	3	4	5	6
Step	X			X		

Count	1	2	3	4	5	6
Step	X		X		X	

If you really want to speed it up, think of your steps as falling on one, five, and three of the next measure.

Count	1	2	3	4	5	6	1	2	3	4	5	6
Step	X				X				X			

You can add a second pattern to this basic pulse by using your hands: snap your fingers, clap, or tape quarters to your thumb and middle finger.

Here's an example of a 6/8 pattern for your hands called the *[African] Short Bell Pattern*:

Snap fingers or clap on beats one, three, five, and six in measure one, and on two, four, and six in measure two.

This pattern can be done vocally using any sound you like.

After you have had enough practice for this pattern become automatic (and you really want to be adventurous), add a third pattern with the voice, or invent a melody over the double ostinato (using either scat syllables or made-up text).

Count	1	2	3	4	5	6	1	2	3	4	5	6
Step	X			X			X			X		
Clap	X		X		X	X		X		X		X

Whatever you do, *Rhythmic Walking* will really put some pep in your step.

African Switchback

Three players. This is similar to *Eight-Count Rhythm Machine*, but for three players plus optional soloist. The added timbre and the quick switch back and forth between timbres gives an interesting layered effect not unlike African drums.

Players have to determine which beats to play ahead of time. Player One picks four numbers to clap (or plays on percussion or their instrument) from a count of eight. Player Two uses a distinctly different timbre and picks two numbers that are different from the four that Player One has chosen. Player Three gets whatever two numbers are left over, and uses yet another distinctly different timbre.

It simplifies things to make a beat template (or a table) of who does what when. TUBS templates can be found in *A Rhythmic Vocabulary*[32] as mentioned in *Eight-Count Rhythm Machine*, or you can simply construct your own using a piece of paper and a ruler or using the table feature of a word processor program.

Example: Player One picks beats one, three, six, and eight. Player Two picks beats four and five, leaving Player Three with two and seven.

Count	1	2	3	4	5	6	7	8
Player One	X		X			X		X
Player Two				O	O			
Player Three		+					+	

Variation 1: Change the distribution of claps. For instance, Players One and Two play three notes each; Player Three plays two.

Variation 2: A soloist may play over the rhythm once it's settled into a comfortable groove.

Variation 3: The game may be played with only Two players.

Variation 4: Regardless of the number of players, don't fill all of the numbers; leave silences. For instance, Player One plays beats one and five; Player Two plays beats two and four; Player Three plays beats six and eight, with silences on counts three and seven.

Variation 5: Allow overlapping of "hits," as in *Eight-Count Rhythm Machine*.

Variation 6: Change the overall count to five, six, seven, nine, etc. Odd numbers are challenging and fun!

Variation 7: Have more than one player per "hit," e.g., double or triple the hits.

Deep in Hocket

Three players. Set up a beat table as in *African Switchback*. This time, use melodic instruments. Each player selects a tone from a pentatonic scale (scale steps 1–2–3–5–6). This game is easier if melodic instruments are supported by a rhythmic accompaniment consisting of steady quarters and/or eighths, or a trio playing its own beat table (not necessarily the same as the melody instruments' table).

---

[32] *Eight-Count Rhythm Machine*: 85.

Variation 1:	One tone only.
Variation 2:	Allow changing tones selected from the pentatonic scale.
Variation 3:	Choose from a wider pitch set, e.g., a major scale, any kind of minor scale, a whole tone scale, or a diminished scale; any kind of arpeggio (major, minor, diminished, etc.).
Variation 4:	Free choice of any pitch in the chromatic scale.
Variation 5:	Free choice of any pentatonic scale note, but each instrument may also choose the key of the scale for a more atonal sound.
Timbre variation:	Sing the pitches! Keep in mind, however, that the main focus here is not on pitch, but on keeping an absolutely solid and precise rhythm.

(Inspired by Phil Tulga's slick online rhythmic pattern program: the Unifix Cube Drum Machine, found at www.philtulga.com/unifix.html.)

Circle Ostinato

Three to twelve players. Player One begins a short ostinato. Player Two adds a second ostinato that shares the same eighth-note pulse, but may or may not be in the same meter (e.g., Player One's ostinato may repeat every four beats, where Player Two's ostinato repeats every seven eighth notes). Player Three then solos over these ostinati, sharing the pulse but not necessarily any set time signature. When finished, Player Three switches to a new ostinato figure and cues Player Four (or going back to Player One if there is no Player Four), who then begins a solo. Continue in this manner so that there are always two ostinato players sitting next to each other with the soloist on one side. When everyone has played (or at a signal from Player One), end with a long tone played by everyone.

Ideas:	Use an agreed-upon key or leave the choice of key open.
Variation:	If the players are able to create ostinati easily, they may add any kind of vocal sounds, such as drones, mouth noises, interjections (e.g., Ha! Gree! Flah! Shhhh! Ooof! Woo! Mmm! Zhhhh! Grrr! Lalala! Fffff!), call-and-response, long tones, extended techniques, etc.

Ostinato

Two-plus players. Player One begins a short ostinato and then other players enter with complementary ostinati until all are playing.

Hint:	Incorporate space into each of the ostinati to leave room for others to come through.

Go around again and have each player change their ostinato and then signal for the next player to begin. After the second time around, Player One signals for everyone to finish on a whole note.

Note:　　　　The ostinati need only have a common eighth-note pulse; a common meter is not necessary.

Variation:　　Players may choose when to change their ostinati.

See also:　　*Mouthing Off* and *Giggle Machine in Timbre* Games; *Morphs in* Accompaniment Games.

Odd Meter Drone Ostinato

Two players. Player One plays the odd meter drone ostinato below. Player Two solos over this in C major.

Variation 1:　　Solo using any of the following chords over the same ostinato: Cm, C7, Cm7, D♭, D, Dm, B♭, Am, A♭, E♭, F, Fm, G, F♯.

Variation 2:　　Repeat Variation 1, but switch keys at will during the solo.

Variation 3:　　Player One's ostinato keeps the same rhythm, but may change the notes to fit a pre-determined chord (e.g., any listed in Variation 1).

　　　　　　Example:　　The ostinato line in C minor could be C–D–E♭–D or C–D–E♭–B. The choice of pitches may vary, but maintain the note values.

Variation 4:　　Transpose the ostinato note to many other keys, repeating the variations above.

Groove + Long Line

Two to six players. All use percussion instruments (or found percussion) to set up a strong, aggressive groove. A brass, woodwind, or string player invents a very simple melody in major mode with longer, sustained notes and repeats it over and over. As he repeats, other non-percussion players join in and play this melody at the unison or octave. As soon as the other players can play the line comfortably, they find and switch to another line that harmonizes with the melody. At some point, after the harmonized melody has been played over the groove for some time, the melody player may signal that he is about to begin a new melody or that a new player will play the melody. Play until the cows come home.

Remember that many of these rhythm games can be combined with other games (Melody, Harmony, Style, etc. Use your imagination!)

Move with the Groove

Three-plus players. The group should sit in a circle or row. Player One invents a short and catchy three- or four-note rhythmic groove. One by one (in order or not), the other players imitate either the groove or the rhythm exactly, and then invent a line that harmonizes with the original.

Idea: After the Player One establishes the groove, the percussion players join in first to help establish a strong rhythmic feel.

Double Trouble

Six players. Repeat *African Switchback* with two separate groups of three playing in alternation. Groups pick numbers independently. It will likely take a bit of practice to pass the count from group to group smoothly without any glitches.

Call-and-Response: Rhythms!

Two-plus players, preferably a Leader and a large group. The leader either claps or plays a one-measure rhythm (e.g., in 4/4 or 6/8) on a percussion instrument, which is immediately played back as exactly as possible by the group (or partner). The tempo and complexity of the rhythm may be gradually increased as the group meets the rhythmic challenges of the call.

Variation 1:   Sit in a circle. Each player gets a one-, two-, three-, or four-measure rhythm (decide beforehand), then passes the turn to the player on the left. Player One starts. If Player Two misses, Player One must repeat. If Player Two misses three times, Player One must start again with a newer, simpler rhythm. Then Player Two invents a rhythm (on a new pitch if using an instrument) etc.

Variation 2:   Sit in a circle. Player One plays a rhythm on one pitch of any length. The rest of the group echoes the rhythm on the same pitch. Player Two then invents a rhythm for the group. The second time around Player One may use two pitches to play the rhythm. The group can decide if it is ready to tackle three pitches, etc. on the next time around.

Idea: The call may be vocal scat syllables instead of percussion. (Source: Christine Stevens, *The Art and Heart of Drum Circles*.[33])

Quarters to Two

Four-plus players; more is better. The group sits in a circle or semicircle and makes a percussive, non-tonal pulse of steady quarter notes in moderate tempo using any means, including small percussion instruments, body percussion, foot stomps, vocal sounds, mouth noises, or extended techniques on instruments. These sounds may be the same for all or individually chosen. The leader designates two players (not necessarily sitting next to each other) to be soloists. They solo using either percussion instruments or body percussion for thirty seconds to a minute as determined by the leader, who indicates when the soloists should finish. The next two soloists begin, continuing until all have soloed. Soloing here means any kind of departure from the basic beat. Novices should use simple rhythmic values, including rests, eighth, quarter, and half notes.

---

[33] Idea from the CD that accompanies Christine Stevens, *The Art and Heart of Drum Circles* (Hal Leonard, 2003).

Variation 1:	Use one or three soloists instead of two.
Variation 2:	Have solos overlap.
Variation 3:	Soloists may solo on their instruments. Solos should be more rhythmic than melodic.
Variation 4:	The group may add occasional random yelps, calls, or other interjections to the steady beat.
Variation 5:	Any group player may add random (but well-spaced) and sudden, forceful interjections of more dense and/or syncopated rhythmic outbursts
Variation 6:	Several group players may be designated to add another layer of rhythm to the quarter-note pulse, such as an eighth-note pulse; or they may add after beats to the basic pulse.
Variation 7:	Change the number of soloists to one or three.
Variation 8:	Have half the group establish the strong quarter-note pulse, the other half doing some or all of the following: random brief but dense flurries of notes, subdivisions of the beat (eighths, triplets, sixteenths), sparse ostinati (e.g., clave only on the second half of beat four), syncopated ("in the cracks") notes.
Variation 9:	Instead of a steady quarter-note pulse, the group may agree to leave some space—free choice of where rests fall.
Examples:	Quarter notes on one, two, and three; one, two, and four; one and three; two and four; one and four.
Variation 10:	Assign half the group to create a quarter-note pulse using any of the variations above. Assign the other half of the group to create an eighth-note pulse by making percussive sounds on any three eighths in a measure (see *Eight-Count Rhythm Machine*).

One-Measure Rhythm Invention

Three-plus players. Form a circle. Establish a beat in 4/4 at a moderate tempo. (Count off, tap toes, assign one or two players to play percussion, etc.). Each player in turn invents a one measure rhythmic motif and performs it by clapping, playing a percussion instrument, singing a vocal syllable, etc. At first the player may repeat the measure several times to become comfortable with it. Later, the pulse must continue unbroken from player to player as each invents a new rhythm. Advanced players may make the game more challenging by gradually increasing the tempo each time around (a metronome or other rhythm source may be handy here).

One-Note Chamber Music

Two players. Trade instruments with any other player or play the piano with one finger. Have your partner show you how to hold the instrument and play one note—any note. Invent a piece that uses only that one note, inventing fascinating rhythms. Join forces with one or more other one-note players and make some one-note chamber music. (Inspired by Keith Hill.)

Echo Rhythm

Two or three players. As with *One-Note Chamber Music*, except that Player One plays a rhythm using one or two notes and Player Two must imitate it as exactly as possible. If Player Two misses, this becomes the new model. If Player Two gets it right, Player Two may make a new model rhythm for optional Player Three.

Foot Music

One to four players. Starting together or adding players one at a time, players stomp and tromp out rhythms with their feet on the floor. It helps if the floor is not carpeted. Wood floors are a plus. Shoes with hard soles make more noise.

Variation 1:	Ostinati only. Change at command or will.
Variation 2:	Start with ostinati, and then switch to free/solo rhythms.
Variation 3:	Move in a circle, alternating solos with ostinati.
Variation 4:	Integrate clapping rhythms with foot rhythms (e.g., stamp on the beat, clap on off beats).
Variation 5:	Along with clapping sounds, add any other body percussion sound or rhythmic vocal noises/sounds, including text.
Variation 6:	For any size group: stand roughly in a circle and take turns making foot rhythms. Try overlapping rhythms.
Variation 7:	Instead of using the arms for percussion, move the arms around in a supportive way that mimics a kind of dance.
"Prepared" Foot Music:	Invent ways to make different sounds with your feet, e.g., tap shoes, ankle bells, crinkly plastic wrap, etc. Perhaps give each foot a different timbre.

(Inspired by the Charaza Quintet.)

What's In a Name?

Two to four players construct a piece based on the rhythms of their names. Use of motivic development techniques (augmentation, diminution, etc.) is encouraged.

Drumalogue/Drumversation

Two players have a dialogue/conversation using only drums (or any source of percussive sound at hand). One way to do this is to imagine a sentence and play the rhythms of the words on the drum. Use lots of accents!

Against the Grain

Two players. Player One plays or claps two quarter notes in 2/4, accenting the downbeat. Player Two claps three quarters against it (i.e., three claps in the space of Player One's two claps).

> *Variation:*   Start the two-beat first and add the triplet. Try three against four, four against five, three against five, four against six, four against seven. Experiment with starting with either number first.

Mixed Meters I

Two to four players. Establish a common eighth-note pulse then have each player enter in a different (pre-selected) meter (e.g., 4/4 + 5/8 + 6/8 + 7/8). This game benefits from percussion accompaniment (especially low drums), such as a steady quarter-note beat, or one or more percussion instruments giving the prominent accents for each meter. Restricting the number of pitches available also helps. A pentatonic scale works well, but using even one to three pitches is good.

> *Variation:*   Leave some spaces (rests).

Mixed Meters II

Two to four players. Try this first with only percussion (instrument or clapping), then with a restricted number of pitches (a pentatonic scale works well) on your regular instrument. Players think of a number from one to five, and then play that number of quarter notes, adding one extra beat of rest.

> *Example:*   If Player One chooses three, she would clap three times and rest once, repeating the pattern. If Player Two choose four against that, Player Two would clap four times and rest once, repeating the pattern. The beats (claps) line up, but the rests in this case only coincide every twenty beats.
>
> With more players and different numbers (i.e. meters), the rests of all players will line up much less often.

(Source: Doug Goodkin's *Sound Ideas*.[34])

> *Suggestion:*   Goodkin suggests that when the rests do line up, players immediately continue with a new number. This may take some practice and require slower tempos at first. Also try this game once with five or six players, assigning the numbers one through five (or six) for a complete set of mixed meters.

Mixed Meters III: 3/4 vs. 6/8

Two players. Player One improvises a tune in a predetermined key in 6/8, accenting the first and fourth eighth notes to emphasize the meter. Player Two improvises in the same key, but in 3/4, accenting the first, third, and fifth eighth notes. Except for accent placement, choice of note value is free.

---

34   Doug Goodkin, *Sound Ideas* (Warner Bros. Publications, 2002): 59.

Variation: At a signal from Player One, players swap meters.

Rhythm Palette

Four-plus players. Notate (or memorize) one, two, or three simple rhythms ahead of time (example: short-short-long), and rehearse them with the group. In the course of an improvisation, use the Soundpainting sign for *palette:* Left hand palm is flat and vertical; right hand fist touches it. *Palette* indicates any bit of rehearsed music. Follow the *palette* sign by holding up one, two, or three fingers to indicate which of the rhythmic palettes is to be played (or make up your own system). The leader then indicates a beat and the players improvise using the rehearsed rhythm. The rhythm may be used in any degree of augmentation (long notes) or diminution (short notes), as long as the basic rhythm is preserved.

Variation: The rhythm palette may be given (on the spot or prearranged) to only one group, such as percussion, brass, the left side of the room, etc., while other players solo in turn.

Rhythmic Canon/Rondo/Palindrome (or Subdivision)

Three players. Player One plays two whole notes in 4/4 at a moderate tempo. Key may be agreed upon ahead of time or not. Player Two then begins with two whole notes as Player One plays half notes. After two more measures Player One plays quarter notes as Player Two plays half notes. Player Three enters playing with whole notes. This continues until Player One reaches eighths or sixteenths (whatever is comfortable). Player One then reverses the procedure, playing ever longer notes until he reaches whole notes again, after which he is either silent or plays a subtle rhythmic pulse in some manner. The piece is finished when the last player is alone. She finishes by playing a *fermata* on the last whole note.

Variation 1: Each player must play every level of rhythmic subdivision, but may choose the order.

Variation 2: Each player must insert some kind of rest (short or long) between or among measures.

Baby Grand Opera

Two players: one singer and an accompanist on piano or mallet percussion. The soloist should mentally assume the role of an opera singer, singing to begin a pulseless "recitative" using either scat syllables or commentary on an event (e.g., "And as I gazed upon the discount cheeses, I said to myself, 'O Self, What Grand Cheese Be This?'").

The accompaniment consists of simple triads built on any diatonic scale step but in random order in any selected key. At some point, the accompaniment becomes pulsed, and the soloist begins her "aria" (e.g., "Gorgonzola, Mi Amor"). End in grand style, and take an elaborate bow when finished. Wave gracefully with great emotion and showmanship to your fans in the balcony; touch your heart as you accept the roses thrown from the loges, blinking back grateful tears.

Move It

One-plus players. Over a solid rhythmic accompaniment set up by several players (or an electronic rhythm source), one or two players solo using a short rhythmic motif. The goal is to keep finding new parts of the measure to enter.

Example: Start the motif on the beat. Then start it on an eighth note before the downbeat, an eighth note after the downbeat, then on beat two, etc.

Swing It

One player. Take any technical exercise (scale, arpeggio, pattern), etude, familiar tune (folk song, camp song, pop tune), classical theme or melody, or invent your own, and play all the eighth notes "swung." If you don't know how to swing, it don't mean a thing; just listen (and sing along) to some big band music from the 1930s and 40s until the concept of swing becomes clear.

Variation: Do it all again with a friend.

Chant

Three-plus players. The group decides on a theme, such as vegetables, household objects, sports, outer space, animals, etc. The leader conducts a steady beat while the group makes up a sentence about the chosen object and begins rhythmically chanting the sentence. Group members take turns soloing over the chant.

Optional: Some players may play percussion ostinati.

Epic Soundtrack

Four-plus players. Half of the group plays rapid percussion ostinati; the other half plays short but energetic ostinato figures in C pentatonic minor (1–♭3–4–5–♭7), using two to three notes each in the middle to lower register. Each player in turn plays a solo over this using only long and very long tones in C Dorian (1–2–♭3–4–5–6–♭7).

Variation: Two players solo at the same time.

Optional: A conductor indicates dynamic levels for the group.

Try to Shake 'Em, or Bucking Bronco

Two players. Player One claps or plays the *Short Bell* pattern from *Rhythm Walking*. Player Two enters and does her utmost to play a variety of complex rhythmic figures against the ostinato, including playing completely out of time, attempting to shake Player One from his ostinato. When Player Two either succeeds or gives up, players switch roles. This may be done with several players in a circle or with a leader and successive players.

Odd Ostinato

One-plus players. Player One (perhaps with some help from a couple percussionists) plays an ostinato in an odd meter such as 5/8 or 7/8. Player Two improvises in over it using only four pitches of the player's choice

Examples:	C–D–E–G
	C–E♭–F–G
	C–F–G–B♭
	C–E–F♯–G
	C–E–G–A
	C–E–G–A♭

Follow That Rhythm

Two-plus players. One player names a familiar tune (e.g., "My Country 'Tis of Thee," "America, the Beautiful," "Yankee Doodle," etc.). All players improvise pitches, freely or within a given key. They must use only the rhythm of the tune (it will sound like a crazy chorale). Use a conductor if necessary.

See also: *Que Será Será* in Technique Games.

Transformation

One-plus players. Transform any familiar tune by playing it in another meter (and perhaps style). For example, play "Stars and Stripes Forever: as a waltz. Play "Yankee Doodle" in 5/8 or "America, the Beautiful" in 7/8.

Sensemaya Step

Two-plus players. While rapidly counting to three or four out loud, step using this ostinato pattern from the orchestral piece *Sensemaya* by Silvestre Revueltas: 4–4–3–3–4–3 (one step for each number). Loop the pattern until it feels comfortable, and then play a rendition on a percussion instrument. Every note need not be played. You might simply play the first note of every grouping.

One player may then play a *cantabile* solo over the rhythm played by the rest of the group, first independently of the beat, then in synch with it.

Suggested scales	Dominant seventh (1–2–3–4–5–♭7)
for soloist:	Lydian dominant (1–2–3–♯4–5–6–♭7)

Ping Pong

Two players. This game emphasizes teamwork and requires absolute concentration and fast reflexes.

Players face each other, eyes closed. Player One plays a G4; Player Two responds with the same note. Player One "serves" another G, ever so slightly faster and Player Two returns it. Player One gradually increases the speed, reaching a maximum speed in which the ping-pong effect is clean and accurate. At some point, the pong will start landing on top of the ping and the game is over. Players switch roles.

Variation 1:   Player One plays two notes: F and G, always starting on F. After the initial F, Player One switches (or not) at random. Player Two must "return" the same note "served." Player One again gradually increases speed until the maximum speed is attained.

Variation 2:   Player One plays three random notes very quickly; Player Two copies as quickly as possible. Although it is nearly impossible (without perfect pitch) to know which note to start on, it is a bit less difficult to catch at least some of the intervals. In any case, Player Two tries to approximate the shape of the motif and reproduce the internal intervals.

(Invented by the magician Ian Savile.)

Different Drummers

Two to four players. Tap out a common pulse. Each player enters with a very rhythmic melody that shares an eighth-note pulse, but the meter may be entirely different for each player.

Example: Player One enters in 4/4, Player Two in 7/8, Player Three in 6/8, Player Four in 5/8.

Tip: Use accents to help delineate individual meters.

Variation: Assign different meters ahead of time.

Drums Everywhere [Technique]

Find ways to turn your particular instrument into a drum (without damaging the instrument, of course). This may mean only gently tapping or clapping keys (e.g., for woodwinds), but some instruments, such as piano, cello, bass, harp, etc., are capable of more robust sounds.

Experiment with all instruments in a trio or quartet, making rhythmic percussive sounds. Remember that your instrument has this capability so that, while improvising, you can switch at any moment to become... a drum!

Personal Percussion [Technique]

Everyone must make a percussion instrument from items in their pockets or handbag, and then do any game in this section.

Room Percussion [Technique]

Everyone must find ways of creating percussive sounds using whatever is in the room, e.g., slapping palms on floors, desks, walls, etc. Use whatever is available. Then play any game in this section.

Rhythm Machine

Four to eighteen players, or two groups of two to nine players each. One by one, players of Group One enter vocally with one of the following scat words:

Tiki   Oh
Taka   Boo
Uh   Dah
Ah   Dot
Chika

All players may use the syllable *Bah* plus their chosen word from the list above.

The scat word may be pitched or un-pitched. Pitch is free. The group must share a common pulse but not necessarily a common meter.

Players are encouraged but not required to create ostinati, and players may add bits of body percussion to the vocal interjections.

Group Two players, one by one, solo (vocally or on their instrument) over the rhythm machine, taking about thirty seconds each.

After all have soloed, players in Group Two choose a scat word and join the rhythm machine as players in Group One gradually drop out. Then Group One players may solo each in turn.

Variation 1:	Solo with voice only.
Variation 2:	Create a rhythm machine with percussion instruments only.
Variation 3:	Create a rhythm machine with melody instruments only.
Variation 4:	Create a rhythm machine with free choice of instrument, percussion, or voice, but stay with it the entire time.
Variation 5:	Rhythm machine players have the choice of switching between instrument, percussion, or voice during the piece.

Rhythm by the Book

One to two players. Using a book with examples of one- or two-line rhythms, such as *Rhythmic Training*[35] by Robert Starer or *Studying Rhythm*[36] by Anne Carothers Hall, Player One improvises a line in a pre-selected key using the rhythms of the top line. Player Two can do the same on the bottom line to create a duet.

Variation 1:	Try all kinds of different keys and types of scales (major, minor, whole tone, pentatonic, blues, diminished, etc.).
Variation 2:	*Start playing without selecting a key and see what happens.*

---

[35]   Robert Staver, *Rhythmic Training* (Alfred Publishing Company, 1999).
[36]   Anne Carothers Hall, *Studying Rhythm* (Prentice Hall, 1989).

Anticipation Angst

One to two players. This may be done by one player alone with a rhythm source (a metronome, etc.) or by adding a second player to lay down a solid rhythmic background. Play any familiar tune, but whenever possible, arrive "too early," i.e., finish phrases by the second half of beat four instead of on the downbeat of the measure in 4/4; or start phrases just ahead of the downbeat.

Variation: After experimenting with a number of familiar tunes using anticipation, make up your own pieces, beginning with the titles "Early Bird," "Who, Me?" and "Don't Mind If I Do."

Experiment with standard scales, arpeggios, and patterns.

Delay Delight

One to two players. This is similar to *Anticipation*. (Don't forget the rhythm source.) Change the familiar tunes rhythmically, delaying entries by an eighth note, which may involve changing or shifting other rhythms in the tune. After experimenting with familiar tunes, make up your own pieces, beginning with the titles "Last One," "I Heard You the First Time," and "Late Again."

Experiment with standard scales, arpeggios, and patterns.

Universe Symphony

Twelve-plus players, as many as will fit in the room. Charles Ives's magnum opus was his *Universe Symphony*, which survives through a heap of sketches and fragments. Several brave souls have put together (very different) performance versions of it. What we want to borrow for this game is the idea of a huge percussion ensemble that "plays the pulse of the cosmos"—rhythms that cycle over and over throughout the entire movement.

Find and listen to a recording to get an inkling of the possibilities, and then form a large percussion ensemble with at least half of the class or group. Create a cycling rhythmic pattern. The rest of the group may play an extended improvisation independently of the percussion that calls up every improvisation/musical technique in the book: long tones, extreme registers, extended techniques, varying densities (including silence), random hits, vocal sounds, etc. Play for as long as you are able. Shoot for an hour, if possible. The group can somehow decide whether it wants to end with a bang or a whimper.

Shifty

Two-plus players. The idea of this game is to take a simple rhythm and shift it forward or back at will.

One or more players should construct a rock-steady accompaniment, e.g., a quarter-note bass line and/or a steady percussion beat. Remaining players select a simple rhythmic motif using any combination of half, quarter, and eighth notes that takes up no more than half the measure.

Examples in 4/4:

The second half of the measure is empty. The group selects a key and each player chooses a chord tone, playing only this one pitch.

Begin with the chosen motif on beat one (beats three and four will be empty in 4/4). Repeat for several measures, and then shift the motif to begin on any other beat, e.g., start on beat two with rests on one and four. Continue in this manner.

Tip:	It may be a bit disorienting at first to keep track of where you are after shifting. Start simply and add complexity as you acquire experience and familiarity with the process. If you feel frustrated or confused (with this game or any other), simplify, simplify!
Variation 1:	Any player may solo in any key, using these shifting rhythms as an accompaniment.
Variation 2:	Shift the motif to any half beat in the measure, e.g., begin the motif on the second half of beat four or one.
Variation 3:	Use any diatonic tone, not just chord tones.
Variation 4:	Use two or three pitches. Choose one or two chord tones and make the rest non-chord tones.
Variation 5:	Use a pentatonic major (1–2–3–5–6) or pentatonic minor (1–♭3–4–5–♭7) scale for pitch selection.
Variation 6:	Add rests in the middle of the motif and expand the repeating unit to fill an entire measure.
Variation 7:	Make a motif length that does not match the meter, e.g., use a motif that is three eighth notes long in a 4/4, such as two eighth notes and an eighth rest. In this case, the motif will repeat several times per measure. This causes the motif to shift automatically. Starting on any other downbeat or upbeat in the measure can also shift it.

Percussion Ostinato

Four-plus players. Player One starts an ostinato in 6/8 with a percussion instrument. One by one the remaining players join in, either on a percussion instrument or on their instruments. When everyone is playing, Player One stands up and takes a solo on his instrument or on a percussion instrument. Players should use extended techniques at some point in the solos as well as in the ostinati.

Sparse Rhythm Machine

Four-plus players. All players create a rhythm machine ostinato (see *Rhythm Machine*) using a very sparse texture (lots of space!) using only voice.

Variation 1:	Use only body percussion.
Variation 2:	Use a free mixture of vocal sounds and body percussion.

Riff Game

One-plus players. Player One invents a short, catchy riff (a one- or two-measure ostinato rhythmic/melodic figure) in 4/4 at a quick tempo. Listen to Motown, funk, Latin, rock, or big band music for examples, or ask friends who have big band experience. Repeat the riff while a soloist goes wild over it. Confine note choice for the riff to the minor pentatonic scale (1–♭3–4–5–♭7; C–E♭–F–G–B♭ based on C). This alone can serve as an accompaniment, but it is more fun to add more players.

Player Two may copy the riff, but then must invent a line using identical rhythms but different notes chosen from the pentatonic scale. These notes usually move parallel to the original riff. If Player Two has trouble, Player One should simplify the riff.

Player Three may then jump in, repeating Player Two's procedure, but using different notes.

Variation:	Try other scale choices: major, major pentatonic (1–2–3–5–6), various minor scales, etc.
Idea 1:	One player may, instead of adding to the riff, add a short phrase to the end that leads back to the repetition of the riff.
Idea 2:	Try layering two different riffs.
Idea 3:	Invent and play over riffs in styles other than pop and jazz, e.g.:

Medieval   Renaissance
Baroque   Romantic
Stravinsky-esque   Schoenbergian
Waltz   March
Samba

Suggestion:	Repeat this in all other keys.

Juice Bottle Beat

Three players. Stand in a triangle. Each player holds a large, empty plastic juice bottle with top. Toss the bottle a short distance into the air and catch it with a slight smack of the hands. Do this together in rhythm, creating a steady beat.

Using spoken directions, players invent new ways to add rhythms to the basic beat one by one, e.g., tossing the bottles to each other, passing them on the ground or from hand to hand, etc.

(Suggested by percussionist Theresa Mckenzie Sullivan and her brothers via a video available at http://vids.myspace.com/index.cfm?fuseaction=vids.individualandvideoID=2024682430.)

Rhythm Combination Game No. 1

Four players. This game combines *The Long and the Short of It* (Rhythm Games) and *Yes, We Sing Bananas* (Timbre Games).

Players One, Two, and Three choose one of the following rhythms: long-short-short), short-short-long, or short-long-short, and make percussive sounds using body percussion or mouth noises. Player Four sings a vocal solo over this groove, using only syllables from the word, "banana," alternating with any extended techniques possible using the voice and/or mouth (e.g., humming, growling, howling, yelping, cooing, grunting, laughing, hissing, whistling, gargling, giggling, crying, rapid-fire nonsense syllables, etc.).

Rhythm Combination Game No. 2

Four players. This game combines *After Beats Only* (Rhythm Games) and *Play the Face* (Energy/Mood Games).

Using the natural minor scale (Aeolian mode: scale degrees 1–2–♭3–4–5–♭6–♭7), Players One and Two lay down a steady line of quarter notes and eighth-note after beats. They may also choose to combine *After Beats Only* with *Gaps* (from Rhythm Games) to leave a bit of space now and then for breathing—a good idea for wind players.

Player Three makes faces that express emotional/physical states (happy, sad, seasick, in love, frustrated, anxious, itchy, drunk, perplexed, sleepy, thoughtful, etc.). Player Three may move from emotion to emotion at will, but must not switch *too* quickly. Player Four "plays the face," i.e., improvises a musical depiction of Player Four's facial expression.

See also: Accent Games.

• • •

I'm the enemy of the conservatory, because it kills music. ...Imagination has been wrung out of these people, and it's tragic. Really, musicians have lousy rhythm.

—Choreographer Mark Morris[37]

---

[37] Quoted in "Music: Let's Play the Music (and Dance)" by Johanna Keller, *The New York Times*, July 11, 2004.

Chapter 13
Accent Games

Using accents is a surprisingly effective and simple way to make an improvisation (solo or accompaniment) interesting and meaningful, perhaps because it mimics the use of stressed syllables in animated spoken language. Instrumentalists, who are often over-concerned with pitch, also surprisingly neglect this technique. Focusing on accents can help correct this and make the use of accents more automatic and natural. Accents make music come alive for both performer and audience.

The need to be right all the time is the biggest bar there is to new ideas. It is better to have enough ideas for some of them to be wrong than to be always right by having no ideas at all.

—Edward de Bono[38]

Accent Solo

Two-plus players: solo plus the group. The group plays a subtle but a solid background pulse of quarters and eighths on any combination of drums, shakers, or bells, etc. Player One improvises a solo that emphasizes shifting accent patterns.

Tip 1:   Don't calculate—just jump in, play what your ear tells you, and have fun. Make the accents very clear!

Tip 2:   Add a judicious sprinkling of accents on weak beats (in the "cracks").

Tip 3:   If you find an accent pattern that has some appeal, repeat it for a while. You don't have to fill the airwaves with originality every second. Sit on a new accent pattern until it becomes easy and comfortable or until you have the urge to tweak it or start a new one.

Accent Template

One player. Make a template with four rows of eight quarter notes per row. "Compose" a piece by writing in accents and dynamics markings.

Tip: You may also use squares instead of quarter notes and simply put a check mark in the squares to be accented.

---

38 Edward De Bono, *Lateral Thinking* (Harper Paperbacks, 1973).

Variation 1:	Add timbre changes to the accented notes.
Variation 2:	Replace some or all of the accented notes with timbral changes.
Variation 3:	Play the accents in canon.
Variation 4:	Repeat with two or three players.
Tip:	Use different timbres.

Accents I

Six-plus players. Half the group (Group One) establishes a solid quarter note beat in 4/4 using a drum, a desk, a cardboard box, or even the floor, using either drum sticks or just hands. The other half of the group (Group Two) plays eighth notes over the quarter note pulse. When Group Two is solid and comfortable playing the eighths, players may then gradually introduce accents, first with the dominant hand, then later with the non-dominant hand.

Practice accenting the strong beats (one and three) then the weak beats (two and four) with each hand. After Group Two has acquired some experience and control of accenting with each hand, Groups One and Two switch roles.

Accents II

Six-plus players. Repeat *Accents I*, this time in 6/8 time with two groups of three eighths per measure. Note that the hand playing the accent changes each dotted quarter beat (**L**RL **R**LR). Spend some time on this until it feels completely automatic and natural. Then have the rest of the group (even if it's only one player) lay down a solid pulse while you accent the after beats only (you tap all beats, but accent only the after beats). Over a rock-steady (but not too loud) accompaniment of dotted-quarter notes from the other drummers, improvise a solo characterized by a mix of regular and irregular accents. Play all night; trade off at will.

Accents III

Six-plus players. This game combines *Accents I* and *Accents II*. This time, players can rap out various subdivisions of odd-meter measures such as 5/8, 7/8, 8/8 (3+3+2). When drumming an odd meter of choice becomes second nature, take turns soloing over the group groove.

| *Variation 1:* | Have Player Two beat the main subdivisions in the measure: two uneven beats in 5/8, three uneven beats in 7/8, three in 8/8 (3+3+2), etc. |
| *Variation 2:* | Have Player Two give a steady, unmetered quarter note pulse on a bass drum, desk top, etc. while Player One plays over it in odd meters. |

Accents IV

One-plus player. Play a steady stream of eighth notes, but add sharp accents and both regular (e.g., every two or three notes) and irregular intervals. Try this with your favorite (and especially your least favorite) scales and arpeggios.

Accents V

Four-plus players. Each player raps steady eighth notes at a moderate tempo on a drum, lap, pot, etc., with a hand or some other object. Assign each player a different number of eighth notes to play before an accented note occurs. For example, the player assigned one beat plays one accented beat and one unaccented beat. The player assigned two beats plays two unaccented beats and then an accented beat. Players with adjacent numbers should not sit next to each other. Players should strive to have as many timbres as possible. The assignment of beat numbers does not have to be consecutive or complete. For instance, numbers assigned might be one, four, six, eleven, and thirteen.

Variation: Free (independent) choice of beat numbers.

Idea: When the group reaches a very steady pulse and accurate placing of accented beats, increase the tempo. See how fast you can go while keeping the clarity as you gain experience and skill.

Scale Accents

One player. When practicing daily scales and arpeggios, add various accent patterns, e.g., accent every other note, every third note, or every fourth note. For a challenge, accent every fifth note or more. The most interesting patterns are those that do *not* coincide with the meter, such as ternary accents in duple meter or vice-versa.

More ideas:
• Combine odd/even accent groups. e.g., 2+3, 3+2, 3+3+2, 2+2+3, and/or 3+2+2.

• Irregular accents. Improvise accent groupings as you go up and down the scale, sometimes duple, sometimes triple, sometimes long groupings.

• Combine accent groupings with various articulations: all staccato, all *legato*, combinations of *legato* and *staccato* within accent groupings.

• Double the fun and make it a duet. Share a pulse. Try both playing exactly the same accent/articulation patterns and independently choosing the accent groupings.

Accenting the Wrong syLAble

One player. Play a familiar tune. Accent all the "wrong" notes.

Tapversation

Two players. Players have a (voice) conversation sitting across from each other at a table, but each taps the table to emphasize syllables, i.e., the accents of the language as well as the emotional content. (Invented by Rosalind Buda and Amanda Maas.)

Super Imposition

One player. Play a familiar tune. Superimpose an accent pattern from a different meter on the melody, e.g., a 3/4 over a 4/4 piece.

Accent Combination Game

Six-plus players. This game is a combination of *Rhubarb Rhubarb* (Miscellaneous Games) and *Accent Solo* (Accent Games).

Half the group mutters the word "rhubarb" over and over (not in synch!). The other half sets up a pulse of quarters and eighths using a combination of all of the following:

- Body percussion
- Mouth noises
- Room percussion (i.e., anything in the room that can make a noise, including objects in handbags, pockets, etc.).

The groups are independent of each other, except that a leader has the power to affect the dynamics of each group (raise or lower one hand for the Rhubarbs, the other hand for the Accents). These dynamics may be the same or opposed, or moving louder/softer together/opposed. After this all goes on for a good while, the leader may give the Synchronize signal (interlocked fingers), and both groups must listen and arrive at a common pulse. When this has been accomplished, the leader signals for a *crescendo*. When it can all grow no louder, the leader gives a clear cut-off to end the piece.

> See also: *Hand Drills and Skills, Drumalogue/Drumversation,* and *Mixed Meters I* and *II* in Rhythm Games.

> *Reading music...whether it involves playing from a score or from memory. It is an important and necessary stage of development, but it is of little ultimate creative value if it does not lead to a capacity for spontaneous musical expression.*
>
> —Bill Dobbins [39]

---

[39] Bill Dobbins, "Improvisation: an Essential Element of Musical Proficiency," *Music Educator's Journal,* January, 1980: 36–41.

Chapter 14
Dynamics Games

Dynamics may be the quickest, easiest, and most effective way to add interest to a piece. Given this, it is astonishing how often improvisations begin and end *mezzo forte* without much dynamic variation in between. Varying volume is something that should be practice early in improv training, and should be the first thing to be considered when examining an improvisation that seems lacking interest.

Simplicity is the key. With just a single facilitation element, such as dynamics...a facilitator can make a beautiful arrangement using repetition and variation.
—Christine Stevens, *The Art and Heart of the Drum Circle*[40]

Dynamics Map

One-plus players. Plan a "map," graphic (e.g., a "mountain range" level indicator) or other plan of variations in dynamics.

Example:	Begin very softly, then gradually (or suddenly) get very loud; at some point return to the initial dynamic.
Variation:	Have each player construct her own map and pursue it independently of the others. (Inspired by an exercise by Tony Wigram.)

Nothing Exceeds Like Excess

One-plus players. Play or sing as loud as you can (without injury). Don't hold back. Let it all out. What did it feel like? How do you feel afterwards?

Wisps

One-plus players. Play a piece as softly as you possibly can throughout. Vary the timbre, note density, and tempo, but remain soft. Fade for a long time at the end.

---

40 Stevens: 40.

Surprise!

Two-plus players. Improvise a piece that uses extreme and startling changes in dynamics. Create a unified piece with other players in all other respects (tempo, style, articulation, etc.), but remain obstinately individual in your choice of when to play very loudly or very softly. Incorporate times of silence.

See also:
- *Developing AB's* (Form Games).
- *Ritual, Opposites, Go Wild,* and *Nothing Succeeds Like Excess* (Miscellaneous Games)
- Energy/Mood Games

Spontaneous Improvisation is a tool that makes every performance unique. Its use makes it impossible for any two players to execute K. 622 the same way, as is, sadly, so often the case today. The tool may be likened to the thing that makes a hockey game interesting: once the puck is thrown down, one has no idea what is going to happen. And that is one of the principal reasons why eighteenth-century musicians improvised: it made every performance of a work measurably different from every other performance of that same work. As such, it was a tool used to create freshness and originality, the very thing that we all want to have in our performances.

—Daniel N. Leeson, Spontaneous Improvisation in Mozart Performance

Chapter 15
Melody Games

Inventing melodies will likely come as a new sensation for many players who have been taught to play the melodies of others exclusively.

Tips for melody creation:

- *Keep the melodies simple.* You should be able to sing what you play.

- *Intent.* Melodies come easily if you are evoking an affect (mental, physical, emotional, spiritual). For example, it is easier to create a melody if you are trying to depict joy, grief, anxiety, love, rage, etc., than if you just try to "play something."

- *Give it a shape.* Melodies, like stories and compositions, should have direction and tell a story, with a beginning, middle, and end, a.k.a. set-up, climax, and conclusion.

- *Let the melody breathe.* Make use of the 13th note: silence. Space frames the content and gives both you and the listener a chance to rest, digest, recover, and be ready for what comes next.

- *Practice contrast in your melody-making.* Try to make use of elements such as dynamics, rhythms, register, articulation, and timbre to give melodies life and interest.

- *Practice making melodies constantly.* Softly sing or whistle to yourself when you are sitting in traffic or walking the dog, and use all the suggestions above. If you happen upon a terrifically catchy tune, notate it in some way on a scrap of paper (or that little music manuscript pad you carry everywhere) or sing it into a recording device as soon as possible. Mentally notate it as a last resort; otherwise, keep singing it to remember it! It might form the basis of a composition that can be constructed later. But record the idea as soon as possible because you *will* (trust me on this) forget it, no matter how vivid it seems at the time.

• • •

Free form expression/improvisation and the removal of musical notation opens an avenue into an individual's expressive center. They become free to listen to what they are playing while making musical decisions about how the melodic line sounds. The significant changes in performance are due to the fact the mind is no longer consumed with a visual response to notation, only listening to the flow of notes being played.

—Edward S. Lisk, in *Intangibles of Musical Performance*

• • •

Glacier Music

One player. Find a resonant space (i.e. very large room) and play very long notes (wind players: an entire breath) with much space in between. Repeat using several short notes; listen as the notes mix and layer in the "wet" space. Experiment with long *crescendi* and *decresendi*. Gregorian chant is one possibility for style.

If a large room is not available, use an electronic device with digital reverb, microphone, and amp to artificially create the extended reverb.

Variation:	Use a digital delay, which will create a series of diminishing echoes of short melodic fragments. Play. Listen. Repeat.
Variation for brass:	Have someone depress the sustain pedal of a grand piano (or use a brick or other heavy weight). With the lid open, play a short series of (loud) tones on the strings. Listen to the soft echo chord it creates. Repeat. Try different combinations of scales and arpeggios, and vary the length.

Son of Glacier Music

Two to four players. Players play long, pulseless tones in C major. Move up or down to a new note by diatonic scale steps—no leaps. Leave a bit of space in between the long notes and listen to the chords created. Decide instinctively whether to ascend, descend, or stay the same.

Variation 1:	Try in other keys.
Variation 2:	Try with no set key.
Variation 3:	Try in minor.
Variation 4:	Have each player pick a different key.
Variation 5:	Have some other players play ostinati on percussion instruments to add a pulse.
Variation 6:	Use whole-and half-note values exclusively.
Variation 7:	In a larger group, sit in a circle. Have three or four players play the long tones; next to them sit three or four percussionists. Every thirty seconds the leader indicates a movement to the right.

Drone

Two-plus players. One or more players play a unison low note as a drone. Each player in turn should experiment playing a slow solo over the drone, noting the effect created by each scale step. Time permitting, try all the major scales over the drone (e.g., over a C drone, try the major scales of C, D♭, D, E♭, E, etc.), but be very aware of what scale step you are on.

Pulsed Drone

Two-plus players. Similar to Drone above, except one or more players play the drone as steady quarter notes on any given pitch. Player Two solos over it, only this time Player Two can have some fun playing with rhythm, e.g. syncopating against the steady beat.

Variation 1:   Leave out some of the quarter notes; e.g. play quarters only on of these patterns:

1 and 3

1 and 4

1, 2 and 4

1, 3 and 4

1, 2, and 3

2, 3 and 4

Variation 2:   Give the pulsed drone some kind of catchy/funky/jazzy/Latin rhythm.

Rainbow Scales

One player. Play any one-octave scale up and down (only!), but instead of playing it the usual colorless way of straight eighth notes, add all kinds of variation: add accents, change the note values, dynamics, articulation, and tempo; add rests. In short: make music out of it—make the scale as musically interesting as possible.

Variation: Do the same with two players, playing both independently and in relation to each other (e.g., one player may lead and the other imitates, mirrors, or matches style; or both intermittently lead and follow).

• • •

Free form expression/improvisation is based upon scale knowledge. ...Within a short period of time your students will naturally experience success when playing free form melodies and find the need for scale knowledge to expand their improvisational possibilities.

—Edward S. Lisk[41]

• • •

Scale Flavors

One player. Classical musicians practice major and chromatic scales almost exclusively; the more adventuresome and ambitious among us may also occasionally dabble with the various minor scales; but once they are mastered, never venturing outside of them deprives us of continued musical and technical enrichment and personal development. If you are reasonably fluent in your major scales, make a point of sampling those other scale "flavors" regularly (see "Patterns and Scales" in Resources, page x). Make an equal point in choosing your *least* familiar keys! Use regular warm-up or workout routines, substituting one of the scales below.

---

[41] *Intangibles of Musical Performance* (Meredith Music Publishing, 1996): 57.

Other scales to sample (numbers represent scale degrees):

Pentatonic major:	1–2–3–5–6
Pentatonic minor:	1–♭3–4–5–♭7
Blues:	1–♭3–4–♯4–5–♭7
Whole tone scales:	1–2–3–♯4–♯5–♭7
Diminished scales:	1. Whole-half: 1–2–♭3–4–♭5–♭6–♭♭7 (=6) 7
	2. Half-whole : 1–♭2–♭3–3–♯4–5–6–♭7
Dorian:	1–2–♭3–4–5–6–♭7
Phrygian:	1–♭2–♭3–4–5–♭6–♭7
Lydian:	1–2–3–♯4–5–6–7
Dominant 7th (Mixolydian):	1–2–3–4–5–6–♭7
Lydian Dominant:	1–2–3–♯4–5–6–♭7
Locrian:	1–♭2–♭3–4–♭5–♭6–♭7
Spanish Phrygian (*Also known as the Klezmer Ahava Raba scale or the fifth mode of the harmonic minor scale.*):	1–♭2–3–4–5–♭6–♭7
Klezmer (Misheberekh; *also known as the fourth mode of the harmonic minor scale.*):	1–2–♭3–♯4–5–6–♭7
Altered (Superlocrian):	1–♭2–♭3–♭4–♭5–♭6–♭7

Ideas: Apply your "new" scale to any game in the book…

Daily Arkady

One player. Russian hornist Arkady Shilkloper is one of the most creative musicians on the planet. When asked how he warms up, he simply says he "plays music"; he investigates simultaneously music, technique, and his needs as a player. He finds a rhythmic or melodic fragment and follows it where it leads, mindful of what the current state of his embouchure needs to warm up. The author of this book named this procedure "Daily Arkady" in honor of this brilliant musician. A Daily Arkady is a refreshing and highly effective integration of technique and musicality, and is different every time. D.A.'s may focus on a certain area if desired: the chord (or chord progression) D.A., the rhythmic D.A., the style D.A., the scale D.A., the arpeggio D.A., the extended techniques D.A. However, most days the best idea is to be alert, aware, adventurous, and let loose.

Document Your Practice! Do not forget to *record* your improvisations both alone and in groups. Listening to what you played provides excellent feedback on what worked and what didn't so that you can learn and improve each time. You may also happen to come up with something that you would like to preserve, revise, and polish to make into a written composition later. The recorder may see intrusive at first, but if you record everything, it will soon become a normal part of the process. While you might not want to save everything you record, if you don't record everything, those spontaneous gems will be gone forever.

Serial Composition

Four-plus players. Player One improvises a short phrase then passes it to Player Two, who continues it and hands it off to Player Three, and so on. Players may decide on key and/or style ahead of time— or not. Players may use nods or other physical gestures to help pass the line along and connect it seamlessly. Players should try to maintain the style and elaborate upon strong ideas; distinct melodic motifs should be continued and developed. See similar games in Aural Games as well.

One-Measure Melody Invention

Three-plus players. This is a variation of "One-Measure Rhythm Invention [Rhythm Games]" (page x), which should be played before this one so that players are comfortable with inventing rhythms.

Form a circle. Establish a beat in moderate 4/4 tempo (count off, tap toes, assign one or two players to play percussion, etc.).

Basic Play:	The group decides on a three-note rhythm (e.g. long-short-short). Each player in turn invents a one-measure melody using the agreed-upon rhythm.
Variation 1:	When the group is comfortable with *Basic Play*, they should then improvise the rhythm and the melody. At first, the player may repeat the measure several times for the sake of comfort. Later, the pulse must continue unbroken from player to player as each invents a new one-measure three-note rhythm plus melody. Advanced players may make the game more challenging by gradually increasing the tempo each time around (a metronome or other rhythm source may be handy here).
Variation 2:	*Basic Play* again, but this time with four notes.
Variation 3:	Like *Variation 1* (invented rhythms *and* melody), but with four notes.

Card Melody

One to four players. Take twelve 3X5-inch note cards and write a note of the chromatic scale on each. Shuffle. Deal each player one card. The players play simultaneously, each soloing (and occasionally resting) using the 'card' note. Repeat the game; this time each player gets two cards and may use only these two notes in their solo. Listen to the other players; relate to them somehow. Repeat for three and four cards (only for three players).

Variation: Repeat, using the card note as the key or scale (so that now each player has a choice of seven notes instead of one). Decide in advance whether the scales will be major, minor, or independently chosen.

Three or Five Only

One to eight players. Players are limited to three or five notes only. Each player chooses the notes for the player next to him. Choices may either be free or from a pre-selected scale. Invent a piece using only these notes. Style may pre-selected or discovered *en route*.

Two by Two

One to eight players. The restriction for this improvised piece is that all melody notes must consist of note pairs. Players must play any melodic pitch twice in a row; however, rhythmic values may vary. The length of each note of the pair may be different.

Variation: Make it three notes.

Whole or Half

Two players. Two players invent a duet in some style (see Musical Styles and Forms for suggestions).

Restriction: Players are not bound to any particular key, but they may move only by step or half step—no leaps allowed.

Half and Half

Two players. The chromatic scale is divided up into exclusive halves: six notes for each player with no common notes. The players then improvise either freely or in a selected style, making the loveliest music they can.

Suggestions for dividing up the notes (feel free to make your own mixes):

1. Player One: C–D–E–F♯–A♭–B♭
   Player Two: C♯–E♭–F–G–A–B

2. Player One: C–D–E–F–G–A
   Player Two: B–C♯–D♯–F♯–G♯–A♯

3. Player One: C–D–E–G–A–B
   Player Two: D♭–E♭–F–G♭–A♭–B♭

4. Player One: C–D♭–D–E♭–E–F
   Player Two: F♯–G–A♭–A–B♭–B

5. Player One: C–D–F–G–A–B♭
   Player Two: D♭–E♭–E–F♯–G♯–B

6. Player One: C–E–G–G♯–A–B♭
    Player Two: B–C♯–D–D♯–F–F♯

Tripartite

Three players. Same game as *Half and Half* above, except that now the chromatic scale is divided up for three players.

Suggestions for dividing up the notes:

1. Player One: C–D–E–G
    Player Two: D♭–E♭–F–A♭
    Player Three: F♯–A–B♭–B

2. Player One: C–C♯–D–E♭
    Player Two: E–F–F♯–G
    Player Three: A♭–A–B♭–B

3. Player One: C–E–G–B
    Player Two: B–D♯–F♯–A♯
    Player Three: B♭–D–F–A

4. Player One: C–D–E–F
    Player Two: B–C♯–D♯–F♯
    Player Three: G–A♭–A–B♭

5. Player One: C–E♭–F♯–A
    Player Two: B–D–F–A♭
    Player Three: B♭–C♯–E–G

6. Player One: C–E–A♭–A
    Player Two: B–E♭–G–A♭
    Player Three: B♭–D–F–F♯

Leaps Aloud

Two players. Two players invent a duet in some style.

Restriction: They may only move by leap—minor third or larger.

Variation 1:   Players must choose and stick to only one interval that plus or minus a half step.

Variation 2:   Players must reverse direction after each leap.

Fitting In

Two to eight players. Start a pulse, then players enter with long tones *ad lib*. The group must find a common tonal area (each player needs to ask: "Is my note fitting in?"). Once players find a note that fits, they should construct a network of notes, a collection of pitches that also work. Explore stepwise. (Source: Ed Sarath.)

Change That Tune

Six-plus players. Player One begins, improvising a melody with a definite feeling or style; it should repeat after roughly ten seconds. Player Two (the group may be in a circle) enters, playing a rough version of Player One's piece along with Player One. When Player Two has it, Player One drops out. Player Two then transforms the melody into something different. Player Three enters, copying Player Two's melody, and play continues around the circle.

Nostalgia

One player. Play any familiar tune, using one or two phrases, a verse or chorus, or the entire tune. If you make any 'mistakes', keep playing, but take note and when you play the tune again, play the 'mistakes' exactly as you did the first time. If you make any 'mistakes' the second time through, repeat the process. Try to remember and play the latest version as exactly as possible. Continue *ad lib*.

Obstinacy

Two-plus players. Set the key and scale ahead of time (C major, D minor, etc.). Each player chooses a three-or four-note motif and must stick with it for the entire piece, although the player may use various techniques of motif development (rhythmic or intervallic augmentation or diminution, transposition, sequence, octave displacement, change of timbre, and so on) to create interest.

Circle Duet

Six-plus players. Players sit in a circle or semicircle. Two players sitting some distance apart (or opposite each other if in a circle) improvise a duet, playing for approximately thirty to forty-five seconds. Then the next pair (moving counterclockwise) plays another duet, making it as contrasting as possible with the previous duet. (Source: Ed Sarath.)

Variation: Players on either side of the soloists may add subtle percussion accompaniment.

Quotes Only

Two to four players. Players construct a piece with one restriction: they may only play quotes (i.e. passages from compositions). Good sources for quotes include folk songs, hymns, Christmas carols, orchestral excerpts, ad jingles, children's songs, symphony themes, Broadway tunes, camp songs, and so on. Players may have a list of songs in front of them while playing (see Familiar Tunes List in Resources).

Twisted Quotes

Two to four players. Repeat the *Quotes* game above, but distort the familiar tunes in as many ways as possible, such as changing the intervals, using an exotic scale, adding or subtracting notes, or keeping the melody while changing the rhythms. Example: play "Mary Had a Little Lamb" in the Phrygian mode (1–♭2–♭3–4–♭5–♭6–♭7) with a Calypso feel. Inspired by Bill Cahn, author of *Creative Music Making*.

Twisted Unison

One player at the piano. The player sings a simple melody (invented or familiar) and plays it in unison at the piano except for one thing: the vocal line is a parallel interval away from the piano line. For example, the piano is playing the melody in C and the voice is singing a whole step above in D major. More advanced players can try this with other intervals: major or minor thirds, perfect fourths or fifths, etc. The ultimate challenge: a half step or a tritone away.

Medley

Two to four players. This one works well with a pre-chosen list of familiar tunes (cowboy songs, children's songs, Christmas songs, etc.). Each player chooses a tune independently and plays the tune or part of a tune in any key. Alternate short solo turns with playing accompaniment figures taken from other snippets or motifs from the tunes. Players should weave in and out of fore- and background, matching rhythms and keys, or contrast in register, dynamics, energy, and so on. Steal other player's tunes and motifs shamelessly.

Mixed Messages

One player, for piano. The left hand plays a simple familiar tune in, say, C major. The right hand plays in unison with the left, but in a different key, say, F♯. Experiment with many combinations of chord pairs, including scale types other than major (any kind of minor, whole tone, diminished, Lydian, Phrygian, and so on.)

Variation: Hands in unison (same key or not), improvising the line.

Walking Melody with Lurches

One player, but it could serve as background for a second player; two players could also play this at once. Choose a comfortable tempo, somewhere between moderate and brisk. Play steady quarter notes. Move stepwise up and down the scale (change direction *ad lib.*), adding sharp accents at regular and/or irregular intervals. Experiment with both *legato* and *staccato* articulation. You may occasionally make a wide leap when you run out of room ascending or descending.

Scale choices: 1. Major

2. Chromatic

3. Minor (any kind)

4. Mix major or minor and chromatic.

5. Other (pentatonic, blues, whole tone, diminished, etc.).

As always, try in all keys.

Hold/Move Duet

Two players. Two players play a duet, with the object being for one to move when the other holds. Start with a slow tempo; experiment with faster tempos as you gain experience. Play the duet in an agreed-upon major key; then repeat in minor.

Hold/Move Chamber Music

Three-plus players. Players may play *Hold/Move*. Each player holds (and then moves to) a different note, creating a contrapuntal texture, which may sound something like a Bach chorale (or not). Experiment using a pre-set major or minor key and then no pre-set key.

Third Time's A Charm

Two players. Improvise a duet in a major key (preferably one of the most unfamiliar). Players alternate between solo and accompaniment roles.

Special limit: Players are not allowed to develop any idea introduced in a solo role or to bring in any new ideas until it has been repeated at least three times.

Far Out

One or two players. Percussion *ad lib.* may be added. Improvise an atonal melody. Emphasize dissonant intervals such major and minor seconds, tritones, and major and minor sevenths. Give the atonal melody coherence by using repetition, sequence, dynamic phrasing.

Tonal/Atonal

Two-plus players. Players begin in an agreed-upon major key. Style (e.g. march, lullabye, dirge, fanfare, etc.) may be set ahead of time or discovered along the way. At a signal from Player One, players transition into playing atonally—but continuing the style. At some point, Player Two signals the return back to the original tonality. Players may end here or repeat the cycle.

Gesture

Three-plus players. Someone invents a gesture or motif consisting of several notes, not necessarily tonal. All players help to develop the motif, repeating it, transposing it, playing it in augmentation and diminution, being silent, using extended techniques, exaggeration, etc. (Source: Ed Sarath.)

Echo

Four-plus players. This works well with a circle of players. Player One plays one note. The player on Player One's right—Player Two—echoes exactly what Player One plays. Continue on around the circle, but if Player Two plays something different, this becomes the new note (or interval) to be imitated. This game can be played with different restrictions depending on the level of the players. As players become more adept, the speed of imitation may become quicker. Use the major scale to start; as players become more proficient, try other scale types, e.g. minors, pentatonic, whole tone, diminished, blues, etc.

Variation 1:   Two notes: first a step apart, then expand into larger intervals.

Variation 2:   Three notes: C–E–G or C–D–E.

Variation 3:   Five notes: C–D–E–F–G or C–D–E–G–A or C–E♭–F–G–B♭.

Variation 4:   Six notes: Start using some easy-to-remember first notes (stepwise or triadic); add more complex interval combinations as proficiency develops.

Variation 5:   More notes: How many can you add?

Variation 6:   Add inflections (e.g. a glissando or slide into the note).

Variation 7:   Change timbre (half-valve, harmonic, etc.).

Yes, and...

Two to 16 players. The first rule of improvisational theatre is that when one player starts something, the other players who join in must accept Player One's premise or set-up and support and continue it. This is called "Yes, and…" The same can happen in musical improvisation: Player One begins a tune, then the next player listens for a few seconds and then joins in, trying to play in the style of Player One as much as possible, also assuming a complementary role as accompanist, duet partner, ostinato, long tone, etc., following and accepting Player One's decisions at every turn. Player One has complete freedom to take the solo line in any direction.

Watching T and V (variation of Replay)

Four-plus players. Players sit in a circle. Player One, beginning on the tonic, plays a measure or two in B♭ major. Player Two replays the notes, but changes it in one or more ways (adding or subtracting notes, ornamenting, changing octaves or meter, using augmentation or diminution, etc.). The next player takes this new product and transforms it further, and so on around the circle.

As You Were Saying (variation of Replay)

Two-plus players. Player One does a short improvisation in a set key or scale (e.g. pentatonic major) at first. At some point, Player One stops, indicating to Player Two a few seconds before stopping to be ready. As soon as Player One stops, Player Two must try to begin an improvisation using the last measure or two of Player One's solo. The game continues as Player Two hands the line off similarly to Player Three (or back to Player One).

Taking It from Here (variation of Replay)

Two-plus players. Larger groups should sit in a circle. Player One plays approximately one measure and hands it off to Player Two, who continues the melody for another measure (or so) before handing off to the next player.

Variation 1:	Vary the size of the melody fragment.
Variation 2:	Have Player Two's melody overlap the end of Player One's by several notes.

Interior Decoration

Two players. Players One and Two improvise melodies together on any major or minor scale. Play mostly stepwise, adding many grace notes and other decorations or embellishments.

Canon 1 (variation of Replay)

Two players. Player One enters, playing a *cantabile* melody. Player Two enters after a measure or two, trying to play precisely what Player One plays. At first they should play only in an agreed upon key. With some experience, Player One can play progressively less tonal music and/or change keys.

Canon 2

Two players. Players pick a key and starting note. Player One begins playing. Player Two comes in a measure later and has to play exactly what Player One played. (Source: Matt Hellenbrand.)

Suggestion:	Keep it simple!

Canon 3

Two players. Pick a key. Player One plays quarter notes. Player Two plays in canon one quarter note behind Player One. (Source: David Hastings.)

Variation 1:	Change rhythms.
Variation 2:	Modulate to a new key.

Round You Go

Two players. Like the *Canon* games above, but limited to four or eight measures, then the melody line repeats (both players will have to remember what the melody is!). Keep the melody very simple and in a major key.

Variation:	Change to a minor key. Vocalists should try to invent text for the round (and remember it for subsequent repetitions!).

Row, Row, Row...

Two players. Players improvise using three to six tones from one of the following:

1. Pentatonic scale (steps 1–2–3–5–6).

2. Major scale.

3. Minor (natural, harmonic, or melodic minor, or Dorian mode).

4. Any note (chromatic scale).

Suggestions: 1. Choose the key ahead of time.

- Same key (e.g. everyone plays in C major).

- Different keys (e.g. Player One plays in C and Player Two in E).

- Different types of keys, e.g.,
  Player One: C major, Player Two: C minor
  Player One: C major, Player Two: E♭ minor

2. No discussion of keys; free choice in the moment.

3. Use one key the whole time or change key at will.

4. Use diatonic and/or chromatic sequences of the tones (easier with only three to four tones).

5. Restrict to this set of tones only, but add variety by changing articulation, dynamics, timbre, or by using silence, extended techniques, and so on.

6. As with number five above, but add retrograde as a possibility.

7. For longer rows, occasionally select smaller cells within the row (e.g. choose three notes and vary them in the above-mentioned ways before moving on).

Mock Audition

Two-plus players. Player One is the Audition Committee and announces (one at a time) the (made-up) composers and the (made-up) pieces that Player Two must perform to "try to win the job."

Examples: Please play the *Cantabile* solo for thirteenth horn from Hank Würstchen's Anxiety Symphony No. 3.

        Play the Long Pizzazz solo at letter B in Wendy Underbutler's tone poem, "The Wretched Duck."

Player Two must respond with convincing but completely fabricated renditions of the fictional excerpts. Player One may add extra instructions before or after.

Examples: Very good. Now, can you play it again, twice as fast, with a lot of jaw vibrato and a *glissando* at the end?

        I hope you brought the crumpled newspaper that Bronfuss asks for as a mute. No? Take mine.

Variation 1:   Use the names of actual composers (Mozart, Strauss, Bach, Beethoven, Brahms, John Williams…) but invent fictional compositions.

Examples:	I'd like to hear the Left-Handed Fugue and Two-Step from Bach's *Die Unglaubliche Käse* [The Unbelievable Cheese] Cantata.
	Please play the exposition from Mozart's "Short Notice" Concerto for Bass Slide Whistle.
	(Now you know how Peter Schickele must have gotten started...).
Variation 2:	Use famous excerpts, but ask for outrageous changes to tempo, dynamics, articulation, etc.
Example:	Please play the *Andante Cantabile* horn solo from Tchaikovsky's Fifth Symphony, but change octaves every phrase and play it twice as fast, swung, in 7/8.

Zip It!

One to three players. Generate a tone row for improvisation using numbers; each number corresponds to a scale step, e.g., in C Major 1 = C, 2 = D, etc., with 8 = C at the octave, 9 = octave D, and 0 = silence. Base a piece on your zip code. Example: 52241 in C major = G–D–D–F–C. Add note values (they don't all have to be the same length). As a duet or trio, players from the same zip code may choose different note values (and/or different keys!).

Try using the same technique with today's date (month, day, and year), your age (two digits are often enough to produce a satisfactory ostinato), your birthday, or part of your telephone number or Social Security Number.

Every Which Way

One player. Take a familiar tune (or a passage from a solo or etude) and keep the rhythms, but change the melody. (Source: Matt Hellenbrand.)

Variation 1:	Keep the melody, change the rhythms.
Variation 2:	Vary the melody.
Variation 3:	Keep the same chord progression, but create a new melody.

Heterophony

Two to four players. The group agrees on a familiar tune. Player One plays the tune very plainly and unadorned. The other players play at the same time as Player One, but they alter the rhythms and add ornaments as they see fit.

Same and Change

Three-plus players. Sit in a circle. Two players begin by entering together, playing quarter notes and half notes only in moderate tempo. When they land on the same note, Player One drops out and Player Three enters. When Players Two and Three land on the same note, Player Two drops out and Player One enters. When One and Three land on the same note, Player Three drops out and Player Two enters.

Variation 1:   Set key.

Variation 2:   Free.

Progressive Tones

Two to eight players. Each player plays a short phrase in an agreed upon key, but each must begin the phrase on a progressively higher scale step until the octave is achieved, i.e. in C major, Player One begins on C, Player Two on D, etc. With fewer than eight players, there will be some overlap or alternation.

Old and New

Two to three players. Player One plays any solo from his instrument's literature, looping the selection after one or two phrases. Player Two improvises a second part to make a duet. A third part may be added, but Player Three should limit this part to an accompaniment only.

Old and Argh!

Two players. Player One plays any solo from her instrument's literature. Player Two invents an accompaniment that is diametrically opposed to it in style.

Anything Goes

Two to three players. Like *Old and New* above, except that the players construct the duet or trio from fragments (free choice) on the printed page. Players are free to play fragments in any length or order, and may apply various kinds of motivic development. Players must keep in mind, however, that although they are selecting fragments individually and independently, they must use their intuition, imagination, and skill to *make the parts fit together as much as possible*.

Tension/Release

Two-plus players. Two or more players improvise a duet in a major key, switching between solo and accompaniment roles as signaled by the solo player. *Soloists must begin and/or end phrases on a "wrong" note,* and then resolve it to a chord tone. Here, "wrong" means a tension or dissonant note. In major, mild dissonance can be obtained using scale steps 2, 4, 6, and 7; in C: D–F–A–B. For sharper dissonance, begin on ♭2, ♯2, ♯4, and ♭6 (in C: D♭–F♯–A♭).

Hare and the Tortoise

Four to twelve players. All players commence with fast, convoluted, high-energy melodies. Gradually all the lines move slower and slower, using longer and longer rhythmic values until finally all players hold one last very long tone. Silence ends the piece. Then...

Tortoise and the Hare

Four to twelve players. Play the above game in reverse, starting with very long tones which gradually become quicker and quicker strings of notes until all players are filling the air with dizzying cascades of notes. All cut off at once at a signal from the leader.

Bumblebee

One to two players. Players use short chromatic segments to depict the wild flight of a bumblebee, playing as fast as their technical level allows. Extended techniques (flutter-tongue, *sul ponticello*, etc.) may be added.

Variation:	One player is a fast bee, the other is a rather slow bee. Switch roles when exhausted.

Great Minds...

Two players. Player One begins any favorite classical solo. At a signal from Player Two, Player One must continue, but improvising in the style of the solo.

Tip:	Steal characteristic motifs and phrases from the rest of the piece (including the accompaniment).
Optional:	At a second signal from Player Two, Player One returns to the written solo.

Inside/Outside

Two to three players. Each player is assigned two tones with which to improvise. Player One may choose only chord tones. Use steps one and three the first time (the tonic chord, in this example)—C and E in C major—to set up an ostinato. Player Two may use three tones, but these must be non-chord tones, i.e., 2, 4, 6, 7. Use adjacent non-chord tones the first time, e.g., two and four (D and F in C major). With three players, Player Three uses only two chord tones, but a different selection than Player One, e.g., 3 and 5 or 5 and 1 or 1 and 5. Player Three's selections do not have to be adjacent; e.g., 5 and 3 (ascending).

Variation:	Player Two may go farther outside the diatonic scale and select tones from another key, e.g., when Player One plays C and E (C major), Player Two may play E♭–G♭–B♭ (1–♭3–5 in E♭ minor).

Inside/Outside Composition

Two to three players. Write out an introduction and theme followed by the game above, which may be repeated in sections (as cued by Player One) so that each player plays in a planned key area.

Ending: Cue the theme once again and then move to a written-out Coda.

Intervals

One-plus players. This games works best on piano, but may be played by other instruments as well. Improvise an interesting melody line using only:

- Unisons or octaves (plus diatonic steps)

- Scale degrees 1 and 5

- Scale degrees 1, 4, 5

- Scale degrees 1, 2, 5

- Choice of 1 (root or tonic) plus any two or three other notes in the major or chromatic scales.

Change octaves with any of these at will. Skilled piano players may assign an accompaniment function to one hand and solo with the other. See also *The Sparse and the Laconic* in Texture Games, page x.

Versatility

Four-plus players. Use a marimba, voice, piano, and some kind of percussion (djembe, bongos, shaker, claves, etc.) and improvise a piece. After about a minute, players switch instruments one by one. Continue until everyone has had a chance to play all the instruments. Finish on the instrument on which you began.

Pathways

Two players. Each player picks two notes some distance apart (an octave is a good start). Player One starts high; Player Two starts low. They begin playing, following a meandering pathway (with varied note values) to eventually reach the other note (a graph of the motion would look like an angled squiggle). Players either hold the final note or go silent when they reach their goal.

Variation 1: Players may choose the same two notes or choose independently.

Variation 2: Players may choose the same key or choose independently.

Variation 3: Try with three or four players.

Round Trip: After players reach the goal note, they reverse course and slowly meander back to the beginning note.

Hide and Seek

Two players. Players pick a note at random. They may move up and down at will, but only by step or half step, using quarter, half, or whole notes in a common pulse. A player may only move when the other is still. A player must move in the opposite direction of the other player. When players reach unison, the game is over.

Variation 1:   Upper voice moves in quarter notes; lower voice in half notes. If a third voice is added, it always moves in whole notes in the low register.

Variation 2a: Each player picks an interval, always moving by a major second or minor third, for example. Players may change direction at will.

Variation 2b: Both players play the same interval, but with a random choice of (starting) note.

Variation 2c: Both players play any interval with a random choice of note.

For all versions of *Variation 2*, players could also start on the same note. The game ends when unison is reached once again.

Eye of the Beholder I

One player. Play the ugliest possible melody for a half a minute or so. Follow it with *Eye of the Beholder II* (below).

Eye of the Beholder II

One player. Play the most beautiful solo you can imagine for another half minute. Do this alone or in a group of any size. Agree on a key beforehand—or not. Add dynamics as needed.

Variation: Use only one or two notes for each version of *Eye of the Beholder*.

Competition

Two to eight players. Divide into two groups. Group One improvises—simply—for about fifteen seconds. Group Two imitates Group One as closely as possible, but tries ways to make the improvisation a bit more exciting. Continue until exhausted. (Source: Azadeh Raoufi.)

Out of Chaos

Four to sixteen players. Without prior discussion, everyone starts playing at once, all independent in keys, styles, moods, tempi, dynamics, etc. Very gradually the sounds find unity and, after some time, synchronize into one unified sound. Stay with it for while, then at some point, make eye contact and end with one big sound.

Sequences

One player. The player decides on a simple one-measure pattern in a major key. Start with quarter and half notes only (the measure may be invented or selected from a solo, etude, or orchestral/band excerpt); then play the measure in diatonic sequence up one octave and down again. Repeating it in all keys is a good idea.

Suggestion: Repeat in a minor key.

Pace Yourself

One to two players. Robert Pace has developed a piano method that incorporates improvisation (any piano teacher interested in improvisation should check out his many books) and this game is based on his method of teaching improvisation. The play:

1. Select a simple familiar tune in any key. Play the tune until you can find the melody without hesitation (thorough individuals may wish to learn it in several or all keys, as well as working to be able to play the chords and chord roots).

2. Vary the melody but keep the same rhythms (to keep it recognizable) while:

- Changing the direction or contour of the melody. For example, if the melody ascends, the variation could descend. Or if the melody were 1–3–1, you could play 3–1–5.

- Simplifying the melody by using fewer notes (e.g. instead of 1–3–5, you could play 1–3–3)

- Compressing leaps into steps. The melodic direction may be kept the same or reversed.

Note: Pace advises to make a plan about what you would like to change *before* playing the variation.

Variation 1:   This procedure can also be applied to any piece of printed music—but the player must know the harmony (chord progression).

Variation 2:   Add a second player to play a bass line that outlines the harmony.

Copy Machine (piano)

One player. The right hand plays one to four notes in any key. The left hand (in the same position but an octave lower) immediately imitates a short gesture, a measure, two measures, a phrase. Keep it up for a while; make it gradually more interesting both rhythmically and melodically. Then switch— left hand leads this time. (Source: Azadeh Raoufi.)

Variation: Repeat the game with two players at the keyboard. Start simple and progress.

Key Quotes (piano)

One player. Using only the black keys on the piano, try to discover as many familiar tunes as possible.

Variation: After discovering a tune, repeat and add an accompaniment on black keys in the bass.

Black Key Duet (piano)

Two players. Invent a duet using only the black keys of the piano. Using black keys only provides an easy way to become acquainted with the major pentatonic scale (scale steps 1–2–3–5–6), in this case, F♯ pentatonic. The pentatonic scale is very useful because everything you play sounds "good"—there are no sharp dissonances available.

Idea:	Players should not hesitate to cross above or below the other player!
Variation 1:	Player Two switches to a different pentatonic scale, such as C pentatonic (C–D–E–G–A). Now there is some crunch!
Experiments:	Try out as many pentatonic scale combinations as you can find. Write short descriptions of your findings in the improv notebook in which you keep ongoing records of all your musical discoveries. Write subjective descriptions of the sounds with ideas for use in an improvisation, e.g., "Left hand, C pentatonic; right hand, E pentatonic. Restless, uneasy, bright, hint of Debussy, mild to sharp dissonance, use for the A section of "Waiting to Go On" or "The Tax Audit."
Variation 2:	Each player must play two notes at a time (which will give rise to some interesting four-note chords, especially if two different pentatonic scales are used).

Alternation (piano)

One player. Improvise a piece alternating single notes in the right and left hands, with the restriction that the left hand may play only black notes and the right hand only white notes. Repeat and switch roles.

Idea:	Find a partner and play as a duet.

Bitonal Bits (piano)

One player. Improvise a simple melody in unison with both hands in five-finger position—but each hand plays in a different key.

Homework Assignment:	Make a chart of all the possible pairings of hands/keys.
Variation 1:	Repeat in the minor mode.
Variation 2:	One hand plays in a major key; the other in a different minor key.
Variation 3:	Use modes (Lydian, Phrygian, etc.).
Variation 4:	Use other scale types: whole tone, diminished, etc.

Modal Transformations

One player. (A second player may be added as accompaniment, and remember, percussion can be added to just about anything). This game takes a familiar tune and goes a step beyond a modal switch by changing the scale to one of the modes. This idea may be applied to any familiar tune.

Consider each modal transformation to the following well-known tunes:

Mary Had a Little Lamb
Lightly Row
This Old Man
Go Tell Aunt Rhody
Twinkle Twinkle Little Star

Suggestion:	Sing the transformations before playing them on the instrument. Make sure the differences are in your ear.
Experiment 1:	*Every day, pick a mode and play it—slowly—in all keys.*
	Example: C Dorian, D♭ Dorian, D Dorian, and so on.
Experiment 2:	Improvise in a mode with a friend at the piano. Have the friend accompany using triads built on the modal scale, or just a 1–5 drone.
Alert:	From now on, listen to every familiar tune and classical theme to determine if it is modal, and if so, which one. Write down your findings in your improv notebook.

Below are suggested titles for improvised pieces in each mode.

Dorian:	Modes can be visualized or quickly found using the white keys on the piano. The Dorian mode is a type of minor scale. A Dorian scale can be played on the piano with white keys only, beginning on D.
	A useful and versatile way to know the Dorian mode is spelling the scale as scale degrees: 1–2–♭3–4–5–6–♭7. In D Dorian, this is D–E–F–G–A–B–C–D. In C Dorian, it is C–D–E♭–F–G–A–B♭.
	The Dorian mode is a very popular improvising scale in jazz. It is played over the iim⁷ chord in jazz progressions (and can be played over the ii–V combination). After transforming the suggested melodies above to Dorian, make up pieces entitled "Wintry Sunset," "Lost My Cool," and/or "Dirge for a Duck."
Phrygian:	The Phrygian mode has a dark, exotic, and/or Hispanic sound to it. It is spelled 1–♭2–♭3–4–5–♭6–♭7. A variation of it with raised third is known as the Spanish Phrygian, and is spelled 1–♭2–3–4–5–♭6–♭7.
	A Phrygian scale can be played on the piano with white keys only, beginning on E.
	C Phrygian is C–D♭–E♭–F–G–A♭–B♭.
	After transforming the above melodies to Phrygian, make up pieces entitled "Spanish Adventure" and "Parthenon at Night."

Lydian: The Lydian mode is a very bright-sounding mode, "more major than major." It is spelled 1–2–3–#4–5–6–7. A Lydian scale can be played on the piano with white keys only, beginning on F.

C Lydian is C–D–E–F#–G–A–B–C.

After transforming the above melodies to Lydian, make up pieces entitled "Fast Race in New Shoes," and "Sun Time."

Mixolydian: The Mixolydian mode is also known as the dominant seventh scale. It is extremely common in jazz, used over the V^7 chord of the common ii–V–I chord progression. It is simply a major scale with a lowered seventh, and is spelled 1–2–3–4–5–6–♭7.

A Mixolydian scale can be played on the piano with white keys only, beginning on G. C Mixolydian is C–D–E–F–G–A–B♭.

This mode will not "transform" any of the suggested tunes because they do not use the seventh scale degree. To hear the transformation, try these: "White Coral Bells," "Joy to the World," "The First Noel," and "A Mighty Fortress." Then make up pieces that use the seventh scale degree prominently entitled "New Car," "Don't Be Late," and "No Upper Limit."

Experiment: Swing the eighth notes.

Aeolian: The Aeolian mode is simply the natural minor mode or the Dorian mode with a flatted sixth degree. It is spelled 1–2–♭3–4–5–♭6–♭7.

An Aeolian scale can be played on the piano with white keys only, beginning on A.

C Aeolian is C–D–E♭–F–G–A♭–B♭.

After transforming the suggested melodies (or others) to Aeolian, make up pieces entitled "Dark of the Moon," "Mountain Chant," and "Chase!"

Locrian: The Locrian mode has a unique, pungent sound because the interval between the root and the fifth is a tritone. It is used in jazz over half diminished (also known as $m^{7(♭5)}$) chords, although often the second step is altered from ♭2 to 2. It is spelled 1–♭2–♭3–4–♭5–♭6–♭7.

A Locrian scale can be played on the piano with white keys only, beginning on B.

C Locrian is C–D♭–E♭– F–G♭–A♭–B♭.

After transforming the suggested melodies to Locrian, make up pieces entitled "Vinegar Festival," "Upset," and "Anxious Moments."

Lydian Dominant: The Lydian Dominant is not a natural scale, but it is a very useful construct with a unique sound and is often used in jazz. It is spelled 1–2–3–#4–5–6–♭7—

just the Lydian scale with a lowered seventh or a dominant seventh scale with a raised fourth. C Lydian Dominant is C–D–E–F#–G–A–B♭.

After transforming the suggested (or other) melodies, make up pieces entitled "Coming Un-Raveled," "Year's Supply of Cool," and "Up to Here."

Whole (Tone) Transformation

One player. The whole tone scale is only six notes: 1–2–3–#4–#5 (♭6)–♭7. The C whole tone scale is C–D–E–F#–A♭–B♭. The D whole tone scale uses the same notes, as do the scales based on the other notes in this scale. A half step lower than C is the B whole tone scale: B–C#–E♭–F–G–A, and the same goes for building scales with these tones. Thus there are only two distinctly different whole tone scales.

As with *Modal Transformations* (page x), transpose the suggested tunes and others by using whole tone scales, then make up a piece using one or more whole tones scales entitled "Impressionist's Picnic," "Clouds' Illusions," or "What?"

Rubato

Two players. Player One plays a scale up and down (change direction at will) in quarter notes of any type in a low register; the notes should be metronomic—dead on the beat. Player Two improvises using the same scale in a higher register, but playing slightly *behind* the beat, or playing partly behind the beat, then hurrying through the latter part of a measure to catch up.

Kool Kopprasch (for brass players, especially horn players)

Two-plus players. Set up a riff (see *Riff Game* in Rhythm Games) or other rhythmic and harmonic accompaniment. Pick a Kopprasch etude and use as a source for improvisation over the riff. Try this in different keys.

Alphorn Solo (horn)

One player. Using only the open F horn overtone series and long tones, create abeautiful, haunting, lyrical adagio solo. Repeat using fingerings of two (E horn), one (E♭ horn), one and two (D horn), and two and three (D♭ horn).

Alphorn duet/trio/quartet (horns)

Two to four players. Repeat *Alphorn Solo* above, this time with two, three, or four players playing at once. Steal as many ideas as you can from your neighbors!

Bebop Alphorn (horn or other brass)

Two-plus players. Using only notes from the overtone series (fingerings: 0; 2; 1; 1–2; 2–3) and jazzy/funky rhythms, invent a catchy, up-tempo solo line

> *Tip:* Stick with a few select pitches; you don't have to traverse the entire overtone series). Add a rhythmic accompaniment, such as the Riff Game in Rhythm Games, page x.

Outside Alphorn (horn or other brass)

Two-plus players. With one or more players playing a riff, pulsed drone, or other kind of groove, the solo "alphorn" improvises using only one fingering (e.g., for horns, use first valve only, which is horn in E♭) as in *Bebop Alphorn* above, but this time add snippets of valve combinations a half step above or below the main key. For example, for horns playing in E♭, add some brief excursions to horn in E (second valve) or D (one and two).

Predictable You

Two players. Player One plays a phrase that is as predictable as possible. (Think repetition, simplicity, lack of contrast, narrow range, no dynamic change, same timbre, etc.). Player Two picks up the phrase at some point and continues it as exactly as possible.

Variation: Time each phrase: Player One plays for ten or twenty seconds, then Player Two takes over. This type of playing is death for a soloist, but works well for an accompanist, whose job is to create a "carpet" to support the soloist and make her stand out.

Melody Combination Game 1

Two players. This combination consists of *Far Out* (Melody Games, page x) plus *Pick One* (Style Games, page x). Player One improvises an atonal melody to an accompaniment generated by Player Two, but both of them must do so in a style chosen from the list (Musical Styles and Forms in Resources, page x) in the back of the book, such as Baroque, Broadway, Fugue, Funk, Gavotte, Habañera, Minuet, Lullaby, Polka, Samba, Tango, Waltz, Yodel, etc.

Melody Combination Game 2

Two players. This combination consists of *Scale Flavors* (Melody Games, page x) plus *Oom Pah* (Bass Line Games, page x). Both players use the whole tone scale based on C (C–D–E–F♯–G♯–A♯). Player One plays an oom-pah bass, for example: 1–♯4–1–♯5 (C–F♯–C–G♯). Player Two invents a Sousa-esque solo over it. If a Player Three should happen by, he can play a suitable percussion part. Switch parts after a bit.

• • •

Musical creativity should be the first and foremost priority in the teaching of music. In every music lesson, there should be a time for improvisation, for invention, and a time for technical training, and development of the tools, which would include improvisational skills based on free and theoretical styles.

—LaDonna Smith[42]

---

[42] "Improvisation in Childhood Music Training and Techniques for Creative Music Making," www.the-improvisor.com/web%20ARTICLES/improvisation%20&%20Education.html

Chapter 16

Form Games

If we play only written compositions, our understanding of form will be much less acute than if we spontaneously create music. We must understand form and other musical elements from the inside out. Improvisation greatly heightens awareness of structure and construction of a successful composition, just as engaging in a debate differs from reading texts aloud.

It is sometimes thought that in improvisation we can do just anything. But lack of a conscious plan does not mean that our work is random or arbitrary. Improvisation always has its rules, even if they are not a priori rules.

—Stephen Nachmanovitch[43]

Developing AB's: Contrast!

Two to four players. It is easy to fall into the trap of playing pieces that sound exactly the same from start to finish without change or contrast. Once a player is comfortable with inventing material, the next focus should be on developing material that contrasts *sharply* with the original material. This game consists of short improvisations (approximately thirty seconds long) that emphasize clear parameters and switching to contrasting material. Use the following pairs as starters, then invent your own.

A	B
Loud	Soft
Fast	Slow
Dense flurries of notes	Very sparse texture (i.e., lots of space or silence)
Long tones, *legato*	Extreme *staccato*
Upper register	Lower register
Major	Minor
March-like	Lyrical love song
Tonal	Atonal
Normal timbre	Extended techniques
Homophonic	*Fugato*
4/4	3/4
2/4	5/8
3/4	7/8
6/8	3/4
Plain	Ornamented

---

43 *Free Play*, 26.

Card Contrast

Two to four players. Write the information from the A and the B columns in *Developing AB's: Contrast!* on 3X5-inch cards. Shuffle the decks and deal two, three, or four A cards, and as many B cards. Use them to construct A and B sections of a piece in AB or ABA form.

> *Variation:* Draw from the A pile, drawing again if two are contradictory (e.g., tonal/ atonal). Improvise the A section from the results
>
> > *Example:* Loud; Long Tones; Minor; Wide Leaps.
>
> Repeat using cards from the B pile.

Contrast Game

Four-plus players. Player One plays a short phrase. Player Two responds with a phrase that contrasts as much as possible in terms of note values, dynamics, tempo, texture, register, style, timbre, or meter. Continue the process around the circle.

Reps

Two to four players. Repeat *Developing AB's: Contrast!* above, adding a repeat of each section (AABB). Keep the sections very short (approximately five seconds). Begins with simple keys and note values. As facility develops, gradually increase the length of each section. Remember to make very clear contrasts between sections!

ABA Warm-Up

Two players. Player One invents a short phrase (A). Player Two plays a wildly contrasting phrase next (B). Player One must then repeat as exactly as possible what he played the first time. For additional interest, add up to three additional players various percussion instruments.

ABA Played (See ABA *Written* in Composition Games.)

Two to four players. Music is always more interesting if there is both unity (do something, then do it again) and variety (do something, then do something different). The simple ABA form has both unity and variety.

Without discussion, begin an improvisation. Listen for a strong idea. Stay with it, establishing and developing it. This is section A. Commit as much of it as possible to memory. When the time seems right, establish a new, contrasting section (B). When section B has run its course, return to section A, repeating it as exactly as possible. With practice it will be possible to remember most of section A, but in first acquaintances with ABA, make each section fairly short to facilitate memory. Longer improvisations will come later.

Song Form

Two to four players. Improvise a piece that uses AABA form. Use gestures or glances to indicate the repeat of section A. Take care to remember as many details as possible about section A! Initial attempts should limit the length of the section A section to about ten seconds.

Rondo

Two players. It takes time and practice to develop the complementary abilities of remembering what was previously improvised and creating contrasting material. Begins with very short material. Diligent practice will enable the memorization of longer sections.

When players have developed some facility in this type of memory, continue the development by trying a piece in rondo form (ABACA), the main material alternating with contrasting episodes. See creating contrasts in *Developing AB's: Contrast!* above. Keep the theme and episodes very short at first. With continued success, increase the challenge by lengthening the sections as well as adding new ones (e.g., ABACADA).

Sonata

One or two players. Using any agreed-upon style, meter, or tempo, improvise a piece using the basic elements of sonata form. Style is open. Begin the exposition (section A) with a bold, forthright theme or themes in a major key. At some point, transition to a more lyrical (or contrasting) second theme in the dominant key.

Next is the development (section B). Take motifs from the exposition and transform them using various motivic development techniques (transposition, sequence, fragmentation, etc.). At some point make a transition to the recapitulation (section A'). This improvised recap might not adhere to the exposition as strictly as a written composition does, but try to remember as much as possible about the opening material of the first and/or second themes. The piece may end after the recapitulation or finish with a coda section.

Etude

One player. An etude is designed to develop a particular technique. Choose a technique that you wish to develop and improvise a piece using the selected technique as much as possible. The technique may be musical (e.g., learning dominant chordal or melodic patterns) or an idiomatic technique of the instrument (e.g., difficult fingering patterns).

Through-Composed

One to four players. Improvise a piece with the form ABCD. No repetition of sections. Make each section contrast vividly with the others in a way that is clear to an audience.

Recommended: Tie the sections together with the use of a repeating melodic or rhythmic motif.

Theme and Variations

One to four players. Decide on a style before beginning. Player One is responsible for establishing a clear and simple theme. After no more than sixteen bars, the variations begin. Each player takes a set of variations. Conclude with a restatement of the theme plus a codetta.

Blues

One to four players. Use the traditional twelve-bar blues structure (three four-bar phrases) to construct a piece. The style does not have to be that of the blues or jazz. You may use the following harmonic scheme (or not):

I^7	IV^7	I^7	I^7
IV^7	IV^7	I^7	I^7
V^7	IV^7	I^7	I^7

See also: Storytelling Games
              Lyrical Piece, ABAC, and *Sea Chanty* in Improv Set-ups

• • •

Today's approaches to theory and notation are often dryly academic and isolated from matters of the spirit and heart. ... Try to connect your practice to your feelings for making music on your instrument.

—Julie Lyonn Lieberman

Chapter 17

Harmony Games

For most musicians, the harmony that we learn in traditional music theory classes is not as deeply rooted as it could be. It is primarily the pianist who experiences harmony through her instrument, and usually only by reciting from the printed page (unless she is fluent in figured bass or baroque ornamentation). To enjoy a deep, meaningful, and lasting understanding of harmony, we need to do as jazz players do and *use* harmony by improvising (although we don't have to play in a jazz style). This will take some time, depending on the player's background and instrument. However, using improv games to learn theory and harmony ensures the best and most expeditious results.

> *Our performing system has been geared toward perfection of execution and polish. Everything is worked out to an extraordinary luster. That produces consistency, but not necessarily creativity.*
>
> —Robert Levin[44]

Descending Scale

Two to plus players. Player One plays a slow descending major scale, repeating it over and over. Player Two solos over this using thirds and sixths whenever possible. Occasional fifths are okay. It is possible to add a third or even a fourth player.

Variation 1: Solo freely, letting your ear guide you from note to note.

Variation 2: Player Two picks a different key than Player One.

Variation 3: Player Two stays in the same key as Player One, but explores landing on notes that are a half step above or below diatonic tones, i.e., "mistakes."

(Source: Charles Young.)

Familiar Tune

One to four players. This game has so many musical vitamins and minerals that it should be done daily, but the best reason to do it is because it is both challenging and fun.

Choose a familiar tune, something that each player already knows *very* well (a children's song, folk song, Christmas carol, etc.) and try to play it by ear. After all players can play the melody easily, one or more players may play the melody while others play any of the following (all by ear, of course!):

---

44   Daniel Delgado, "Lost Art," *Harvard Magazine* [online], May–June, 2000, http://72.47.194.143/2000/05/lost-art.html

Chord roots
Harmony part(s)
Countermelody
Variations on the melody

It is best to add these one at a time. Give everyone a chance to try them all if possible, and then turn everyone loose to play any of the roles they like. Do this in an easy key (e.g., C major), and then gradually try it in other keys until they *all* become easy.

Variation: Switch modes. Play the tune in a minor key (or in major if the original tune is minor. For the daring, add some dissonant notes to the harmony.

See also: *Happy Birthday* (Improv Set-Ups, Chapter 33).

Improv on the Chords

Two to four players. Repeat *Familiar Tune*. When all players are comfortable playing the various roles/parts suggested, abandon the melody and do the following:

One or more players play the chord roots.

One player may play a long tone accompaniment (e.g., the third of the chord).

One or two melody instrument players may improvise an ostinato accompaniment.

One or two players may add a percussion accompaniment of any kind.

One player improvises a solo over the chords.

The only necessary chords are I and V. Others are nice but optional.

The Mismatch Game

Two players. Player One plays a simple diatonic melody; Player Two invents any kind of chordal setting to accompany it: diatonic, quartal, atonal, jazz, etc.

Variation: Player One plays a complex melody of any kind: atonal, jazzy, quartal, etc. Player Two invents a very simple diatonic melody.

Change of Mode

One player. Play any familiar tune in a major key. Play it again in minor. Repeat in many other keys.

Variation 1:   Play any technical exercise or pattern with which you are familiar (such as the Herbert L. Clarke cornet technique exercises). Repeat in every major and minor key.

Variation 2:   Seek out familiar tunes and exercises in minor keys. Play them in the major mode.

Mode Mix

Two players. Player One improvises in any major key; Player Two improvises in the same key, but in a minor mode. The version of minor for Player Two may be freely chosen at the time.

Possible combinations: Ascending melodic minor (1–2–♭3–4–5–6–7).
Descending melodic minor (♭6–♭7).
Harmonic minor (♭6–7).
Dorian (6–♭7).

Drifting

One player. The player invents a simple melody in C major. At some point a chord tone is chosen as a common tone between C and a new key. The player continues in the new key, repeating the procedure *ad libitum*.

Example: The median (third scale degree) in C major (E) becomes the tonic (first scale degree) of E major; then the dominant (fifth scale degree) of E major (B) becomes the subdominant (fourth scale degree) of F♯ minor, etc.

Variation 1:   Any scale step of the old key may be the common tone in the new key.

Example: The submediant (sixth scale degree) in C major (A) becomes the subdominant (fourth degree in E minor.

Variation 2:   Use arpeggios only.

Variation 3:   Mix arpeggios and scales.

Make Over

One player. Play any familiar tune or technical pattern, changing from major to other kinds of scales, such as dominant seventh, whole tone, chromatic, diminished, altered, Phrygian, Lydian, etc.

Crunch Time

Two players. One player plays any familiar tune (e.g., "Mary Had a Little Lamb", "Twinkle, Twinkle, Little Star," etc.) in a chosen key. Player Two plays simple triads on piano or mallet percussion to accompany, but instead of playing the third of the chord, the accompanist plays either a ♭2, 2, 4, ♯4, or ♭6. Use any kind pulsed pattern for the chord or arpeggiation of the triad.

Double Crunch

Two players. As with *Crunch Time*, but the accompaniment is completely atonal. Player One should bravely try to play the tune as "straight" as possible.

Reverse Crunch

Two players. In this variation of *Crunch Time*, Player Two uses simple basic triads to outline the chords of the familiar tune while Player One uses the rhythm of the melody, but plays the tune as atonally as possible.

Add-on Flats and Sharps

Two to three players. Confine the range to one octave, C to C. Improvise something between these limits as a duet or trio. Each player in turn announces how many flats or sharps will be applied.

Variation 1:	Apply flats and sharps in the usual order: one flat = B♭, two = B♭ and E♭; one sharp = F♯, two = F♯ and C♯, etc.
Variation 2:	The player choosing accidentals may assign flats or sharps to any note.
Variation 3:	The player choosing accidentals may add both flats and sharps in the usual order or at random.
Variation 4:	Players decide how many sharps or flats (or both) to add.
Variation 5:	Change the range to an octave between any notes other than C to C.
Variation 6:	Play without the octave limit.

Higher and Higher

Two to four players. Each player takes a turn soloing in a set key with the other players supporting. The soloist cues the next soloist when ready. The new soloist must play in a key that is a set interval higher than the previous key.

Examples:	One half step higher (start in C, move to D♭).
	One whole step higher (start in C, move to D).
	A minor third higher (start in C, move to E♭).

Suggesting Harmony

One or two players. Pick a simple chord progression (use V–I to start), meter, and tempo. Play several times through using arpeggios only, first ascending, then descending, and then both. Repeat this procedure with scales. Finally, do this using both arpeggios and scales, but always in a way that the underlying chords are clear.

Suggestions:	Use several chord tones, especially on strong beats.
	It is possible to artfully suggest a two-line dialogue with a single line.
	Experiment with other and longer progressions.
	Extract chord progressions from chorales and other pieces and improvise melodic lines over them as above.

Repeat everything with a partner, who may play any of the above roles as well as playing a bass line (roots or roots plus chord tones).

Models: Bach cello suites and violin partitas.

(Inspired by Charles Young.)

• • •

In a world where most music is heard electronically in highly edited, "perfect" performances, such high technical standards place a considerable burden on live performers. The technical achievements made possible by the electronic media are rarely, if ever, attained in live performance, because people are simply not perfect. The inherent risk for performers in such an environment is that the pressure to be technically perfect will have a dehumanizing effect if not balanced by humanizing concerns and activities.

—William Cahn, *Creative Music Making*[45]

• • •

Invention, the Mother

One player. Pick a chord of any type (major, major seventh, minor, minor seventh, dominant seventh, augmented, diminished, etc.) and an affect of any type (see the article "On Affect" by Keith Hill and Marianne Ploger at www.musicalratio.com). Marry the two in an improvised melody that is both tuneful, memorable, and clearly spells out the chord.

Chord/No Chord

Two to three players. One or more players set up a one-chord background in any major key. If the accompanist is a pianist, she may play a rhythmic background based on simple diatonic chords in that key. The soloist, however, is under orders to play a *cantabile* solo that is almost entirely *not* in that key: either highly inflected, in another key, or atonal. On the other hand, the soloist should relate to the accompaniment (and vice-versa) as much as possible in other ways (dynamically, rhythmically, stylistically, etc.).

One Chord: Major

Two to three players. One or more players set up a one-chord background in C major playing rhythmic ostinati on chord tones (such as scale degrees 1–3–5 for the I chord). Keyboard, guitar, marimba players, etc., are well suited for creating an effective chordal background over which to solo.

The soloist plays any and all known scale and arpeggio patterns over this background. (If desired, explore more unfamiliar sounds by trying other major or minor scales e.g., D7 over a C chord). Next, invent short three- to four-note patterns and melodic fragments and play them in sequence diatonically up and down the scale. After doing this for some time, improvise a solo in C major.

---

45   Routledge, 2005: 9.

The solo can be simplified by via restrictions, such as using only a couple of notes of the scale), an evocative title ("The Thoughtful Anaconda"), tempo, style (sea chanty, dirge, ragtime, etc.), and/or mood (jealous, anxious, sleepy, drunk, impatient, angry, giddy, eager, pensive, sad, irritated, fearful, etc.).

Variation 1:   Enrich the chord by adding another note to the triad such as the second, sixth, or seventh scale degree, creating in C major CADD^9, C^6, and Cmaj^7 respectively.

Variation 2:   Try in all major keys.

One Chord: Minor

Two to three players. One or more players set up a one-chord background in D minor playing rhythmic ostinati on chord tones (e.g., 1–3–5). A soloist uses the D Dorian scale (scale degrees 1–2–♭3–4–5–6–♭7, or all white keys on the piano beginning with D).

Other chord types: Dominant seventh
Scale degrees 1–2–3–4–5–6–♭7
In C major: C–D–E–F–G–A–B♭
Chord: 1–3–5–♭7

Whole tone
Scale degrees 1–2–3–♯4–♯5 (♭6)–♭7
Triad: 1–3–♯5

Lydian
Scale degrees 1–2–3–♯4–5–6–7

Lydian dominant
Scale degrees 1–2–3–♯4–5–6–♭7

One to Two/I-ii/Major to Dorian Minor

Two to three players. Repeat *One Chord: Minor* using the tonic (I) and supertonic (ii) chords. In C major, the chords are C major and D minor.

Play each chord for four measures. Once soloing over that length feels comfortable and automatic, reduce the solo length to two measures, then to one, and then to half a bar each. The soloist's comfort level determines the tempo and number of measures spent on each chord. Learn this progression in all keys.

More Two-chord Diatonic Progressions

Two to three players. Repeat *One Chord: Minor* and *One to Two* using two-chord progressions other than I–ii.

Examples:

	ii	V⁷
C major	Dm	G⁷
G major	Am	D⁷
F major	Gm	C⁷

	ii	vi
C major	Dm	Am
G major	Am	Em
F major	Gm	Dm

	I	vi
C major	C	Am
G major	G	Em
F major	F	Dm

	I	IV
C major	C	F
G major	G	C
B♭ major	B♭	E♭

	I	iii
C major	C	Em
F major	F	Am
E♭ major	E♭	Gm

	I	V⁷
C major	C	G⁷
F major	F	C⁷
E♭ major	E♭	B♭⁷

See *Two-Five* for additional information.

One-Four-Five

Two to four players. The I–IV–V⁷ progression is very common in popular and folk music. Set up a bass line and/or rhythm background (e.g., guitar or piano chords) of one measure in 4/4 for the tonic chord (I), another measure for the subdominant chord (IV), and two measures for the dominant seventh chord (V⁷).

Percussion is welcome.

Each player solos in turn over the progression. Make sure that each chorus (i.e., four-measure phrase) is different from the last in some way (e.g., melody, ornaments, rests, rhythms, dynamics, articulation, etc.). Add different styles (e.g., Latin) *ad libitum*. Soloists make a silent gesture to the next in line to indicate they are done.

Variation 1:	The accompaniment player may change chords at any time, not necessarily following any set number of measures.
Variation 2:	The accompaniment player may change meter (e.g., 4/4 to 3/4) at will.

The soloist must listen and adjust to the change in either variation.

Sad One-Four-Five

Two to four players. Repeat *One-Four-Five*, in the minor mode: i–iv–V7$^{(\flat9)}$ In C minor, the chords are Cm–Fm–G7$^{(\flat9)}$.

Variation:	Reduce the pattern from four measures to two, with i–iv in the first measure and V7$^{(\flat9)}$ in the second. The tempo may be quite brisk (e.g., a cut time feeling).

Oom Pah

Two players. This is a variation of *One Chord*, but in march style. Player One plays I–V in a relatively unfamiliar key (e.g., D$\flat$, F$\sharp$, etc.) in cut time, mimicking the tuba part in a march. Player Two improvises a march in the same key. More experienced players may improvise a solo line in a different key, such as soloing in D over an accompaniment in C.

Variation:	Use this game to practice I–V and I–IV–V^7 progressions.

Two-Five (ii–V7)

One to four players: a soloist plus accompaniment. As with the preceding games, some players create an accompaniment background on piano/guitar, bass, drums, or with a recorded play-a-long (e.g., a computer program such as Band-in-a-Box), using a ii–V7 progression. Practice techniques such as scales, arpeggios, patterns, and various licks as well as improvising freely. Take your time. It takes considerable time to become comfortable playing in each key in the examples below.

Tip:	If you are interested in jazz style:
	1. Find a friend to work on it with you.
	2. Find a teacher or mentor to help guide your study and listening.
	3. Start listening to many kinds of jazz soloists.
	4. Make transcriptions of the solos you like (software programs such as The Amazing Slow Downer can help) and learn them by heart.
	5. Read a good history of jazz.

Examples:

	ii	V^7
C major	Dm	G^7
F major	Gm	C^7
B♭ major	Cm	F^7
E♭ major	Fm	B♭^{7}
A♭ major	B♭m	E♭^{7}
D♭ major	E♭m	A♭^{7}
G♭ major	A♭m	D♭^{7}
B major	C♯m	F♯^{7}
E major	F♯m	B^7
A major	Bm	E^7
D major	Em	A^7
G major	Am	D^7

Two-Five-One (ii–V^7–I)

One to four players: a soloist plus accompaniment. As with the preceding games, some players create an accompaniment background on piano/guitar, bass, drums, or with a recorded play-a-long (e.g., a computer program such as Band-in-a-Box), using a ii–V^7–I progression. Practice techniques such as scales, arpeggios, patterns, and various licks as well as improvising freely. Take your time. It takes considerable time to become comfortable playing in each key in the examples below.

The ii–V^7–I progression is the basis of most jazz standards. The length of the ii–V^7 is typically the same length as the tonic (I) chord alone. So, if ii–V^7 (In C major: Dm–G^7) is one measure long, the resolution on C (the I chord) is one measure long. If ii (Dm) and V^7 (G^7) are each one measure long, then the tonic chord (C) is two measures long. Learn the ii–V^7–I progression in all keys.

Examples:

	ii	V^7	I
C major	Dm	G^7	C
F major	Gm	C^7	F
B♭ major	Cm	F^7	B♭
E♭ major	Fm	B♭^{7}	E♭
A♭ major	B♭m	E♭^{7}	A♭
D♭ major	E♭m	A♭^{7}	D♭
G♭ major	A♭m	D♭^{7}	G♭
B major	C♯m	F♯^{7}	B
E major	F♯m	B^7	E
A major	Bm	E^7	A
D major	Em	A^7	D
G major	Am	D^7	G

Chord Hopping

One player. Perhaps as part of a *Daily Arkady* (Melody Games), freely improvise back and forth between two chords. This can be fun and effective chord practice. At first improvisations may seem halting and full of hesitation. Stick with it until movement between the chords feels automatic, familiar, and fluent.

Suggestions:	Begin with major chords a half step apart (e.g., C to D♭ or C to B) or a whole step apart (e.g., C to D or D to E).
	Chord types may be mixed, e.g., C to E♭m, C to A♭7, etc., but any two chords will do.
Tip:	Limit play at first on each chord to scales, arpeggios, or short melodic patterns, such as 1–2–3–1 (in C major: C–D–E–C). Then mix several types at once.

Chord Hopping à Deûx

Two players. Players reasonably adept at *Chord Hopping* may try this as a duet in a more structured setting.

At first, spend considerable time on each chord and switch on the signal of Player One or Two. Then try varying lengths of chord duration, switching progressively sooner: Eight bars, four bars, two bars, one bar, half a bar.

Try non-diatonic major/minor progressions such as C to E, A to E♭m, D♭m to B♭m, etc.

More players may join on percussion.

Variation:	Use progressively longer progressions made up of the same or mixed types. Vary the number of measures spent on each chord as described above.
Examples:	Three chords: C–F♯m–B
	Four chords: B♭m–E–F♯–Dm
	Many chords: C–F♯–Fm–B–D♭m–E–B♭–Am–D

Spicy Progressions

One to two players. Repeat *Chord Hopping* à Deux using chords with different kinds of extensions.

Examples:	Short strings:
	Cm^6–E^9
	$E♭^6$–$B^{6/9}$
	Gm^{11}–$C7^{(♯11)}$
	A long string:
	$C^{6/9}$– $F♯^6$– $F°$–B^{ADD2}–$D♭7^{(♯9)}$–$E^{ø7}$– $B♭^{SUS}$–Am^9–$D7^{(♯5)}$

Non-triadic Chords

Two-plus players. Experiment with non-triadic chords (i.e., chords with notes that do not spell out major or minor triads). These will likely emphasize intervals other than thirds, such as fourths and seconds.

Examples:

Chord tones	In C Major
1–2–5	C–D–G
1–2–6	C-D-A
1–2–♭7	C-D-B♭
1–2–7	C-D-B
1–4–5	C-F-G
1–4–♭7	C–F–B♭

Construct an ostinato accompaniment using these chords. Write out parts for instruments available in class, transposing if necessary; rehearse the ostinato once, then improvise a solo over it.

(Idea from "The Tyranny of Triads" by W.A. Mathieu in *The Listening Book*.[46])

Transposition Map

One player. This is a good game to play after acquiring some proficiency with *Chord Hopping*. Pick a short series of tones (e.g., 1–2–3–5). Write down a random series of keys, (e.g., C, E♭, B, A, F♯, D, B♭, D♭, A♭, G). Play the tone series without pause through each key on the "map."

Tip:	When the switch between any two chords seems hesitant, loop between the two until the transition is smooth.
Variation 1:	Play the map backwards
Variation 2:	Create a tone series based on other scale types, such as:

> Minor
> Dominant seventh
> Diminished
> Augmented
> Whole tone
> Blues
> Pentatonic

Random Chord Sounds

Three to four players. Play long tones on random notes, changing at will.

Variation 1:	Pick a common key to limit the note choices.
Variation 2:	Each player picks different keys.
Variation 3:	Leave the choice of notes completely free.

---

46 Shambala, 1991: 159.

This game will sound better if players are occasionally silent. In fact, silence improves almost any group game. The more players, the more each should rest.

Random Chord Hits

Three to four players. Repeat *Random Chord Sounds* using a series of short "hits" (eighth notes) instead of long tones. Remember to leave random bits of space now and then between strings of notes.

Variation: Mix long tones and hits.

Four Hands

Two players. Players One and Two improvise a duet at the piano with four hands in ABA form. The section A is in D minor. Section B is in a major key chosen silently by each. Player One signals when to move to section B. Player Two signals the return to section A. Repeat with other players in other keys.

Pentatonic Chant

Five to six players. Players One and Two sing a vocal ostinato on nonsense syllables (e.g., coma sala picky packy ama nana bala—or make up your own). The chant is two measure long. All syllables are an eighth note in duration. Sing odd-numbered words on F, even-numbered words a step higher on G. Any low instrument plays an pentatonic ostinato based on F (F–G–A–C–D). Other players may add additional sparse ostinati. Percussion may be added. Remaining players play soli in F major, with or without inflections (adding sharps or flats).

Longitude

One to three players. Write out a set of chord changes (invented, from jazz standards, classical, or folk literature, etc.). Invent a short motif that moves to a new register with every new chord and alters as few notes as possible (e.g., when going from major to minor, only the third scale degree must be lowered). Percussion and a bass line playing the roots works well as an accompaniment.

Latitude

One to three players. Write out a set of chord changes (invented, from jazz standards, classical, or folk literature, etc.). Invent a short motif that keeps its shape as much as possible (making only the alterations necessary to fit the current chord) as it stays approximately in the same range (e.g., in the middle of the treble clef staff). Percussion and a bass line of chord roots work well as an accompaniment.

Chord Melody

One player. Choose any simple, yet familiar tune in any key. Using the rhythms of the familiar tune, create a new melody using only chord tones (scale steps 1 3 5). **Idea:** Two can play at this game— make it a duet.

Rhythm Chord

One player. This is similar to *Chord Melody*, but combines an ostinato rhythm with changing chords.

Decide on a number of notes and their note values for one measure of 4/4. The simplest is one whole note, but two half notes, four quarter notes, a half plus two quarters, etc., are all possible.

Find or invent a succession of chords. Use folk songs or other familiar tunes, one of the cycles (all keys) from Cycles (in Resources), jazz tunes (see *Real Book* in Improvisation Books, Articles, and Links in Resources), or classical solos.

Start with major chords only.

Play the same pattern of note values in every measure. Pitches may be chosen from chord tones at will. Start with triadic patterns (e.g., 1–3–5) only. When comfortable with this in all keys, add extensions to the triad chord notes (e.g., the sixth, seventh, or ninth above the chord rood).

Tip:	When including more notes per measure use fewer pitches than notes, or reuse a pitch.
Examples:	Quarter-quarter-half might be played as

C–C–C
C–C–E
C–E–E
C–G–C

Use a metronome or a friend with a percussion (or percussion-like) instrument. Software programs such as Band-in-a-Box can be programmed to play your chord progression as well.

Variation 1:	Repeat in minor. Later add extensions.
Variation 2:	Use freely mixed major and minor chords.
Variation 3:	Use ii^7–V^7–I chords exclusively (see Patterns in Resources for a listing in all keys).
Variation 4:	Introduce smaller note values, such as eighths and sixteenths. Remember the tip about using fewer pitches.
Variation 5:	Use syncopated rhythms.
Variation 6:	Construct rhythms over a two-measure unit.
Variation 7:	Use more exotic chords, such as:

Diminished
Augmented
Half-diminished
Altered dominant (see Scale and Chord Chart in Resources).

Rhythm Scale

One player. Repeat *Rhythm Chord*, making any note in the scale fair game to play in the rhythm selection.

Variation: After you are comfortable in the basic major, minor, and pentatonic scales (this will take a while), try more exotic scales, including modes, such as:

> Phrygian
> Lydian
> Altered dominants
> Whole tone
> Diminished
> See Scale and Chord Chart in Resources.

Chromatic Challenge

One player. Repeat *Rhythm Scale* using the Chromatic Scale. This atonal approach can be very challenging, especially at a faster tempo. Remember the tip about using fewer pitches. Perhaps begin using only half the chromatic scale (the first six stepwise notes), as too much choice can be daunting at first. Next repeat, using the remaining six notes. This will work with any tritone grouping (e.g., D to A♭ or E♭ to A).

Double Your Pleasure

Two players. *Repeat Rhythm Chord, Rhythm Scale,* or *Chromatic Challenge* as a duet. Both players may use the same rhythm, but it is more interesting to use independently selected rhythms.

Harmony Combination Game

This game combines *Spicy Progression* (Harmony Games) and *Half and Half* (Melody Games).

Two players. Players decide on a suitable spicy chord (suggestions below) and divide up the notes of the scale into chord and non-chord notes. Player One plays only chord notes; Player Two plays only non-chord notes plus the scale's tonic note.

Improvise, tying over common tones between chord changes whenever possible. Begin in 4/4 at a moderate tempo, using two measures for each chord.

Examples: Spicy Chord Progression No. 1
C minor with major^7–E7$^{(♭9)}$

Cm^{MAJ7}

Player One: C–E♭–G–B
Player Two: C–D–F–A

E7$^{(♭9)}$

Player One: E–G♯–B–D
Player Two: E–F–A–C♯

Spicy Chord Progression No. 2
F6/9–B7(♯5)

F6/9

_____

Player One: F–A–C–D
Player Two: F–G–B♭–E

B7(♯5)

_____

Player One: B–D♯–G–A
Player Two: B– C♯–F (Note: This chord is based on the
                whole tone scale, and so has only three notes.)

Variation: Use the same kind of chord twice, just transposed.

                Example: C6–B♭6

Idea: Make the piece more interesting and easier to play by adding a percussion
                ostinato and/or bass line.

Suggestion: If spicy progressions don't agree with your musical palate, choose something a
                little plainer. Straight major chords (e.g., C–B♭ or E–G) or a combination of
                major and minor (e.g., Dm–A) are fine.

● ● ●

*Most of us were taught within a framework of a traditional and replicative performance
pedagogy, but students in this new century are best served through preparation for real
world experiences.*

—Judith Coe

Chapter 18

Bass Line Games

Although low-range instruments are more suitable for these games, it is all relative: a flute trio could play these games just as well.

> Tip: *Many of the bass lines below can be ornamented or embellished in various ways to add pizzazz. With imagination and judicious choices, a bass line can be a bit different almost every time, without affecting the harmonic function.*

I consider improvisation to be an essential skill in reaching a level of contentment as a musician, because improvisation requires you to know music.

—Robert Zollman[47]

Oom-Pah March

Two players. Player One plays an oom pah rhythm on beats one and three of a measure in cut time using scale steps one and five. Player Two improvises a march over this. Try different kinds of marches: slow, fast, quirky, minor. Later, give the oom pah more interesting rhythms, such as the 3+3+2 clave or other Latin rhythms.

The Low Down

Four players. Player One improvises a short, catchy (i.e., rhythmic) bass line. One by one the other players join in exact imitation. When all can play the bass line, Player One begins a solo. At some point Player One nods to Player Two, who then solos as Player One rejoins the bass line. Continue until all have played.

Spanish Bass

Two to four players. Player One plays C–B♭–A♭–G (or some transposition thereof) in half notes and then repeats ad libitum. Other players solo over it, using either the C natural minor scale (1–2–♭3–4–5–♭6–♭7) or the C Spanish Phrygian scale: 1–♭2–3–4–5–♭6–♭7. As always, move to other keys when C minor feels fluent and familiar.

---

47   "Improvisation: Chasing the Mystique," www.wholelearning.com/IMPRintro.htm

Plain Descender

Two players. Player One plays the following descending bass: C–B–A–G (8–7–6–5) in half notes. Player Two solos over it using the C major scale. When soloing in C becomes very easy, add interesting rhythms, syncopations, and rests. Try putting chromatic or diatonic notes on strong beats (such as beginning on F♯ or D♭) and then resolving to a chord tone. Try this game in all keys.

Heart and Soul

Two players. Player One plays the following bass line in half notes: C–A–F–G and repeats. Player Two solos over it using the C major scale. Work through all keys.

Walking Bass

Two players. Player One plays a walking bass in quarter notes using the diatonic scale of any chosen key. Player Two solos over it. Start with major scales, and then repeat the game exploring minor, whole tone, diminished, and other scales.

Taking a Walk Outside

Two players. Player One plays an atonal walking-bass accompaniment. Player Two solos above it. Most important is the continued quarter-note pulse.

Chaconne à son goût...

Two-plus players. Player One plays a repeating bass line consisting of four half notes that may or may not outline a key/chord. Other players solo over it in turn.

Examples:	C–E–G–A♭	C–E–D–D♭
	C–A–A♭–G	C–F–B♭–A♭
	C–D♭–C–G	C–E–F–G
	C–E♭–F–B♭	C–F♯–G–D♭
	C–D♭–D–G	C–F–G–B♭

Follow the Lieder

Two or three players. Player One decides on a chord progression and outlines it. Player Two solos over it. If there is a third player, he may play a background of long, connecting notes, moving as little as possible (e.g., stepwise) between chord changes.

Bach Bass

Two players. You will need a book of Bach chorales for this game. Player One plays a distinctive bass line chosen from a Bach chorale over two to four measures and repeats it over and over while Player Two solos over it. (Idea by Matt Hellenbrand.)

Pachelbel Bass

Two or three players. The bass line of the famous Pachelbel canon is:

C–G–A–E–F–D–G–G

In C major, the chord progression is:

C–G^7–Am–Em–F–G^7–G^7

Player One plays this bass line. Player Two solos over it. A third player may be added, who may choose solo like Player Two or wish to try a greater challenge: play what Player Two plays in canon!

• • •

All European improvisation ensembles, regardless how they understand their goals, have one tendency in common: they are concerned with discovering and developing those territories that have been repressed by a thousand years of notation-dependent music. More accurately speaking, not simply by notated music, but by music notated with five staves and the well-known rhythmic symbols which no doubt has produced marvelous results but which has with equal certainty prevented the development of different musics.

—Erhard Karkoschka, Aspects of Group Improvisation

Chapter 19

Aural Games

Sharp and efficient aural skills are essential in all types of improvisation. Aural Games concentrate on developing aural skills in ways that benefit the improvising performer.

Ear training is traditionally done with the piano, students being required to notate melodies and rhythms they hear and learn to identify intervals. The aural training required and supplied by improvisation is much more intense, effective, and meaningful.

Being able to instantly identify notes (pitch, rhythm, and articulation) and play them back on the instrument is a very different task than having several passes at notating them on paper. Traditional ear training drills are invariably done on piano only; it is important to identify aural challenges in other timbres, beginning with the student's own instrument.

Many musicians are fabulously skilled at playing the black dots on the printed page, but mystified by how the dots got there in the first place and apprehensive of playing without dots. Music theory does not help here; it teaches rules of the grammar, but not what to say. When people ask me how to improvise, only a little of what I can say is about music. The real story is about spontaneous expression, and it is therefore a spiritual and a psychological story rather than a story about the technique of one art form or another.

—Stephen Nachmanovitch[48]

Double Telephone

Four players in two pairs. One pair plays a duet for ten seconds, and then the other pair must play back what they heard as exactly as possible. The first pair must then play back what Pair Two played, attempting to capture the differences with the original. Continue the cycle as each pair continues to remember and play back what they hear.

Variation: The time may be shortened or lengthened for more or less memory challenge.

Replay

Two-plus players. Divide the group in half. Group One plays a very short improvisation—start with a length of five seconds or so. Group Two plays back as exactly as possible what was heard: melody, harmony, timbre, dynamics, style, tempo, etc. *Nothing sharpens the ear more than the intention to repeat what is heard.* Gradually extend the length of the improvisation to be repeated.

---

48 *Free Play:* 9.

Variation 1:	Group One tries to repeat Group Two's rendition of Group One's improvisation as it was played.
Variation 2:	The entire group plays a short improvisation and then plays back as exactly as possible the piece just improvised.

Monkey Mirror

Two players. Player One is the soloist, Player Two is the copist. Player One may play anything she likes. Player Two must instantly copy Player One as closely as possible (like a mirror, or like the irritating junior high trick of repeating everything someone else says immediately afterwards). Player One may change key, meter, tempo, and/or dynamics at will. Player Two attempts to stay with the changes.

(Idea from Evan Mazunik.)

Follow That Timbre

Four-plus players This may be assigned to each player of a large group.

The Leader plays a recording of a piece that features in some way a variety of timbres. Players select a timbre (bass line, snare drum, piccolo, etc.) that approximates their primary or a secondary instrument and listen carefully to the short selection (it may be only a portion of the whole piece).

This process is repeated one to three times. One player is selected for each timbre, and these players improvise an approximate rendition of the piece.

Repeat. Then assign a new set of players to each timbre and repeat.

Continue until all have played.

Tip:	Make the recorded selection fairly short at first. Use longer selections as progress is made.

Play It Again, Sam

One player. Improvise a bit of music—anything from a short motif (three to four notes) to an entire phrase—then immediately play it back as exactly as possible. If the improvisation is too long or complex to remember exactly, shorten and/or simplify.

As facility is developed, gradually increase the complexity (key, tonal/atonal, rhythm/meter, etc.) and length.

Variation:	Two players do this as a call and response game (see below).

Play It Again, Sam, Again

One player. Play any snippet of music from a solo, etude, excerpt, warm-up, or any familiar tune and immediately replay it transposed up or down a half a step. Repeat *ad libitum*.

Variation:	Two players do this as a call and response game (see below).

Play It Again, Sam, One More Time

One player. Play any snippet of music from a solo, etude, excerpt, warm-up, or any familiar tune and immediately replay it in another mode (e.g., if the original was in major, play it in minor).

Variation: Two players do this as a call and response game (see below).

Sing It, Sam

One player. Sing a measure of made-up melody and then play back exactly what you sang on your instrument.

Variation 1:   Make the melody several measures long, up to a whole phrase.

Variation Two: Reverse the process by playing a measure or more on your instrument and then sing it back.

How long a melody can you successfully repeat?

(Inspired by David Hastings.)

Try to Remember...

Three to six players. All sit in a circle.

Player One plays a C. Player Two plays the C, plus any note in the C major scale. Player Three plays both of those notes and adds another note from the C major scale. Continue adding players and notes.

If a player cannot quite remember the sequence or is unsure which notes were played, the preceding player repeats the line until the new player can remember and play all of the notes.

At some point the string will be too long to remember, but see how far you can get.

For groups with really good ears (those who can remember strings of fifteen to twenty notes), repeat this game in other keys and/or with other scale types (minor, dominant seventh, whole tone, blues, diminished, etc.).

Monkey Hear, Monkey Do

One player in a practice room. Listen to the player in the room next to you. Copy snippets of what you hear. Leave spaces. Be aware that this could be extremely annoying, so play softly and/or use a mute. Repeat in other environments and in other ways (e.g., while walking in the city, sing back the sounds of car horns). Listen to the world everywhere, play it back, transform it into music.

What You Hear Is What You Get (To Do)

Four-plus players. One or two players are designated as soloists. They may play anything they wish. All others are designated as listeners and may play only what they hear a soloist play or a variation of it. Motivic development techniques (e.g., augmentation, diminution, sequence, transposition, etc.) may be applied. The Leader may reassign the soloist function at any time.

Pass the Notes I

Four-plus players. The group sits in a circle.

Player One plays *two* notes: the first must be C; the second must be in the C scale. Player Two takes up the second note, making it the first note of a new group.

If Player Two misses the interval of Player One's notes, Player One repeats them until Player Two finds them.

When everyone becomes proficient at this, the tempo may be increased to boost the challenge. Try different keys and kinds of scales.

Pass the Notes II

Four-plus players. As with *Pass the Notes I*, but with Player One passing *three* notes, the last servings as the first of Player Two's three notes.

Play the Shape

Two players. Two players alternate short improvised bursts of two to six notes, perhaps changing the number of notes each time. The melody may be tonal, atonal, or include extended techniques. Player One leads.

Player Two's goal is not necessarily to play back exactly what Player One played, but to play something that has the same melodic *shape*: the rhythm and phrasing should be as exact as possible, though (i.e., Player Two may not know the starting note or be able to identify several quick intervals, but should play a similar string of notes in a rough approximation).

Example: If Player One plays four notes and the directions are up-down-up-up, Player Two should play notes that copy this shape, playing large intervals when the interval is large, and vice-versa.

Player Two is copying Player One, but is relieved of the responsibility of being exact. It is more important to be quick and decisive. This allows Player One to play some rather rapid strings of notes and not worry that they are way out of reach for Player Two because Player Two can always come up with something that resembles the basic shape of Player One's phrase.

Round Robin

Four-plus players. The group sits in a circle. Player One plays a three-note motif. Player Two sits to Player One's right and must imitate the motif exactly. Move around the circle in this way.

The second time around, Player One creates a new four-note motif. Continue until the motif is too long to remember.

Hint: Keep the motifs simple until the aural and technical skills of the players develop. Gradually add complexity, new keys, wider intervals, and challenging rhythms. Highly talented groups may edge toward atonality.

Name that Tune

Four-plus players. Just like the old TV show, one player plays three notes from memory from some fairly well known tunes in any style or genre. Anyone in the group who thinks they know the tune raises her hand, and, when called on, plays the entire tune. Three attempts to play the tune more-or-less correctly are allowed. If a player is considerably off the mark, another may try, but that player gets only two attempts.

Variation: All players raise their hands at the beginning. Player One repeats the melody, adding one note each time. Players put down their hands as soon as they recognize the tune. Continue until all hands are down.

Teach that Tune

Two-plus players. Player One teaches the group a new tune, repeating the first phrase before going on to the next, until the entire group has learned the whole tune. This should take less and less time with practice.

Steal that Tune

One player. Select a tune on a CD that you like—any style of music. Isolate a phrase from that track and listen to it over and over. Hum that phrase until confident enough to sing it and then sing along (making up words if you with) with the recording. This may be easier with a software program like The Amazing Slow Downer, which can change the tempo of a CD track without changing pitch, and allows looping of any segment of the music.

Now find the tune on your instrument. Work until able to play it by heart, then make it yours by changing the phrasing in subtle ways to reflect your taste. Go back and learn a few more phrases, even the entire tune, if you are so inspired.

Possibilities: Play *Teach That Tune*, teaching what you've learned to other players and working up an arrangement (which does not have to be a copy the original; it's yours now).

Learn a new tune.

Transcribe what you learned into standard notation and chords, if you like, as appropriate to the tune. Once it is down on paper, make up and write down accompanying parts for a duet, trio, or quartet for whatever instruments your friends play. If they read music, you can all perform your opus. If they don't, you can play *Teach That Tune* until they get it.

Write chords that go with the tune to play on the guitar while you sing.
Play some kind of drum part (which could also be on made-up percussion instruments from objects in your kitchen, garage, or office) while you and/or your friends sing the tune.

Write lyrics to the tune, or, if it came with lyrics, write new ones.

Repeat the entire process with a new tune you made up yourself while walking the dog or singing in the shower. Why not? It's fun and free. Paying 99 cents to iTunes is quicker, but why give up all that fun?

See also: *Playing Along* (Style Games).

Familiar Tune

One to four players. This game has so many musical vitamins and minerals that it should be done daily, but the best reason to do it is because it is both challenging and fun.

Choose a familiar tune, something that each player already knows very well (a children's song, folk song, Christmas carol, etc.) and try to play it by ear. After all players can play the melody easily, one or more players may play the melody while others play any of the following (all by ear, of course!):

Chord roots
Harmony part(s)
Countermelody
Variations on the melody

It is best to add these one at a time. Give everyone a chance to try them all if possible, and then turn everyone loose to play any of the roles they like. Do this in an easy key (e.g., C major), and then gradually try it in other keys until they *all* become easy.

Variation: Switch modes. Play the tune in a minor key (or in major if the original tune is minor. For the daring, add some dissonant notes to the harmony.

See also: *Happy Birthday* (Improv Set-Ups).

Nostalgia

One player. Play any familiar tune, using one or two phrases, a verse or chorus, or the entire tune. If you make any mistakes, keep playing, but take note and when you play the tune again, play the mistakes exactly as you did the first time. If you make any mistakes the second time through, repeat the process. Work to remember and play the latest version as exactly as possible. Continue *ad libitum*.

Improv on the Chords

Two to four players. Repeat Familiar Tune. When all players are comfortable playing the various roles/parts, abandon the familiar tune melody and do the following:

1. One or more players play the chord roots.

2. One player may play a long-tone accompaniment (e.g., the third of the chord).

3. One or two players of melody instruments may improvise an ostinato accompaniment.

4. One or two players may add a percussion accompaniment of any kind.

5. One player improvises a solo over the chords.

Only chord tones one and five are necessary. The others are nice, but optional.

Twisted Unison

One player at the piano. The player sings a simple melody (invented or a familiar tune) and plays it at the piano in a different key in parallel with the voice (e.g., the piano is in C major, the voice is in D major). More advanced players can do this at more challenging intervals (e.g., major or minor thirds, perfect fourths or fifths, etc.). The ultimate challenge: a half step or a tritone away.

Lightning Arrangements

Two or three players. When players have some experience figuring out familiar tunes by ear, they should play together, trying different roles. Player One plays the melody while Player Two plays (i.e., figures out aurally through experimentation) the roots of the underlying chord, and Player Three plays a part that is in harmony or counterpoint (or both) with the melody. Switch so that each player can experience all roles. Start with easy tunes with few chord changes in easy keys. Progressively take on more complex tunes and less familiar keys.

Question and Answer

Two players. Player One plays a phrase that seems like a question, that is unfinished in some way (e.g., it may end on the dominant). Player Two responds with an answer that completes Player One's phrase.

Tip: Start simply. Melodies may become more complex as players acquire experience.

Copy Cat

Two players: a teacher and student. This works best for young students at the piano. Older students may try this with other instruments, as they are able.

The teacher plays a single note and asks the student to copy it, and then the student leads as the teacher copies. Gradually add notes one at a time.

(Idea by Azadeh Raoufi.)

Copy/Counterpoint

Two players: teacher and student. After the student is comfortable with *Copy Cat* and *Copy Machine* (Melodic Games), repeat *Copy Cat* with Player Two playing long tones while Player One plays a short melody.

(Idea by Azadeh Raoufi.)

Stolen Moments

Two to four players. Each player brings a short, interesting rhythm heard the day before from any source (e.g., recorded or live music, machinery noises, ambient noise indoors or outdoors, etc.). Players jump in together and create a piece that combines the use of these rhythms.

Tip: Steal each other's rhythms as much as possible!

Variation: Repeat with snippets of melody heard the day before. Shorter is better. Using only melodies from non-composed sources (e.g., bird song, someone whistling, machinery sounds, etc.) will make this game especially challenging.

Grand finale: After playing the game and its variation, repeat, combining rhythms and melodies.

• • •

Call and response games are a genre all their own and comprise an excellent and enjoyable way to train the ear both tonally and rhythmically in the framework of a game with its inherent intrinsic motivation.

NB: the call-and-response games are for two or more players. They work best with larger groups.

Suggestions for Call-and-Response Games

• Players might try closing their eyes or play the game with the lights off. We all hear better without the distraction of visual input.

• Player One (the caller) may introduce extended techniques (*glissando*, flutter tongue, etc.) now and then to stretch the other players, and also for the sheer fun of it.

• The leadership role (the call) of Player One may be taken by students at some point after they have some experience playing in the game. The instructor, however, should watch for the tendency of the less experienced to make the calls too difficult too soon.

• The standard length of the call is four beats (one measure), but as players develop aural skills, this length may be increased to eight or more beats.

• To work on quicker reaction times, decrease the call measure to three (in 3/4 meter) or two beats (2/4 meter).

• Using odd meters (5/4, 5/8, 7/8, etc.) can deepen the aural experience by adding another layer of rhythmic challenge.

• Use a moderate tempo at first. Gradually increase the speed as players advance.

Call-and-Response: Voice (only)

Two-plus players. Using the voice (scat, nonsense syllables, throat or mouth noises) is a good way to begin call and response training. It may be less threatening for novices to answer with the voice rather than trying to find the notes on an instrument. Vocal call and response can later be mixed with instrumental call and response as well.

(Source: Christine Stevens, *The Art and Heart of Drum Circles.*[49])

___

49   Stevens. Idea from accompanying CD.

Call-and-Response: Rhythms!

Two-plus players, preferably a Leader and a large group. The leader either claps or plays a one-measure rhythm (e.g., in 4/4 or 6/8) on a percussion instrument, which is immediately played back as exactly as possible by the group (or partner). The tempo and complexity of the rhythm may be gradually increased as the group meets the rhythmic challenges of the call.

Variation 1: Sit in a circle. Each player gets a one-, two-, three-, or four-measure rhythm (decide beforehand), then passes the turn to the player on the left. Player One starts. If Player Two misses, Player One must repeat. If Player Two misses three times, Player One must start again with a newer, simpler rhythm. Then Player Two invents a rhythm (on a new pitch if using an instrument) etc.

Variation 2: Sit in a circle. Player One plays a rhythm on one pitch of any length. The rest of the group echoes the rhythm on the same pitch. Player Two then invents a rhythm for the group. The second time around Player One may use two pitches to play the rhythm. The group can decide if it is ready to tackle three pitches, etc. on the next time around.

Idea: The call may be vocal scat syllables instead of percussion.

(Source: Christine Stevens, *The Art and Heart of Drum Circles.*[50])

Call-and-Response: Basic

Two-plus players. Player One plays one measure in 4/4; all other players echo Player One exactly in the subsequent measure. Player One should begin simply, gradually adding more challenging tonal and rhythmic material. If players miss any notes, Player One repeats the measure, perhaps making the addition of more difficult material more gradual. Start in C major and then begin again in another key.

Call-and-Response: Intermediate I

Two-plus players. As with *Call-and-Response,* but with Player One adding nonharmonic tones (i.e., "wrong" notes) on both strong and weak beats and parts of beats.

Examples: A tonic triad (I) going to a nonharmonic tone: C-E-G-A♭
#4 resolving to the tonic triad: F♯–G–E–C.

Call-and-Response: Intermediate II

Two-plus players. As with *Call and Response: Basic,* but Player One may change to a key a half step higher or lower at some point. If the responders miss, simplify the call material tonally and/or rhythmically.

---

[50] Ibid.

Call-and-Response: Intermediate III

As with *Call-and-Response: Basic*, but Player One may change to a key a half or whole step higher or lower at some point. If the responders miss, simplify the call material tonally and/or rhythmically.

Call-and-Response: Advanced I

Two-plus players. As with *Call and Response: Intermediate I*, but Player One may change to any other key at will. If the responders miss, simplify the call material tonally and/or rhythmically.

Call-and-Response: Advanced II

Two-plus players. Repeat any of the dall and response games above with Player One playing scales other than major (e.g., any minor mode, whole tone, diminished, pentatonic, blues scale, Spanish Phrygian, Klezmer, or altered). See Appendix for a chart of unfamiliar scales.

Call-and-Response: Advanced III (Atonal)

Two-plus players. Player One emphasizes and juxtaposes intervals that are less likely to spell out keys (e.g., tritones, whole and half steps, major and minor sevenths, etc.) so that the effect is atonal. It may be advisable to initially slow the tempo and to reduce the difficulty of the rhythms, since atonal material is more challenging (e.g., the first call might be a half note and two quarters: C–F#–B.

Call-and-Response: Completion

Two-plus players. Player One plays a short phrase that sounds unfinished (e.g., it ends on the dominant); Player Two plays an answering phrase that completes what the first phrase began.

Call-and-Response: Decoration

Two-plus players. Player One plays one measure of a brief and very simple diatonic melody (two to four notes). Player Two plays the melody back with any kind of elaboration or decoration, (e.g., grace notes, trills, turns, mordents, chromatic or diatonic approaches or connecting tones, etc.).

Call-and-Response with Variations

Four-plus players. Player One plays one measure in an agreed-upon key. Player Two plays it in minor. Player Three plays it in retrograde. Player Four plays it in inversion. Player Five plays variations. It may be useful for Player One to repeat the original measure after each response.

After all have played, Player One may go to new material. If there are fewer than five players, players may take the other roles.

(Source: Matt Hellenbrand.)

Call-and-Response: Overlap

Two-plus players: best with one caller and one responder. This may be applied to any call-and-response game. Instead of a clean break after a measure, the caller continues for a second measure. The responder listens and remembers the second measure *while playing the first measure*. It does not matter whether the repetition is perfect; this is meant to be an ear sharpener.

Call-and-Response: Sequences

Two-plus players. Players agree on a major key. Player One plays a simple two-note motif based on the scale (e.g., C–E in C major). Player Two plays the same *shape* as Player One's motif, one diatonic step higher (e.g., D–F in C major).

If Player Two misses it, Player One repeats the motif. If Player Two is successful, then Player One plays another motif, also beginning on the tonic. As Player Two gains experience and skill, Player One may play a motif that begins on a note other than the tonic and/or play a three-note motif. The first note is always the tonic. Later another scale tone may be used as the starting note). Player One should make the progression of difficulty very gradual, tailoring it to Player Two's ability. Very skilled players may use other scales (e.g., minor, whole tone, blues, chromatic, diminished, etc.) and add more notes.

Call-and-Response: Arpeggios Only

Two-plus players. As with *Call-and-Response: Basic*, but limited to arpeggios. This may be used as desired with any of the appropriate basic, intermediate, or advanced call-and-response games.

Begin with three-note, triadic major arpeggios and add rhythmic interest and then go to other chord types (e.g., minor, diminished, half-diminished, augmented, etc.). Repeat using four-note arpeggios (e.g., chords with added sixth, major seventh, dominant seventh, minor seventh, half-diminished seventh, full diminished seventh, etc.). Go on to five-note arpeggios, adding the ninth over the seventh chords.

Variation: Play one kind of arpeggio (e.g., CMAJ7) and then repeat it, changing one or more notes but staying in the framework of a C-based arpeggio. Add rhythms at will.

       Examples: C–E–G–B
                       C–E♭–G–B♭
                       C–E–G♯–B♭
                       C–E♭–F♯–A
                       C–E–G–B♭

       Play notes ascending only at first. As proficiency develops, try descending only, and then non-consecutive orders of notes. Extend this exercise to all keys.

       Adventurous and advanced players may also investigate non-triadic arpeggios, such as chords in fourths (e.g., C–F–B♭–E♭), fifths (e.g., C–G–D), suspended chords (e.g., C–F–G–C), or chords without thirds (e.g., C–G–B♭–F).

Call-and-Response: Inversions

Two players. Player One begins with a simple one-measure call (e.g., quarter and half notes only). Player Two plays back the measure in inversion, (i.e., Player One's line ascended, Player Two's line should descend).

Call-and-Response: the Ultimate Challenge

Two-plus players. Once players are comfortable with all of the above games, Player One may play any combination of them, again keeping tempo and rhythm simpler at first when combined with challenging tonal material.

• • •

If an idea strikes me as beautiful and satisfactory to the ear and heart, I would far rather overlook a grammatical error than sacrifice what is beautiful to mere pedantic trifling.

—Joseph Haydn[51]

---

[51] James Cuthbert Hadden, *Haydn* (J.M. Dent & Co., 1902).

Chapter 20

Nontraditional Score Games

> Nontraditional scores (such as those using graphic notation) can be another great halfway house on the road from conventional notation to free invention. It is a quick and easy way to create inspiring improv starters, and everyone is capable of creating simple drawings as well as interpreting these drawings in sound. Graphic notation can be used early in improv studies.

The range of notational practices employed to present my work as a composer includes conventional staff notation, graphic notation, metaphors, prose, oral instruction and recorded media.

—Pauline Oliveros, *The Roots of the Moment* [52]

A solo chart, commonly used in improvisational music…has two important functions. First, it can be used as a performance guide to indicate to all of the players where, generally or exactly, the improvisation is going at any moment. Second, it can be used to unify the written and improvised parts of the music. A chart which integrates the two parts cohesively and meaningfully can be a work of art in and of itself, deriving from theoretical knowledge, interpretive insight, creative imagination and a sense of form. Whether simple or complex, the chart must embody, in a musically logical way, the essence of the writing, and at the same time afford freedom of expression, and independence, to the improviser.

—Composer Rhoda Averbach on the CD *Souls and Masters*

The most important aspects of music cannot be translated into symbols on the printed page.

—Edwin E. Gordon [53]

Squiggle Quartet

Two-plus players. Players make quick, rapid squiggles of any sort on pieces of blank paper with pens, pencils, or colored markers. They immediately exchange pieces of paper and play the "piece" without discussion.

---

52   Drogue Press, 1998: 5–6.
53   *Improvisation in the Music Classroom* (GIA Publications, 2003): 1.

Playing the Gallery

Two-plus players. A small group of players arranges with an art museum to provide an updated and improvised version of Pictures at an Exhibition. The group selects a number of paintings from the current exhibition and creates pieces to match on the spot. Make arrangements in advance so that gallery-goers can plan to attend the concert.

Nontraditional Score I

Four-plus players. Each player goes somewhere in the building and makes a score of what they hear using any kind of made-up graphic notation (e.g., squiggles, dots, slashes, geometric figures, etc.). No normal music notation is allowed. Scores should be constructed on one page of blank paper. Time is measured from left to right; ambient noises are marked from top to bottom, (e.g., a fan whooshing, a car door slam, people talking, the hum of neon lights, footsteps, a bus stopping outside, laughter, etc.). Return to the room after ten minutes. Four or five players should then "play" each score, independently deciding which line to play and how to play it.

The interpretations need not have any correspondence with the original noise.

Suggestions:	Have different groups of players play the same scores.
	Have players play the same piece again, but differently.
	Exchange the scores and play again.
Variation 1:	Have players write words and/or short phrases on the sheet instead of drawing.
Variation 2:	Have some players write words and others draw.

Nontraditional Score II

Two to four players. Players construct any sort of a one- or two-page graphic score, using ink, pencil, paint, paper collage, photos, or anything imaginative.

Nontraditional Score III

Two to four players. Using a ruler or a music notation software program such as Finale, construct a blank score consisting of one line for each player. Leave enough room between "staves").

Bar lines signify a new section.

Give instructions for each section using words, dynamic and tempo markings, and suggestions (if any) for key.

Examples:	Any note in F minor.
	Free—any key.
	Emphasize the interval of a fourth using the notes of the C major scale.

Indicate whenever necessary which player should cue the next section. Indicate who (if anyone) has a solo. Traditional notes may be used to suggest rhythms. You may specify pitches occasionally (e.g., to create a unison), but generally pitch choice is governed only by a key suggestion and/or direction of time (e.g., quarter notes alternating over and under the line to suggest back-and-forth movement). You may use squiggly lines and other graphics to suggest activity, direction, extended techniques, etc.

The score should be no longer than one page. Have different combinations of instruments play the score, and encourage players to create very different versions of the score each time through.

Rembrandt

Four-plus players. One group (two, three, four, or more players) improvises freely. While they play, the remaining players draw (or otherwise construct) some kind of map, graphic, text string, or combination thereof to represent the music as it unfolds. After the piece is complete, take the scores and perform them. The performance does not have to sound anything like the original, although it may.

(Idea from Evan Mazunik.)

Skyline

Four-plus players. One player passes out a sketch of a skyline, or better, draws a large-scale version on a blackboard or whiteboard.

Example:

Player One uses the skyline as a map to indicate the dynamic range. Player Two uses it as a map for the key center. Player Three uses it as a map for register (i.e., high, midrange, or low). Additional players are free to interpret the skyline in other ways, or they may join one of the other players.

Players freely improvise together, following the skyline map only for their particular parameter. Stop at the end of the graphic. Most likely they will not end exactly together, which is okay.

Variation 1: Each player freely decides what the skyline graphic represents, and may switch to a different parameter at any time.

Variation 2: Abandon the graphic but keep the concept. Have one player raise and lower a hand or stick to indicate changing levels which will affect one or more parameters during the improvisation.

(Idea from Evan Mazunik.)

Mixed Notes

Two-plus players. Compose a score using one to four staves and conventional notes (e.g., quarter, eighth, half, etc.), but the staves are "invisible" with visible bar lines. Players are thus free to decide the intervals (and key, if not assigned) between the notes. It may help to have someone conduct the piece to ensure that players stay together. Add occasional fermati and dynamics *ad libitum*.

(Inspired by a game by famed Russian improvising hornist Arkady Shilkloper.)

Ad Music

Four players. Player One has spent some time at home going through various magazines, cutting out the most graphically interesting advertisements. Two, three, or four other players sit or stand before a music stand as Player One places an ad before each player as a score. At a signal from Player One, they all begin, each playing her advertisement. During the playing of the piece, Player One may elect to switch ads between players, replace any ad with a new one, or rip an ad in half.

Collage Music

Two to four players. This game takes a bit of preparation. At home players cut out interesting words and pictures from various magazines. Select from these and glue them to a piece of letter-sized cardboard (better than paper). The cutouts and words may or may not relate to each other, and may be humorous or not. These collages are used as graphic scores.

Players may start at the same place or begin interpreting where they wish. The number that can crowd around the score may limit the number of players. Alternately, the collage maker may make photocopies (preferably in color) and give one to each player.

With a Little Help from Our Friends

One-plus players and audience. The audience is invited to make use of supplied paper and crayons or pencils to create one-page drawings, doodles, or sketches of any kind that will then be used as scores for a piece in the concert.

Interactive Art

Three-plus players. Invite a visual artist to the class session or concert. She should bring a rather large white piece of paper placed on an easel. The piece commences with a stroke of paint by the artist; the players (any size group will work, but some kind of chamber group is best) watch and react, interpreting colors and shapes. The artist then responds to sounds of the group, letting them guide her next brush strokes. The group reacts to this, and the pattern continues. The piece is finished when the "canvas" is filled.

Play the Face

Two to four players. Player One makes facial expressions that depict emotional states (e.g., joyful, sad, perplexed, irritated, etc.). The other player or players invent music to reflect the perceived feeling.

Tip: Change faces, but not too quickly. Give players time to establish a musical emotion before changing to a new expression.

Doodle Music

Two to four players. Player One makes flamboyant doodles on a piece of paper, then Player Two adds to the drawing. Take one minute or less in total. Next both play the piece, giving it an evocative title such as "The Mysterious Life of a Humpback Whale" or "My New Shoes Are Too Small."

Repeat with three players, using "Revenge of the Bacteria" as the title.

Repeat with four players, using "Cobras, Pythons, and Me" as the title.

Repeat all with new titles.

School Art Music

One to two players. Go to an elementary school and plan to have a class make artwork that you then set to spontaneous music.

Variation 1:	Improvise and have students paint or draw what they hear.
Variation 2:	Have them make quick drawings while you're there and turn them into music on the spot.

Mona Lisa

Two-plus players. Player One passes out pictures (e.g., reproductions of famous artwork) to each player. Each player then depicts the picture in music.

Variation 1:	Use different pictures.
Variation 2:	Use the same picture for each player (unbeknownst to the players if possible).
See also:	Storyboards (Storytelling Games).

• • •

Musicians used to reading notes and rhythms often are shocked by the bareness of the scores compared to familiar conventional scores which direct their attention to specific pitches and rhythms which to them seem predictable and repeatable. What I value is the more unpredictable and unknowable possibilities that can be activated by not specifying pitches and rhythms. I prefer organic rhythms rather than exclusively metrical rhythms. I prefer full spectrum sound rather than a limited scalar system. I sometimes use meter and scales within this fuller context of sound oriented composition.

—Pauline Oliveros[54]

---

[54] *The Roots:* 4–5.

Music without notation is not limited to a scriptless society. Many ancient notation systems were merely devised by priests and cantors and some were even kept secret. While in religious music notation had a definite place in order to prevent the present and future generations from breaking sacred traditions, secular music relied on free invention and memory, in Western civilization as well as those of the East. Notation became indispensable only under the pressure of worked-out polyphony.

—Curt Sachs[55]

---

[55]   *The Wellsprings of Music* (Martinus Nijhoff, 1962).

Chapter 21

Conducting Games

In the usual process of making music in a group the conductor is responsible for uniting all technical and musical parts while the players read notes prepared for them by a (distant) composer. Players in this system do not have a say in what is played or how it is played.

It may seem at first that a book like this has little to offer conductors in this top-down system. Why share all that power? However, open-minded conductors who sample the possibilities described here may discover that some improv games make enjoyable and effective supplements to the usual musical fare and routine.

Improv injects high-octane interest and variety by asking players to *think, feel, and use their imaginations*, and as a result players are refreshed, motivated, inspired, and excited about making music again. (Let's face it: the routine of rehearsals can become boring after a while.)

The conductor has two main options: He can encourage players to try some of these improv games, (which develop all kinds of skills: technical, musical, aural, ensemble playing, and more); or he can take time out from the regular rehearsal routine and lead the players in some of these games.

This is bold, daring, and different. And it's addictive. Once improvisation games have been added to regular rehearsals, you won't want to be without them.

> *The improvisational attitude toward music, so familiar in swing, affects all of [Charles] Ives's mature work. It affects his conception of performance and composing… Ives leaves a great deal to the mercy of the performer. In his compositions, the notation of a work is only the basis for further improvisations, and the notation itself, frequently of music first conceived many years before, is a kind of snapshot of the way he played it at a certain period in his life.*
>
> —Elliott Carter[56]

A Word about Soundpainting

The first time I saw a Soundpainting performance, I was flabbergasted, astonished, and nonplussed. I had never heard anything like it. It wasn't classical; it wasn't jazz, or folk, or avant garde atonal. The music was extremely varied, occasionally chaotic and/or funny, but it was organized (how, I could not imagine at the time): there were solos, accompaniment, ostinato figures, harmonies, long tones, even vocal sounds, and players making physical movements in synch. At one point there were

---

[56] *Collected Essays and lectures: 1937–1995* (University of Rochester Press, 1996).

even two conductors! The players seemed completely alert and attentive, their eyes riveted to the conductor, but they were obviously improvising. There was both madness and method, and the music produced by this chamber ensemble (about a dozen wildly assorted instruments) was always fresh, engaging, and fascinating.

My thought was "I have got to learn how to do *this!*" Other players and conductors have experimented with rudimentary forms of gestural control of improvisation, but Soundpainting represents the most widespread and detailed system. It was first invented by Walter Thompson in New York more than twenty years ago.

There are several professional Soundpainting orchestras in Europe, New York, Chicago, and many more amateur Soundpainting conductors and groups at several colleges and universities around the country. Soundpainting is an ideal way to introduce classical musicians to non-jazz improvisation. It is a language with a syntax, the most basic form of which is *Who Plays? What to Play? When to Start? When to Stop?*

A well-trained ensemble will be fluent in a hundred to two hundred gestures, but a rank beginner can begin within one minute after learning just three gestures: *Play, Long tone, Exit.* Like a spoken language, additional gestures are learned one at a time.

You might start with "Me. Coffee. Now," but with practice you can say, "I would like a grande mocha skinny decaf with extra whipped cream and cocoa powder sprinkles on top."

In any case, Soundpainting can be used with any and all instruments and at all ability levels, from elementary school to professional. It is still probably easier to get conductor training in parts of Europe (where Walter Thompson lives at least half the year; the Europeans can't get enough of this system) than in much of America, but anyone and everyone can learn the forty basic gestures from the DVD and manual available at www.soundpainting.com.

Daring and progressive conductors of bands, orchestras, and choirs will quickly master the basic gestures and find Soundpainting to be an indispensable rehearsal brightener. And, with practice, some conductors may dare to program an entire Soundpainting piece on a concert, or use some Soundpainting techniques within a piece. Conductors who compose may also be tempted to add windows of Soundpainting in their compositions.

Soundpainting also offers a unique opportunity to involve audiences as well. Audiences usually catch onto some of the basic signs, and after a while, the conductor may *turn around* and give the audience, say, a long tone gesture. They usually get it, and join in (vocally) in astonished delight. If not, a conductor can simply turn back to the group and sign *Long Tone* to demonstrate, then turn back to the audience and try again. Audiences will join in on the back-and-forth (ensemble and audience) duel with unconcealed glee.

Conductors, you will get more compliments than usual after these concerts, because the audience actually gets to do something besides the usual prescribed behavior of sitting silent and motionless. Want to get more audience members to return? Add some Soundpainting (and other improvisation) to your programming.

While Soundpainting is not the only way to combine improvisation and conducting, and whether or not you decide to use it in a concert, it remains rich with possibilities for classical musicians to become familiar with improvisation. The conducting games listed below are mostly derived from Soundpainting. Even if you don't have the Soundpainting manual and DVD, the suggestions here and the list of basic gestures in Resources may help you come up with ideas on how to invent your own conducting games. Why not?

Play What You See

Four-plus players. Decide on a scale. The conductor directs each note of the scale, moving either quickly or slowly from note to note. Players observe closely and react, following the scale up and down while staying exactly with the erratic beat of the conductor. The objective is for the whole ensemble to stay exactly together with unexpected, unpredictable beats.

Conducted Scale Games

Two to four players plus conductor. All players play a common major scale with free choice of note values. A conductor beats the pulse. Players decide when to enter; be sure to include rests. Play one of the following variations.

Variation 1:	Players move only stepwise on the scale but decide when to change direction.
Variation 2:	Each player picks one note value from eighth to whole note and sticks to it. Change direction at will.
Variation 3:	Alternate any two-note values (e.g., quarter and half note, or whole note and eighth note).
Variation 4:	Players independently choose Variation 1, 2, or 3, and move to another variation when they wish.
Idea:	At a set gesture from the conductor, players switch to the parallel minor key.
Also possible:	By previous agreement, flash card, or vocal indication, players switch to a different key.
Crazy idea:	Players pick the new key independently.

Shapeline

Four-plus players plus conductor. Shapeline is a Soundpainting gesture.

In this game, movement makes the score. The conductor is the "living" score, making a mixture of wild and subtle movements using the face, arms, legs, etc. Players interpret all movements as they wish, or may focus on one feature (such as the right hand). This works well with large groups. Standing straight up and being still is the neutral position, which indicates silence.

Point-to-Point

Four-plus players. This is an adaptation of a Soundpainting gesture.

When the leader points to a player she plays, stopping only when the leader stops pointing. What is played may be preset.

Examples: Only long tones.
Only "hits" (short notes)
Only long (or short) chord tones in C major.
Any tone in C major.
Any note at all.
Extended techniques.
Air sounds.
Mouth noises.
Laughter.
Free solo.

The pointing gesture may also be adapted to indicate more than one person at a time. Players have to remain very alert because the pointing may switch between players very quickly.

Point-to-Point Chamber Music

Eight-plus players. The conductor points to a player to indicate an improvised solo. One at a time, the conductor points to up to four players. The players must then relate to each other and create a high degree of unity.

At some point after four people are playing, the leader gives the *Finish Your Idea* Soundpainting gesture (trace a downward squiggle in the air) to one of the four, and points to a new player to join the quartet. The conductor continues replacing the original players, continuing the process until all have been part of the quartet.

Optional ending: Reduce the number of players from four to three, then two, and then one, finally fading out.

Cell Point-to-Point

Eight-plus players divided into duets, trios and quartets. The title and idea of this game comes from Soundpainting. Each group decides what to play.

Examples: Long tones.   Extended techniques noises.
Sparse textures.   Ostinati.
Pointillistic stabs.   Cantabile melodies.
Dense flurries of notes.   Vocal sounds.
High/low range.   Body percussion.

One player acts as the conductor and points at a group which plays only as long as the conductor is pointing directly at it; it is silent otherwise. The conductor may use both hands to point to two different groups at the same time.

Other Soundpainting gestures may also come in handy here, such as *Continue, Louder/Softer, Faster/Slower, Freeze, Memory,* etc. Conductors may use these or invent their own, demonstrating them to the players before beginning this game.

Variation: This game can more closely resemble the Soundpainting gesture *Play/Don't Play* if the players in each group decide independently what to play, giving up the idea of a unified cell sound. Players in this variation should pick a different type of playing each time the conductor points at them.

Idea: At some point the conductor indicates that all groups should synchronize with the sound of one particular group using the Soundpainting gesture for *Synchronize* (interlaced fingers held horizontally).

Conducting a Chorale

Five-plus players. Player One conducts each beat of an improvised chorale, played by four players (this is *Shapeline Conductor* in Soundpainting).

Players may add passing tones. Start with a key, and then try free choice of key. With practice, the conductor can add dynamics, swells, etc. This may be done entirely with the voice as well as with instruments.

Freeform Conducting

Four-plus players. Player One conducts any way she wants (e.g., light-heartedly, heavy-handedly, in three, four, or seventeen), cueing solos or accents and throwing in cutoffs and entrances at will. Players must do their utmost to give the conductors anything and everything she asks for. The conductor may also appoint anyone in the ensemble to take over as the new conductor at any time . Continue until all are exhausted.

Variation: The conductor may shout additional information along with the gestures.

Examples: C major!
No, minor!
Staccatissimo!
Lowest register!
Voice only!
Everyone hum!
Brass, be quiet!

Crossover

Eight-plus players. Divide the group in two equal sections or select two instrument groups from within the larger ensemble (e.g., brass and woodwinds, horns and percussion, trumpets and flutes, saxes and tubas, etc.). Have each group select a basic Soundpainting activity (e.g., long tones, *ostinato* figures, extended techniques, etc.).

At will, give the Crossover sign (sharply point and move index fingers in opposite directions past each other in a wide arc), which is the sign for both groups to instantly switch to the activity of the other group.

Three-Headed Conductor

Four players. Player One improvises, or perhaps just plays a scale up and down. Three other players each assume different conducting roles.

Player Two indicates the beat or pulse. Player Three uses hand gestures to indicate dynamics (the Soundpainting *Volume Fader* comes in handy here: loud, soft, *crescendo*, *decrescendo*). Player Four uses a hand gesture to indicate when Player One should be silent. Player One will have to play close attention to follow all the directions at once!

See also: Concerto! (Miscellaneous Games).

                   Play the Face (Nontraditional Score Games)

• • •

Improvisation is a way of achieving identity.

—Alfred Nieman, composer

The petrifying effect of European classical music on those things it touches, jazz, many folk musics, and all popular musics, have suffered grievously in their contact with it—made the prospects of finding it pretty remote. Formal, precious, self-absorbed, pompous, harboring rigid conventions and carefully preserved hierarchical distinctions, obsessed with geniuses and their timeless masterpieces, shunning the accidental and the unexpected, the world of classical music provides an unlikely setting for improvisation.

—Derek Bailey[57]

---

[57] *Improvisation: Its Nature and Practice in Music* (Da Capo Press, 1933): 19.

Chapter 22

Energy/Mood Games

Another way to break free of written notation and the usual concentration on pitch accuracy alone is to focus on emotion or mood. It is very difficult to notate emotion, but not at all difficult to invent music that expresses it. This gives players a chance to explore and use extended techniques in a very meaningful context.

Note: Some of these games are repetitions of games from other sections, included here for convenience.

Improvisation is the most natural and widespread form of music making. Up until the last century it was integral even to our literate tradition in the West. Leonardo da Vinci was one of the great pioneers of improvisation on the viola da braccio, and with his friends put on entire operas in which both the poetry and the music were made up on the spot. In Baroque music, the art of playing keyboard instruments from a 'figured bass'...resembled the modern jazz musician's art of playing over themes, motifs, or chord changes. In classical times, the cadenzas of violin, piano, and other concertos were meant to be improvised—a chance for the player to put his own creative display into the total artwork. Both Bach and Mozart were renowned as very free, agile, imaginative improvisers, and many stories, both moving and amusing, are attached to their exploits in the field. Beethoven, when he first came to Vienna, became known as an outstanding improviser on the piano, and only later as a composer....

—Stephen Nachmanovitch[58]

Matching

Note: *This is a term and technique from music therapy improvisation. According to Tony Wigram, it is "One of the most valuable of all the improvisational methods"[59] in music therapy.*

Two players. Player One begins; player Two listens carefully for a few moments, then joins in, attempting to play music that "fits together with and matches" Player One's music. Player Two's music is not necessarily identical to Player One's, but is the same in "tempo, dynamic, texture, quality and complexity" (as per Wigram).

Repeat several times, experimenting with a wide variety of moods, energy levels (e.g., tempo/density of notes/dynamics), and degrees of order/chaos.

---

58   *Free Play:* 6–7.
59   Tony Wigram, *Improvisation* (Jessica Kingsley Publishers, 2004): 83.

Reflecting

Note:　　　　　　　*This is a term and technique from music therapy improvisation.*

Two players. Player One begins; player Two listens carefully and then joins in, "matching the moods, attitudes, or feelings" (as per Kenneth Bruscia[60]) of Player One.

The difference between reflecting and matching is that in matching, Player Two's music sounds very much like Player One's, whereas in reflecting, Player Two's music may be quite different from Player One's, but it will nevertheless be very similar in mood.

Feelings

Four-plus players. The group brainstorms a list of emotions, moods, emotional or energy states, etc. The list should include at least a dozen terms, both positive (e.g., love, pity, proud, eager, jolly, bold) and negative (e.g., lethargic, regretful, timid, frightened, crazy, hateful, angry, lonely).

Don't edit. Write down everything the group comes up with without worrying whether it fits exactly. The list is a resource for the players, but a word not on the list may also be choosen at any time if inspiration hits.

The group sits in a circle. Player One silently selects a term and creates music that embodies it. Player Two listens for a moment, then plays music that either matches or reflects Player One's. They continue for about twenty seconds, then end.

Player Two then selects an emotion and plays music embodying the term for Player Three. The process is repeated until all have played.

Play the Face

Two to four players. One player makes facial expressions that express emotional states (e.g., joyful, sad, perplexed, irritated, etc.). The other player(s) invent music to reflect the perceived feeling.

Tip:　　　　　　　Change faces, but not too quickly. Give the player time to establish a musical emotion before changing to a new expression. This may be done entirely with the voice.

Oh Yeah?

Two to four players. As with *Feelings,* but each responding player plays music that is as contrasting as possible. For instance, if Player One's music is slow, soft, and mournful, Player Two comes in with music that is frantic, loud, and wildly exuberant.

Nice to See Your Back

Four players. Player One writes a feeling, mood, emotion, or other psychological or physical state on a three-by-five card and tapes it to Player Two's back without letting Player Two see it. Player Two

---

60　Kenneth Bruscia, *Improvisational Models of Music Therapy* (Charles C. Thomas Publications, 1987): 540.

turns his back and the rest of the group plays that feeling. Player Two then tries to guess what the feeling depicted was.

(Suggested by Stephanie Holmes.)

Hare and the Tortoise

Four-plus players. All players commence with fast, convoluted, high-energy melody lines. Gradually all the lines move slower and slower, using longer and longer rhythmic values until finally all players hold one last very long tone. Silence ends the piece. Follow with *Tortoise and the Hare*.

Tortoise and the Hare

Four-plus players. Play *Hare and the Tortoise* in reverse, starting with very long tones, gradually becoming quicker and quicker strings of notes until all players are filling the air with dizzying cascades of notes. All cut off at once at a signal from the leader.

Fortississississimo

One-plus players. Play or sing as loud as you can without injury. Don't hold back. Let it all out. Examine how this feels during and after the improvisation.

See also: Dynamics Games.
                           Ritual, Cave Celebrations, and *Rhubarb Rhubarb* (Miscellaneous Games).

• • •

It is becoming general knowledge that the simple appearance of much Baroque music is deceptive and that what is seen on the printed page was often merely an outline to be amplified and in performance according to regularized patterns or improvised embellishment.

—Imogene Horsley[61]

---

[61] "Improvised Embellishment in the Performance of Renaissance Polyphonic Music." In *Journal of the American Musicological Society*, 4 (1951): 7.

Chapter 23

Texture Games

Texture here describes the number of instruments playing at any moment.

Beginning ensemble players typically play too much for the good of the piece when they first start to improvise (it's hard to miss out on the fun and be silent). *Not playing* is an extremely important part of creating music in a group, but it takes iron discipline and experience for players to know when not to play. Even one "show-off" who will not stop playing (and often, is not listening) can drain a piece of interest as other players find it difficult to sit out while one person hogs the airwaves. Learning to vary the texture by alternately contributing and being silent is a very important skill for every improviser.

To extend one's flexibility and imagination in improvising is ever important; stretching toward and through variety replaces potential tedium with fresh challenge and discovery.

—Gerre Hancock[62]

Students should be given the tools for thinking. Students should be given the permission for feeling. Students should be given the opportunity for invention.

—LaDonna Smith[63]

Time It

Four-plus players. Not playing too much may be the most difficult thing for players in any ensemble larger than a duet to learn. This game uses a smidgen of technology to help the process.

Each player brings a small hourglass egg timer, stopwatch, or other silent timing device (or enlist a partner with a watch). To help get the feeling of when to play and when to be silent, each player is allotted a set number of minutes, typically no more than half the piece.

Players start the timer when they start playing and stop it when they stop. This is slightly cumbersome, but getting some experience in the process of "reduced" playing is so useful that it is worth the effort. Once a player's minutes are up, he may not play again for the rest of the piece. The allotted minutes may be used up all at once or spaced out. Players must listen carefully for the best time to join in and use their minutes judiciously.

---

62 *Improvising: How to Master the Art* (Oxford University Press, 1994).
63 "Improvisation in Childhood Music Training and Techniques for Creative Music Making." In *Improvisor* [online journal], www.the-improvisor.com/web%20ARTICLES/improvisation%20%20Education.html

Suggestions:

Length of Piece	Playing Time
One minute	Thirty seconds
Two minutes	One minute
Four minutes	Two minutes
Five minutes	Two minutes
Eight minutes	Three minutes
Ten minutes	Six, five, four, three, two, or one minute

Players really begin to choose notes carefully when they realize they may only play a total of one minute out of a ten-minute piece, or ten seconds out of a one-minute piece!

Number of Notes

Four-plus players. This is a different solution to the problem of playing too much, but instead of limiting playing time, each player plays only a certain number of notes, usually a mix of short and long tones. This works best for fairly short games.

Example: For a one-minute piece, each player may play three short notes and two long tones. Free choice of notes.

Count Up

Six-plus players. A variation on the game Red Light, Green Light. Best played in a large space with players spread out in different directions, but roughly equidistant from a facilitator, who stands in the middle of the room.

Players may play one short tone at any time, and may take one step toward the Facilitator afterward. If two players enter at the same time, both must go back to the beginning. The game ends when a person reaches the Facilitator. It is recommended that players keep their eyes closed except when stepping forward or back.

Variation: The game ends when the *last* person reaches the facilitator.

I Need My Space

Three-plus players. Player One plays a very sparse solo (one in which there is more "air" than notes) over any kind of rhythmic accompaniment. No notes are allowed on the first downbeat. Add a second soloist, who is allowed to play on the downbeat.

Clockwork

Six-plus players. Player One or a leader stands in front of the group with one arm and the other hand pointed straight up to indicate twelve o'clock. The player makes one slow circle around the minutes of the imaginary clock. The rest of the players play only one long tone and two short tones of their choice. The piece is finished when the clock hand points to twelve once again.

Variation: Go around the clock two or three times with different rules for subsequent rounds, such as more notes, different timbres, a rhythmic motive, extended techniques, etc.

Floating Duet

Eight-plus players. This game comes from the Soundpainting gesture *Coming and Going*, and is a useful way for large groups to play without the music becoming too dense.

Players enter and exit at will, trying to keep approximately two voices going at all times. Players do not have to wait until someone drops out; it is permissible to charge right in and force a player to drop out. Be bold. When the texture thickens, drop out and when it is too thin, join in.

Variation: Make a different number of voices the goal (e.g., one, three, four, five, etc.)

Hello/Goodbye

Four-plus players. Player One begins. One by one the other players randomly join in until all are playing. Then all randomly drop out one by one until one player is playing alone; this player brings the piece to a satisfactory conclusion.

Suggestion: Players do not have to keep up a continuous stream of notes after they enter. Keep in mind that liberal sprinkles of silence invariably improve a piece, especially one with many players.

The Fast and the Furious

Four-plus players, or one player soloing at a time in a group of four or more. Players play as many notes as they can per second at varying dynamics in a dramatic outburst. The length of each outburst should vary. The space between outbursts should be about as long as the last outburst. The group decides whether to have an accompaniment; if so, it should be sparse.

Variation: Do this in a circle. Players fills the air with as many notes as possible one by one, cueing the next soloist with a nod.

The Sparse and the Laconic

Four-plus players. Players may play only one or two notes at a time with generous amounts of rest between them. Experiment to discover how sparse a solo can be while still making some melodic sense.

This game, like many others, would benefit from some steady percussion accompaniment, such as a regular bass drum pulse in moderate tempo.

Idea: Compose a piece in ABA form, with A being The Fast and the Furious and B being The Sparse and the Laconic, or vice-versa. Switch to the new section at a signal from the leader.

At the Abyss

Two-plus players. Players make this piece as sparse as they can stand it to be. Tension/anticipation is maintained by holding instruments at the ready, but much less sound than silence. Are five to ten seconds of silence between sounds possible for the group as a whole? This is harder than it sounds. Vary the dynamics and other parameters dramatically, but play only a little, waiting long time between each short burst.

Waterfall

Four-plus players. All play rapid swirls of notes at low volume. Either individually or at a signal from the leader, dynamic swells and falls are introduced.

Soundpainting gestures may come in very handy here, especially *Volume Fader* and *Level Fader* (pitch fader). Drum circle veterans might also use typical drum circle arm indications for volume. Everyone else can make up their own signals.

| *Variation:* | Players may slow down the speed of the melodic swirls together or individually. Soundpainters should experiment with *Tempo Fader*. |

Density Combinations

Not playing constantly is a very important yet difficult concept for new improvisers to assimilate. This helps the overall group sound by varying the texture of the instrumentation, avoiding the deadly "everyone's playing all the time" block of sound. Varying density allows individual lines and colors to come through and provides welcome rest and variety to the ears of both players and audience. This game provides a framework to vary the combination of instruments playing at any given moment.

Four players. Give each member of the quartet a number from one to four. As used below, 1–2 is short-hand for Players One and Two to play while Players Three and Four are silent. Style, tempo, and key, for each piece may be decided beforehand or discovered while underway.

Play approximately for ten seconds each in the following combinations. A leader gestures when to switch.

Variation 1:	*Quartet and Trios.*
	1–2–3–4
	1–2–3
	1–2–4
	2–3–4
	1–3–4
	1–2–3–4

Variation 2:	*Quartet plus Duets.*
	1–2–3–4
	1–2
	1–3
	1–4
	2–3
	2–4
	1–4
	1–2–3–4

Variation 3: Quartet-Solos.

1–2–3–4
1
1–2–3–4
2
1–2–3–4
3
1–2–3–4
4
1–2–3–4

Variation 4: Grand Mix.

1–2–3–4
1–2
3–4
1–2–3
1–2–3–4
[one measure of silence]
2
1–4
1–2–3–4
3
2–4
1
2–3–4
1–2–3–4
4
1–2–3–4
1–2–4
1–3
2–3
1–2–3–4

Variation 5: *Texture Rondo.* In this variation 1–2–3–4 is used as the default ritornello density, but any other combination is also possible, as well as episodes that are trios, solos, or a mix of solos, duets, and trios.

1–2–3–4
1–3
1–2–3–4
1–2
1–2–3–4
1–4
1–2–3–4
2–4
1–2–3–4

Variation 6:	Repeat Variations 1–5 with each player experimenting with different densities of notes (e.g., extremely dense, dense, moderate, sparse, extremely sparse).
Variation 7:	Make up your own density sequences or rearrange the ones given above.
Variation 8:	*Percussion Switch.* Repeat any of the above variations, but have everyone play a percussion instrument.
Variation 9:	*Vocal.* Repeat any of the above variations with all singing.
Variation 10:	*Kitchen Sink.* Repeat any of the above variations. Everyone has a choice of playing his main instrument, a percussion instrument, or singing.
Variation 11:	*Kitchen Sink No. 2.* Any player may switch from her main instrument to percussion or voice at any time.
See also:	*Sparse Rhythm Machine* (Rhythm Games).

Percussion Accompaniment Option

The densities above count only for main instruments. Anyone not playing may freely continue playing on percussion instruments, with body percussion, mouth noises, percussive extended technique, vocal drone, etc.

Example:	Players One and Two play while Player Three makes air sounds and Player Four creates an ostinato by drumming fingers on a drumhead.
Variation:	Freely move back and forth between percussion for those not playing their principal instrument and only main instruments playing.

• • •

It cannot be denied that the emphasis on playing techniques, especially in the study of instrumental music, has raised the general level of performance to ever-greater speeds and complexities, which is a good thing. However, the question arises, is that all there is?

—William Cahn [64]

---

[64] *Creative Music Making, 9.*

Chapter 24

Timbre Games

Of all resources available to improviser, timbre is the most-often neglected by beginners. Almost every instrument is capable of a wide variety of colorful sounds, from subtle pitch shadings to wild combinations of extended techniques. New improvisers should make it a regular habit to explore the timbral palette of their instruments to increase the number of available colors and to make the use of different timbres fluent and automatic.

> *Improvisation is the basis of learning to play a musical instrument. But what usually happens? You decide you want a certain instrument. You buy the instrument and then think to yourself, "I'll go and find a teacher, and who knows, in seven or eight years' time I might be able to play this thing." And in that way you miss a mass of important musical experience... a person's own investigation of an instrument—his exploration of it—is totally valid.*
>
> —John Stevens[65]

Rainbow X-Tech

Four-plus players. The ensemble improvises a piece without pulse, using exclusively extended techniques (anything goes except the instrument's normal tone). See how many different kinds of sound you can create!

Ambient Rainbow Soundscape

Four-plus players. The ensemble plays either long tones of variable length or short interjections with any timbre. The result should be a wash of sound without a pulse. Dynamics may rise and fall; there may be gleams and glimmers of various timbral mixes; but there should be no regular or definable pulse.

Rainbow Groove

Four-plus players. Repeat either *Rainbow X-Tech* or *Ambient Rainbow Soundscape*, but establish a steady pulse, either right away or after the piece has begun at a signal from a facilitator See *Entrainments* in *Rhythm Games*.

---

[65] Quoted in Derek Bailey, *Improvisation: Its Nature*: 98.

Rainbow Accelerando

Four-plus players. Repeat *Rainbow Groove*, but start with a slow pulse and very gradually increase the tempo until no further acceleration is possible. The group then finds a place to end using eye contact or other gestural signals.

Scat!

Three-plus players. Using voices only, create a peppy ostinato groove with short scat (nonsense) syllables. Take turns soloing over the groove, singing long tones.

Off the Beaten Timbre: Unusual and Homemade Instruments

Aside from conventional instruments (including extended techniques), found percussion, and body percussion, the imaginative outside-the-box performer might also look into different kinds of musical instruments when searching for new timbres to enliven improvised performance. Consider some of the following sources:

Lark in the Morning. Self-billed as the "world's largest selection of ethnic musical instruments," this company offers nearly every kind of ethnic instrument at their fascinating website and in their print catalog. www.larkinthemorning.com

The Oddmusic Gallery. This website includes descriptions, photos, videos, and audio clips of many amazing and unusual instruments, from the Aeolian Wind Harp and Amazing Pencilina to the Vienna Vegetable Orchestra and Windform. They have a terrific set of links to similar sites as well. www.oddmusic.com/gallery/index.html

Homemade Percussion and Junkmusic. Don't wait! Make your own instruments! This website has a good selection of books on making homemade instruments. www.rhythmweb.com/homemade/

Experimental Musical Instruments. "Books, CDs and more." Provides information on unusual instrument making and makers and a catalog of products. www.windworld.com/index.htm

---

Howl at the Moon

Four-plus singers. The group makes soft, low sounds that gradually become louder, shorter, and begin swooping up in pitch until all are howling in full voice.

At a signal from a leader, the group begins whispering, punctuated by occasional yelps, throat noises, clucks, pops, growls, etc.

At another signal, the group returns to howling, then, with long falling *glissandi*, returns to the initial low sounds.

The piece ends with airy throat noises, dying away. It goes without saying that you can add to or change any of this during the improvisation.

(Inspired by the vocal improvisations of Lydia Busler-Blais and friends.)

Yes, We Sing Bananas

Three-plus singers. Create interesting vocal textures using only the word, "banana." Each singer decides how much of the word to use and what note value to assign to each syllable. Everyone shares a common pulse and key, but all other choices are individual.

Examples: Singer One sings a low note on "ba."

                         Singer Two sings quick 2/4 patter using "ba-na, ba-na."

                         Singer Three sings quarter notes in 3/4 using "ba-na-na" over and over.

                         Singer Four creates an ostinato using "na-na [pause] ba na-na."

Singer One may signal for all to switch to a new syllable(s), or it may be pre-decided that all may switch at will. At some point Singer One signals for all to hold out a note and end the piece.

Mouth-to-Mouth

Four-plus players. The group begins with any kind of non-vocal mouth sounds. At some point players gradually switch to vocal sounds. Continuing the independent decision making, players move to instruments. After all have switched to instruments, reverse the process, and finish the piece when everyone is making mouth sounds again.

(Source: John Stevens.)

Mouthing Off

Three to six players. In this game of improvised chamber music, each player creates an ostinato using only mouth noises. In turn, each player takes a solo using mouth noises plus body percussion if desired.

Idea: In the midst of group rhythmic improvisation, everyone switches at a signal from a leader to vocal scat syllables (e.g., bu, la, dah, dot, bah, be, doo, etc.), using the same rhythms. (Source: Christine Stevens, *The Heart and Art of Drum Circles.*)

Giggle Machine

Three to six players. Repeat *Mouthing Off,* but create the ostinato using various kinds of laughter. Solo with laughs in turn.

Variation: Sprinkle bits of crying in the middle of the laughter solo.

Unfamiliar Tune

One to three players. Play any familiar tune using only extended techniques.

Halloween

One to four players. Use extended techniques to create a piece that is creepy, spooky, chilling, and frightening. (See *Holiday Time* in *Style Games*.)

Noise Quartet

Four players. Improvise chamber music using the following sounds (preferably created on instruments):
    Player One: air sounds.
    Player Two: rapping sounds.
    Player Three: humming sounds.
    Player Four: rubbing or scratching sounds.

Variation: *Add eerie vocal sounds to the noises.*

Something Borrowed

Two to eight players. All players must bring something from home that can be used to affect the timbre of their instruments.

Examples: A brass player might make use a plastic bottle as a mute.

        A string player might weave a strip of paper through the strings to create a buzzing sound.

The resulting new sounds can be used with any other game.

Attractive Opposites

Two players. The highest and the lowest pitched instruments of the group (e.g., bassoon and flute, tuba and oboe, etc.) play a duet. Each emphasizes, even exaggerates, extremes (register, dynamics, etc.) in this "extreme: dialogue.

X-Tech Ostinati

Two to four players. Each player plays an ostinato, sharing a pulse and using an extended technique. Stay with it for a while, then at some point, change to a new extended technique.

Variation 1:   One player solos over the ostinato.

Variation 2:   Any player may play a long tone between *ostinati*.

Variation 3:   Add a section of pulseless, extended-technique playing.

Variation 4:   All players switch rapidly back and forth between as many extended tech-
                      nique sounds and noises as possible.

See also: *Timbre!* in Improv Set-Ups and *Follow That Timbre* in Aural Games.

Different Strokes [Technique]

When playing any drum or object functioning as a drum, use two different kinds of drumheads or drumsticks (e.g., one hard, one soft) for the purpose of having two timbres instead
of one. Experiment with accents and different sticking alternation patterns.

• • •

*The world needs both the enriching effect of the preservation of its musical heritages and
the stimulating effect of new innovations.*

—Matthew Montfort[66]

---

66   *Ancient Traditions, Future Possibilities* (Panoramic Press, 1985): 1.

Chapter 25

Composition Games

Although composition is frozen improvisation, it still has a place in the study of improvisation. The process helps players become accustomed to generating, developing, and refining ideas. It is also useful to be able to create "framework" pieces with windows of improvisational opportunities (since most composers deny us this).

Note: All written compositions should have titles, key and time signatures, instrumentation, and tempo.

When improvisation regains its former position at the centre of Classical music-making, perhaps the gap between composer and performer, between old and new music, between vernacular and art music, and between Classical performer and audience will narrow.

—Robert Levin[67]

Composing is like writing prose or poetry, except that we are not all immersed in music as a way of thinking early enough for it to seem natural.

—Bruce Adolphe[68]

An improvising musician gains many advantages over the non-improviser. The improvising musician has an expanded melodic imagination that contributes to composition and arranging skills.

—Edward S. Lisk[69]

I use improvisation for many reasons. It can spark rich ideas for composition, for it gives us a more intimate sense of raw materials of sound. It provides an astonishing physical and emotional release, and helps develop the kind of spontaneity that can transform the way we play Bach or Mozart or Bartok. It creates a more direct personal relationship with an instrument that can melt square-shouldered bravado into keen-eared listening.

—Eloise Ristad[70]

---

67   *Mozart Piano Concertos No. 5, 14, 16.* The Academy of Ancient Music, Christopher Hogwood, director (Decca: DDD 00289 466 1312). CD liner notes.

68   *Of Mozart, Parrots and Cherry Blossoms in the Wind* (Limelight Editions, 1999): 171.

69   *Intangibles*: 65.

70   *A Soprano on Her Head* (Real People Press, 1982): 190.

Bricolage [Aural Composition]

[Bricolage is defined as making do with what you have, i.e., composing with found percussion.] Five players (a leader plus quartet). Each member of the quartet brings some shop, kitchen, or household objects that can produce some kind of sound. Examples: power drill, towel, stapler, umbrella, bowl & spoon, rice in Tupperware, crinkly plastic, etc. The leader has previously invented (interlocking) ostinato rhythms for each player and teaches each one in turn aurally. Leader, conducting, brings them in one by one. When all are playing, leader points to a Soloist, who then abandons the ostinato and plays freely and extravagantly against the other *ostinati*. Each player becomes the soloist in turn. The leader signals a final hit to end the piece.

Body Percussion Chamber Music [Aural Composition]

Two to three players. Repeat *Bricolage* as a duet or trio, using only body percussion sounds.

Variation: Use mouth noises only.

Basketball Piece

Materials needed: music paper, pen or pencil, trashcan.

Four-plus players. The class forms a circle of chairs around the trashcan. Compose as much as possible for two minutes. No stopping, no erasing, no crossing out. When time is up, crumple up the paper and toss in the trashcan. Repeat. Repeat again. Do it all with a smile on your face.

Variation: Crumple and toss after each page. Do three, four, or five pages.

(Source: Charles Young.)

Quantity Is King

Four-plus players. Write as many notes as you can in one minute. No stopping, no erasing, no crossing out allowed. Repeat in various keys and scale types.

(Source: Charles Young.)

I Got Rhythm

Four-plus players. Using Xs for note heads and writing them only in the third space of the treble clef, write as much as you can in one minute, varying the rhythms. No stopping, no erasing, no crossing out.
At the end of the time:

1. Throw the paper away. Repeat.

2. Perform the composition while several other players outline a steady beat on percussion instruments (or tap their feet, or knock on desktops, etc.).

(Source: Charles Young.)

We Got Rhythm

Two players. Repeat *I Got Rhythm* in duet form. Use two staves. Then add another part and make it a trio.

Scored Rhythms

One composer plus two to five players. Write a piece for two, three, four, or five parts without giving any specific instrumentation. Write only rhythms for each part—no pitches. Don't forget to include unisons, rests, and *ostinati*. You may include opportunities for improvisation.

ABA Written

    Note: *See Miscellaneous Games for ABA: Played.*

Two-plus players. Write a short piece with the form A (four measures) B (one measure) and A (four measures). Over B (measure five), write "Improvise in the style." Taking no more than thirty seconds, fill the A section measures with a mixture of whole notes, half notes, and quarter notes using only the C pentatonic major scale (C–D–E–G–A). Choose two or three percussion players to accompany you.

    Variation 1:   Repeat, this time taking up to one minute and making it a duet.

    Variation 2:   Repeat, taking up to one minute this time and making it a trio. Use half notes and quarter notes in the top two voices and whole notes and half notes in the bass.

Minor Pentatonic

Two-plus players. Write a short piece using the ABA form described in *ABA: Written*. The entire piece should use the C minor pentatonic scale (1–♭3–4–5–♭7, or C–E♭–F–G–B♭); eighth notes may be used. Perform as with *ABA: Written*.

Whole Tone

Two-plus players. Write a short piece using the ABA form described in *ABA: Written*. The entire piece should use the C whole tone scale. Perform as in *ABA: Written*. Repeat using the B whole tone scale.

Dorian Composition

Two-plus players. Write a short piece using the ABA form described in *ABA: Written*. The entire piece should use the Dorian mode (1–2–♭3–4–5–6–♭7). You may use any Dorian key, but D Dorian (D–E–F–G–A–B–C) might be a good start. Perform as in *ABA: Written*.

Dare to Be Bad

One player. Write as badly as you can for two minutes, breaking as many rules as possible. No stopping, keep the pen (preferred) or pencil going at all times. Take the result home and frame it.

(Source: Charles Young.)

Write Something You Can Sing

One player. In one minute, write a melody that you can easily sing at sight. Now write words to the melody in thirty seconds.

> *Theme:*   Things you see or do on a farm (or any other topic of your choice). The words do not have to rhyme or make sense together.

(Source: Charles Young.)

Variation Game

Four players. Compose eight measures on one or two systems. Pass the paper to the composer on your right and take the paper of the composer on your left. Write a variation of the first eight bars. Continue for six variations.

(Source: Charles Young.)

Poem Piece

Two-plus players. Each player selects a favorite poem, which must be a "traditional" poem with regular meter (rhyming optional). Translate the rhythm of the poem into musical rhythmic notation. Using only these tones: C–D–E–F–G–A♭, apply pitches to the notated rhythms. Perform with additional improvised percussion (one or two players).

Triad Composition

One player. Write a piece using triads only. Include one or more opportunities to improvise using triads.

> *Variation 1:*   Major triads only.
>
> *Variation 2:*   Minor triads only.
>
> *Variation 3:*   Mixed major and minor.
>
> *Variation 4:*   Diminished only.
>
> *Variation 5:*   Augmented only.
>
> *Variation 6:*   A mix of any or all of the above.
>
> *Variation 7:*   Non-triadic three-note chords (i.e., triads without major or minor thirds, e.g., 1–2–5, 1–4–5, 1–4–♭7).

Card Chase!

One-plus player. Write the twelve notes of the chromatic scale on 3X5 cards or identical pieces of paper. Mix them up, and then choose four at random. Write "chase" music (as for a television movie soundtrack) using only these four notes. Leave a window for improvisation. Perform in class or for friends.

Piles of Fun

Two or three players. Take the same twelve pieces of paper from *Card Chase!* divide them randomly into two piles. Write a duet for any two instruments, assigning a pile to each. Each instrument may only play notes from its pile. Add un-pitched percussion *ad libitum*.

Variation: Repeat with three piles and write for a trio.

See also: *Constructing Improvisation Compositions* in Resources and *Inside/Outside Composition* in Melody Games.

When the performer is the partner of the composer, there is no limit to the invention and variety possible.

—Jeffrey Agrell

Many musicians are fabulously skilled at playing the black dots on the printed page, but mystified by how the dots got there in the first place and apprehensive of playing without dots. Music theory does not help here; it teaches rules of the grammar, but not what to say. When people ask me how to improvise, only a little of what I can say is about music. The real story is about spontaneous expression, and it is therefore a spiritual and a psychological story rather than a story about the technique of one art form or another.

—Stephen Nachmanovitch[71]

I'm still from a generation which has experienced it being a sin for improvisers to compose—or, for composers, to improvise.

—Reinhold Friedl[72]

---

[71]   *Free Play:* 9.
[72]   Online interview in *MusikTexte* 93, http://hjem.get2net.dk/intuitive/igold.htm

Chapter 26

Depiction Games

Depiction games are good ways to break away from worrying about making mistakes. The purpose here is vivid expression by any means, not reproducing a perfect sequence of notes.

This type of game works well with audiences. Have listeners make suggestions when input is needed by calling out adjectives, nouns, emotions, etc. Remind the audience (and yourself) that, as with all improv games, *the suggestions here are just starters*, and that the important thing is the direction of the piece. You may start with apples and end up with oranges, or start with a puppy and end up with Godzilla—it doesn't matter. The main focus is on inventiveness, a balance between unity and variety, and the effectiveness of telling the story.

Improvisation has played a prominent role throughout the history of world musics. Until quite recently we have tended to ignore the fact that European classical music from 1600 to the present comprises only a small fraction of the world's music. Furthermore, our general neglect of improvisation as a creative discipline stands in direct contrast to the rest of the world, where improvisation has thrived in virtually every cultural region.

—Bill Dobbins [73]

Adjective/Noun

Two players. Two players depict an adjective-noun combination in music. Flamboyant or evocative word choices are encouraged, as are incongruous juxtapositions.

Examples: *The Lovelorn Refrigerator*
        The Paranoid Pancreas
        The Drunken Robot

You may also use two or three adjectives plus the noun, as in *The Stinky, Love-Starved, Free Range Trout*. Construct (many!) more improv starters like these using the Improv Starter Generator in the Resources section (feel free to add to the list). A short list is provided below to get you started. Mix and match! Remember, these are just starters; you don't have to stick with your first idea. Improvisations

---

73 "Improvisation: an Essential Element": 36–41.

often turn into something else once they get underway. Follow your inspiration wherever it leads regardless of where you started.

Grumpy	Cheese
Flamboyant	Cow
Bewildered	Burp
Dyspeptic	Lasagna
Harvard-educated	Paramecium
Love-starved	Great white shark
Chartreuse	Pirate
Stinky	Porcupine
Seasick	Lumberjack
Drunken	Banana
Free range	Anchovy
Debonair	Corn Flake
400 lb.	Festival
Blue	Cockroach
Organic	Trout
Greasy	Fire Truck
Peppery	Octopus
Meditative	Pancreas
Itchy	Pit bull
Forgetful	Frog
Thrilling	Fahrvergnügen
Gelatinous	True Love
French Fried	Sea Urchin
Furtive	Chicken
Indolent	Philosopher
Pensive	Economist
Furious	Talk Show Host

Adjective/Animal

Two players. Same as in *Adjective/Noun*, but the noun may only be an animal.

> *Examples:* *The Philosophical Warthog*
> *The Flamboyant Platypus*
> *The Rapturous Hippo*
> *The Constipated Baboon*

Adjective Only

One or two players. Same as in *Adjective/Noun*, but take inspiration from a single, flamboyant adjective.

> *Examples:* Festering   Quixotic
> Sensuous   Archaic

Cavernous	Repulsive
Anxious	Aloof
Boastful	Quivering
Enigmatic	Odiferous

Add your own!

Conversation

Two players. Two instruments have a conversation, and exchange "talk" back and forth, by responding to rhythms, pitch, and expression.

Variation:	Have an argument!

Emotional Symphony

Six to twelve players. Players are assigned different emotions (e.g., fear, love, grief, joy, etc.) and must depict them on their instruments. A conductor cues the entrances. The emotions played one at a time or simultaneously. This game may also be done entirely vocally.

In the Mood

Six to twelve players. This is a variation of *Emotional Symphony*. Player One begins a tune with a mood, emotion, or psychological/physical state in mind. The other players join in and try to match the mood.

Note:	Player One does not say what the mood is in words; she must clearly express the mood through the instrument.

Examples:	Sad	Angry
	Bitter	Frustrated
	Drunk	In love
	Paranoid	Confused
	Dyspeptic	Anxious
	Sluggish	Swaggering
	Ravenous	Itchy
	Puzzled	Irked

This may be done entirely with vocal effects (but without words).

Oooh Music

Two-plus players. The inspiration for this game comes from the book *Return to Child*,[74] a wonderful improvisation method distilled from several decades of experience at David Darling's Music for People workshops. Play soft, gentle music to communicate tenderness, kindness, and love. This may also be done entirely with vocal effects.

---

[74] James Oshinsky, *Return to Child* (Music for People, 2004).

Yea! Music

Two-plus players. Also from David Darling, this game is the partner and opposite of *Oooh Music*. This time, play loudly and powerfully to communicate extremes of joy, passion, anger, or excitement. Use any and all means available on your instrument, and remember: nothing succeeds like excess. This may also be done entirely with vocal effects.

Soundtrack or Silent Movie

Two-plus players. This needs to be done while watching a TV show or movie with the sound turned off. Players watch the on-screen action and try to depict the drama in music.

Variation 1:   Use a conductor to select players.

Variation 2:   Players listen and watch and decide when to enter.

Shakespeare Soundtrack

Two-plus players. Players select their favorite passages from Shakespeare's plays and sonnets. A leader picks an ensemble to improvise music as the selection is read aloud. This may be done in several ways:

1. Soundpainting.

2. The leader points to those who should play, letting them choose what to play.

3. The group improvises without a director, simply listening and reacting.

4. Try all of these on successive passes.

A vocalist acts as reader, and may sing—improvising—the text. If there is no vocalist, the leader reads.

Suggestions: To be or not to be (*Hamlet* II,I, 56-61).
O Romeo, Romeo! Wherefore art thou Romeo? (*Romeo and Juliet* II, ii, 33).
Tomorrow and tomorrow and tomorrow (*Macbeth* V, v, 19).
Now is the winter of our discontent (*Richard* III (I, i, 1).

Random Depictions

Two to four players. Depict the following in music: white water rapids, a hummingbird, walruses in love, a fast ride on a motorcycle, a swarm of bees. Time: thirty seconds.

Suggestion Box

Two-plus players. Various playing suggestions are written on slips of paper. Players select several slips at random and construct a piece based on the selections. Players may play the piece alone, or select a partner from the group to help. Pairs of players may play their separate instructions simultaneously.

Examples: Style: march, lullaby, elegy, children's song.
Dynamics: *p*, *f*, hairpins.
Miscellaneous: Imitate the style of another player and rest as much as you play.

Once Upon a Time

Five-plus players. One speaker plus four players and/or conductor (optional). The audience contributes a protagonist, setting, and problem. One player makes up a story based on these elements, leaving space for the other players to invent appropriate music to illustrate the text. A conductor may be useful to cue the players and/or select who is to play each excerpt.

Son of Once Upon a Time

Three-plus players. One speaker plus two players, depending on the particular story. The narrator tells a familiar fairy tale and assigns various players to portray the parts. The assignments do not have to be stereotypical.

Example: Little Red Riding Hood
        Red: Tuba
        Wolf: Violin
        Grandma: Trombone

Bride of Son of Once Upon a Time

One to four players. Tell the story of a well-known fairy tale through music in one minute. It should have a beginning, middle, and end.

Headlines

One to four players. Pick a headline from today's paper (tabloids are good sources) and depict it in music, e.g., "Elvis Seen Landing in Alien Spacecraft in Kansas."

(Inspired by Charles Young.)

Ad Music

Four players. Player One has spent some time at home going through various kinds of magazines, cutting out the most graphically interesting advertisements. Two, three, or four players sit or stand in front of a music stand as Player One places an ad before each player as a score. At a signal from Player One, they all begin, each playing her advertisement. During the playing of the piece, Player One may elect to switch ads between players, replace any ad with a new one, or rip an ad in half.

Come to Your Senses

One to two players. Depict in music the following:

Sounds: Baby crying   Lion roaring
       Train passing Waterfall
       Cricket   Whispering

Smells:	Bacon frying	Garbage rotting
	A bouquet of roses	Coffee
	Perfume	

Tastes:	Orange juice	Cotton candy
	Buttered popcorn	Champagne
	Strawberries	Chocolate

Sights:	The Grand Canyon	Clouds
	Tropical fish	The full moon
	A sunset	A sweet smile

Feel (touch):	A first kiss	Velvet
	Sandpaper	A shower
	Warm wind	Silk
	Brick	

Brainstorm with other players and add to the list!

Variation: *Two to five players. Construct a piece with each player using a different sense experience.*

Dictionary Game

One to four players. Pick a word at random from the dictionary and depict it in music.

(Inspired by Charles Young.)

Radio Show

Two-plus players: One speaker plus one or more other players, depending on the story depicted. A conductor is optional. Player One reads a short story, preferably a horror story or science fiction. In a pinch, a children's story (e.g., The Three Bears, Hansel and Gretel, etc) will do. One or more other players illustrate the tale (on the conductor's command).

Suggestion: Use Soundpainting gestures.

Geographical Depictions

One-plus players. Take a map of a city, state, country, or the world. Pick a place at random. Depict that place through music.

(Idea from Heather Anderson.)

Diverse Conversations

Two players. Depict conversations between:

> A black widow spider and her new beau.
> An NFL linebacker and a ballerina.
> A philosopher and a chicken who have been paired up by a
> computer dating service.

Invent more conversations of your own!

Country Music

Two or three players. Play music that evokes the sound of a certain (unmentioned) country. The only discussion or planning allowed is the selection of the country. Listeners must guess the country. No quotes allowed except as a last resort.

Guess the Animal

Two to four players. Depict an animal. Afterwards, listeners must guess what animal was being depicted.

Examples:		
	Blue whale	Octopus
	Slug	Turtle
	Greyhound	Pit bull
	Snail	Piranha
	Lamb	Tiger
	T. Rex	Paramecium
	Vulture	Ostrich
	Eagle	Grizzly bear
	Skunk	Race horse

Guess the Job

Two to four players. Depict an occupation. Listeners must guess what it is afterwards.

Examples:		
	King	Farmer
	Race car driver	Computer programmer
	Deep sea diver	Astronaut
	Movie star	Opera singer

Guess the Emotion

Two to four players depict an emotion. Listeners must guess what it is.

Improvisation Games for Classical Musicians

Guess the Machine

Two to four players. Depict a machine through music. Listeners must guess what the machine is when the piece is complete.

Examples:

Rocket ship	Clock
Sports car	Biplane
Typewriter	Cell phone
Conveyor belt	Toaster
Espresso machine	Tractor
Submarine	Mars rover
Bicycle	

[to start improvising] Forget, if you can, everything you ever learned about music and music-making.

—James Oshinsky[75]

---

[75] *Return to Child: 2.*

Chapter 27

Technique Games

There is no better way to practice technique than to improvise. Suddenly all those routine ways of going up and down scales take on new life and become interesting again. You can practice the same content as before (scales, arpeggios, patterns), but now they are used in a meaningful context. The benefits of this type of training include motivation, flexibility, and quantity of practice.

See also: Melody Games

Imagination is more important than knowledge.

—Albert Einstein[76]

The requisite variety that opens up our expressive possibilities comes from practice, play, exercise, exploration, experiment. The effects of non-practice (or of insufficiently risky practice) are rigidity of heart and body, and an ever-shrinking compass of available variety.

—Stephen Nachmanovitch[77]

Scale Plus Delay

Two to three players. Player One plays a major scale up and down for one octave in eighth notes at moderate tempo. Player Two enters one, two, three, or four eighth notes after Player One. If there is a third player, Player Three does the same thing after Player Two.

Variation 1: Player Three may use a different amount of delay than Player Two.

Variation 2: Players may elect to use different keys (e.g., Player One: C major, Player Two: E♭ major, Player Three: G major), or different scale types (e.g., Player One: C minor, Player Two: E major, Player Three: D♭7).

Variation 3: Each player may decide independently when to reverse direction in the scale.

Variation 4: Each player may choose any note value for any note.

---

76   *On Science.*
77   *Free Play:* 44.

Variation 5:	Players may introduce rests of any length at any time.
Variation 6:	Players may add accents, regular or irregular, to their scale.
Example:	Player One accents every third note; Player Two accents every fourth note; Player Three alternates accents every two or three notes.

Que Será Será

One player. Take a passage from a solo, etude, or excerpt that you know. Play through it completely, disregarding the indicated note values and inventing your own as you go. You may also change the tempo dramatically from crawlingly slow to breakneck speed and anything in between. Dynamics may go from whisper to jet engine.

Repeat this a number of times, making the approach completely different each time. It may help to think of a style when creating new rhythms. Pitches could be played as an ostinato rhythm (play only long-short-short all the way through).

Style examples:	*Sarabande*	Chorale
	Cakewalk	Jig
	Rag	Serenade
	March	Reel
	Bossa nova	Stop-time soft-shoe number
	Fanfare	Recitative
	Boogie-woogie	Swing tune
	National anthem	Waltz

Variation:	Try this as a duet. Pick the same style and play from the same printed page, but invent note values independently. Players may also begin in different places.

Practicing a passage this way will greatly deepen your physical knowledge and mastery of the notes, increase expressiveness, and/or restore vitality to a passage in danger of becoming over-practiced and lifeless.

From an idea presented in William Westney's marvelous book, *A Perfect Wrong Note: Learning to Trust Your Musical Self*.[78]

Thirds: A Charm

Two players. Players pick a major key, preferably one less familiar. Players are only allowed to play a diatonic scale in thirds (e.g., in C major, C–E, D–F, E–G, etc.), but they may change every other parameter: note value, articulation, register, dynamics, note length, meter.

Player One is free to adopt a style (e.g., lyrical, choppy, breakneck, plodding, etc.); Player Two must match that style, but attempt to always be moving in a contrary direction whenever possible. Both players should make sure to add rests. Do not play all the time, but studiously maintain a steady pulse, even if both rest at the same time. Percussion accompaniment is welcome (Player Three, Player Four, etc.).

---

[78] Amadeus Press, 2003.

Variations: Change the interval to a major second, minor third, perfect fourth, or perfect fifth.

Zig Zag

One player. Pick a major key (an unfamiliar one is better, e.g., F♯, D♭, etc.). At a comfortable tempo and starting anywhere in the scale, play three ascending stepwise notes ascending using whatever durations are comfortable (e.g., all half notes, quarter notes, eighth notes, etc.). Make a leap of any size and play three descending stepwise notes. Loop the pair until you can play without hesitation. Repeat with a new pair, then loop the two pairs together. Continue.

Experiment with leaps of all sizes in all registers. Increase the tempo gradually until you begin to feel tension or start missing notes. Stay in control, stay relaxed, maintain accuracy. Repeat in a different key.

Variation 1:   Use other numbers of notes (e.g., two, four, five, six, etc.).

Variation 2:   Keep the ascending notes the same but vary the order of upper notes (e.g., ascending diatonic sequence). Then reverse this procedure: keep the top notes the same and change the order of the alternating descending notes on each alternation.

Variation 3:   Try ascending/ascending and descending/descending patterns.

Variation 4:   Vary durations (e.g., instead of three eighth notes, try long-short-short, short–short–long, short–long-short, etc.). Keep the new assorted note values the same each time, or for additional challenge, change them each time.

Variation 5:   Start with a third and increase the leap interval each time.

Variation 6:   Change keys every four bars.

Variation 7:   Use different scale types (e.g., dominant seventh, all minors, chromatic, whole tone, diminished, altered dominant, modes, etc.).

Variation 8:   Use different meters (e.g., 4/4, 6/8, 5/8, 7/8, etc.).

Double ZZ

Two players. Repeat Zig Zag with a partner. Try with the following variations (and invent more of your own!):

Variation 1:   Reverse mirror: one plays up, the other plays down; one plays up and down, the other plays down and up, etc.

Variation 2:   Try using both the same note values and independent note values.

Variation 3:   Use the same or independent keys.

Variation 4:   Use the same or independent scale types.

Variation 5:   Use the same or independent leaps.

Variation 6:   Add percussionists, either alternating or as ostinato accompaniment.

Leapin' ZZ!

One to two players. Repeat *Zig Zag* and *Double ZZ* using arpeggios instead of scale strings, strings of notes that include both adjacent notes and leaps such as 1–2–4, 1–3–4, 1–2–5, 1–4–5, 1–2–7, etc.

Fanfare

One to three players. Pick an arpeggio of any chord type in any key (e.g., major, minor, augmented, diminished, etc.). Play alone, as a duet, or trio using notes from the chord (which may include the seventh or ninth) in fanfare-style figures (duple, triple, or both).

See also: Scale Accents (Accent Games)
Rubato (Melody Games)

• • •

I want to facilitate people to improvise as well. Music in our society has been degraded. Most of our society can't even sing anymore. Because of massive media saturation and its takeover of the silence of our souls, people rely on external sources for their information. Making one's own music can put one in touch with the internal self and empower one to come from a place of deeper soul power and compassion. In this forum even the beginner is not disadvantaged; he is in a position of being the true improviser, because when one knows little, one must explore. The skilled musician brings with him his experience as vocabulary to contribute to the mutual language. Through group improvisation, music can return to a role in the life of our society as a shared interactive expression, as a kind of collective artistic recreation and release.

—LaDonna Smith

Chapter 28

Accompaniment Games

Every improviser is at times a soloist or accompanist, either leading the ideas and energy or supporting the ideas of others. Most of us spend the lion's share of our practice time working on "solo chops" so we can shine when it is our turn to step into the limelight. More neglected but equally as important is the ability to know what to do when someone else is soloing—which, in improvisation, is more often the case. It is essential therefore that a player be fluent in various accompanying techniques (these will vary somewhat depending on the instrument). Following is a summary of some basic accompanying techniques:

Unison:	Play the same melody and the same rhythm, either at pitch or an octave lower. This is possible only in written-out or rehearsed and memorized sections, or if a short passage is repeated a number of times.
Unpulsed Drone:	Hold out one long (and usually low) tone.
Pulsed Drone:	Play one tone but repeat it, as in a steady stream of quarter notes, to create a pulse.
Ostinato:	Take a short idea and repeat it and repeat it and repeat it... An ostinato is often improved by using a catchy rhythm. The rhythm may be derived from part of the melody.
Countermelody:	Move when the melody rests, hold when the melody moves.
Arpeggios:	Outline a chord.
Bass line:	Play mostly chord tones in the lower register.
Imitate:	Echo what you hear.
Don't play!:	Silence is an important part of music. Silence puts a "frame" around the melody.
See also:	The Art of Accompaniment in Improvisation.

This is what classically trained musicians feel when they discover that they can play without a score. It is like throwing down a crutch. ...it can be debilitating to depend on the creativity of others. When this creative power that depends on no one else is aroused, there is a release of energy, simplicity, enthusiasm.

—Stephen Nachmanovitch[79]

Foreground/Background

Two players. Improvise a duet with minimal discussion beforehand. The goal is to quickly fall into a soloist or accompaniment role. At some point the soloist will switch to play accompaniment; the accompanist must remain alert and switch immediately to a foreground/solo role. The soloist must be aware of the accompaniment that is being played and take over in that style when switching roles. The accompanist may switch accompaniment styles, but the soloist must take over in the same style.

Initiator/Responder

Two to four players. One player is chosen as the initiator. The others listen closely to the initiator and respond in some way, which may include:

Playing something very similar
Playing something that contrasts sharply
Playing a rhythmic/melodic background (ostinato)
Answering sporadically (call-and-response)

Initiator/Responder Soup

Four-plus players. With minimal discussion, all players begin playing simultaneously. Players listen carefully and attempt to relate to each other. An initiator will emerge from the chaos at some point; all others will then gradually identify and match the style of the initiator.

Familiar Tune Accompaniment

Two to four players. Player One plays any familiar tune (see Resources for a list) by heart in various keys (preferably a less familiar key), and all other players play accompaniment. Player One plays variations on successive passes, and may add decorations, elaborations, or ornamentation each time. Accompaniment players should experiment with a different kind of accompaniment role each time.

Examples:	Drone	Ostinato
	Countermelody	Arpeggios
	Imitation	Bass line
	Pedal point	Sparse texture (including silence)
	Playing "opposites"	

---

[79] *Free Play*: 50.

218

Sidekick

Four-plus players, but it must be an even number. Players pair off. As in Yes, *and…*, one player of each pair is the soloist, the other is the sidekick, who follows the lead of the soloist.

Variation 1:   All pairs play independently.

Variation 2:   Set a hierarchy of soloists (i.e., the soloist in Pair Two listens to the soloist and follows the style, tempo, etc. of Pair One, while the soloist in Pair Three listens to the soloist of Pair Two. Alternately, all soloists may follow one selected soloist.

Triad Accompaniment

Two to four players. The soloist plays a familiar tune of any kind. The accompaniment must be triadic (i.e., chord tones, such as 1–3–5), such as the famous Alberti bass.

Variation: Chords may be non-triadic (i.e., notes not thirds apart, e.g., 1–2–4, 1–4–7, etc.).

See also: *Medley* and *Yes, and…* (Melody Games).

Medley

Two to four players. This game works well with a pre-chosen list of familiar tunes or subset (cowboy songs, children's songs, Christmas songs, etc.) of tunes. Each player chooses a tune independently and plays the tune or part of the tune in any key. Short solo turns alternate with accompaniment figures that are taken from other snippets or motifs from the tunes. Players should weave in and out of foreground and background, matching rhythms and keys, or may contrast in register, dynamics, energy, etc. Steal other players' tunes and motifs shamelessly.

Morphs

Two players. This game requires you to buy *Morphs: Etudes for Improvisation*, by New York improvising pianist Mikael Elsila (see www.cafepress.com/morphs). Elsila has composed a book of short cells two to eight measures in length (206 in all). The cells are usually fairly straightforward harmonically, with a *soupçon* of rhythmic interest. The intention is that the cell be repeated *ad lib.* under a solo.

Although there is an accompanying CD of the cells, it is more useful to have Player One play a cell on the piano (the cells are not particularly difficult) while Player Two solos, then switch after a while. It is not indicated, but I recommend repeating the cell in other keys, and perhaps later transforming it with a change of mode (e.g., to minor), tempo, or register, adding ornamentation, etc. *Morphs* is a barrel of fun and possibilities waiting to happen. You can take this great idea of Elsila's a step farther and profit even more from his book if you like: After you have done a number of these, start creating your own morphs, perhaps introducing more styles, chord progressions, meters, and so on that pique your fancy and stretch your abilities. Morph away!

Derived Accompaniment

Two players. Player One uses sheet music to improvise a solo, using motifs from the piece. Player Two (who does not necessarily play the same instrument as Player One) listens to Player One and constructs an accompaniment from what she hears.

Variation 1:   Player Two also uses the same page to construct the accompaniment.

Variation 2:   Player Two uses a sheet of music to construct the accompaniment, but it is from a *different* composition than Player One's! The accompaniment must be made to fit Player One's solo.

Accompanists That Don't Need to Eat or Sleep

GarageBand. This nifty program makes constructing an accompaniment a drop-and-drag process. Select the preprogrammed loop of percussion, bass, etc., and drag it to a track. Click the loop icon and set the measures to loop, and you have a playing partner that never gets tired (well, it doesn't respond terribly well to what you play, but you'll never need to feed it pizza to keep playing for you). GarageBand works better for one-chord improv; for chord progressions, see below. (GarageBand is for Macintosh computers only, and is part of the iLife software suite. http://www.apple.com/ilife/garageband/.

Band-in-a-Box. This rather ugly and clunky program (try to loop a few measures, for instance, and compare that to GarageBand) is very good at mimicking a jazz rhythm section (piano, bass, and drums). Chords to a tune can be input very quickly. Band in a Box will play up to forty different choruses of accompaniment before repeating itself. The program could use a new user interface, but it is great help to practice playing over chord progressions. (Band-in-a-Box is for both Macintosh and PC computers. http://www.pgmusic.com/.)

Free Play. 13 Musical Landscapes (Volume 104 in the Aebersold Play-a-long Series of CDs) serves as accompaniment tracks for free solos. They are described as breaking down "traditional boundaries of rhythm, melody, and harmony to present a blank canvas of sounds, pulses, and colors to excite imagination." Don't forget to browse among the endless acres of play-a-long and improvisation CDs, references, and methods at the Aebersold site. (http://aebersold.com/Merchant2/merchant.mvc?Screen=PROD&Product_Code=V104DS &Category_Code=AEBALL.)

Musician's Practice Partner: Cello Drones for Tuning and Improvisation. *The website for this product describes it as "an effective and enjoyable way to develop your ear and improve your intonation." It contains cello drones on all twelve chromatic pitches—a much more user-friendly sound than any synthesizer drone. These are useful as improvisation accompaniments and for practicing scale material. (http://cdbaby.com/cd/mpp.)*

Various. Many method books come with accompaniment CDs that are useful for various sorts of improvisation, including those by Christine Stevens, Kalani, Alice Kay Kanack, Azzara & Grunow, Dworsky & Sansby, and others. See Improvisation Books, Articles, and Links (Resources).

Any good jazz player has innumerable tricks he can fall back on whenever he gets stuck. But to be an improviser you have to leave these tricks behind, go out on a limb and take risks, perhaps occasionally fall flat on your face. In fact, what audiences love most is for you to go ahead and fall. Then they get to see how you manage to pick yourself up and put the world back together again.

—Stephen Nachmanovitch[80]

---

80 *Free Play*: 22.

Chapter 29

Style Games

Although this book emphasizes style somewhat less than other areas, any improviser would do well to learn as many musical styles as possible. Limits make playing improvisations easier, and style is, in a sense, just a set of agreed-upon limitations that produce a certain effect. Although free improvisation in jazz attempts to be entirely style-free, the author is of the opinion that improvisers benefit from knowing many styles and should be ready to play any style at any time. A larger vocabulary is always an advantage. Learning styles is very worthwhile, and should be an ongoing project in the larger aim of facility in improvisation and is thus encouraged in this book.

Doesn't it strike you as odd that we can spend many years teaching an art that is totally inaccessible to our students unless they are staring at dots on a page, playing someone else's musical creation?

—Julie Lyonn Lieberman[81]

Matching

Two players. This term and technique is from music therapy improvisation, and, according to Tony Wigram, is "one of the most valuable of all the improvisational methods"[82] in music therapy.

Player One begins. Player Two listens carefully for a few moments, then joins in, attempting to play music that fits together and matches Player One's music. Player Two's music is not necessarily identical to Player One's, but is the same in "tempo, dynamic, texture, quality and complexity" [Tony Wigram][83] —in other words, the same style.

Reflecting

Two players. This term and technique comes from music therapy improvisation. Player One begins. Player Two listens briefly and then joins in, "matching the moods, attitudes, or feelings" [Kenneth Bruscia][84] of Player One.

---

81   *The Creative Band and Orchestra*: 42.
82   Wigram, *Improvisation*: 83.
83   Wigram, *Improvisation*: 84.
84   *Improvisational Models*: 540.

See also:　　　　*Replay (Aural Games)* and *Quartet Duets (Improv Game Techniques)*.

Monkey Mirror

Two players. Player One is the soloist; Player Two is the copier. Player One may play anything she likes. Player Two must instantly copy Player One as closely as possible (like a mirror). Player One may change key, meter, tempo, and/or dynamics at will. Player Two must mirror the changes.

(Idea from Evan Mazunik.)

Pick One

Two-plus players. Pick a style from *Musical Styles and Forms* (Resources). Player One solos. Player Two (or the rest of the players) improvises a harmonic and rhythmic accompaniment. After a bit, pass the solo role to a new player.

Variation:　　　With three or four or more players, try having two soloists at the same time.

Idea:　　　Use only percussion that you make using household objects for rhythmic accompaniment.

Fusion

Two players. Pick a style from *Musical Styles and Forms* (Resources). Each player picks a style with which they are familiar, preferably styles with some sharp contrasts.

Examples:　　　Baroque plus Calypso
Fanfare plus Lullaby
Chorale plus Boogie-Woogie
Drone plus Bluegrass
Dirge plus Sousa March
Madrigal plus Mambo
Chaconne plus Cakewalk

Pick a common key and use a common eighth-note pulse (the meters might not match). Players play fairly simple versions of their styles simultaneously. At some point, they begin to steal elements of each other's music. The goal is for both players to arrive at a new "fused" style.

Idea:　　　Pick a style that you know little about. Research that style, listen to recordings, become an expert, then play this game.

Academy Awards

One-plus players. Play a familiar tune, a solo from the literature, or an improvisation the way you imagine a famous person might play it, going on the assumption that a person's personality comes through in their playing.

Examples (add your own):

Superman	Indiana Jones
Bugs Bunny	Rocky
Abraham Lincoln	Betty Crocker
Marilyn Monroe	Big Bird
Elmo	Shrek
Prince Charming	Wicked Witch of the West
Daniel Boone	Frodo Baggins
Lassie	Groucho Marx
James Bond	Oprah
Hamlet	Carmen (of the opera)
Muhammad Ali	Attila the Hun
Napoleon	Don Corleone
Elvis	Queen Elizabeth (I or II)
Lancelot	Guinevere
Romeo	Juliet
Captain Kid	Frankenstein
Darth Vader	Homer Simpson
Ebeneezer Scrooge	Santa Claus
Wonder Woman	Tarzan
Gromit	

This game may be played with several supporting actors, who, after careful listening, establish an accompaniment for the Oscar winner.

Variation: Depict the chosen star in music.

Let's Talk

Two players. Each selects an Oscar winner from Academy Awards or invents her own, and then carries on a musical dialogue, remaining in the style of their character, but responding appropriately.

Watch Out

One player. Play one or more note(s), but make it the ugliest, most awful sound possible. Play music to:

Make paint flake off a wall
Make babies cry
Cause a stampede
Make dogs bark
Make your mother take a swing at you
Curdle milk

Puttin' on the Style

One player. Play music to:
>   Make a small child laugh
>   Put a pit bull to sleep
>   Not scare a flock of songbirds
>   Improve digestion
>   Please your mother
>   Make someone fall in love with you

Playing Along

One player. Play along with any CD. Try playing different parts:
>   Melody
>   Bass line
>   Harmony line
>   Counterpoint
>   Ostinato

>   *See also:*   *Steal That Tune* (Aural Games).

Dirge

One player. Create the saddest piece you can. Try using minor keys, extended techniques, low register, long tones, dynamic contrasts, dissonance, or a slow tempo. Give it a name (as you should do for all your pieces) and/or dedicate it to a departed loved one.

>   *Variation:*   Add a second player for accompaniment.

Where Are We Going with This?

One player. Play a piece from the standard repertoire, such as a Mozart concerto. At some point spontaneously break away from the piece and continue, with an entirely invented line, playing as much in the style as possible. Later, rejoin the original to finish the piece.

>   *Idea:*   Have another player or a random event (e.g., bird chirp, knock at the door, phone ring, etc.) determine the switchover point.

Fanfare

One to three players. Pick an arpeggio in any key and of any chord type: major, minor, augmented, diminished, etc. Play alone or as a duet (or trio) using notes from the chord (which may include the seventh or ninth) in fanfare-style figures.

Serenade

One player. Create a beautiful song for the one you love.

> *Suggestions:*   Major key
> Beautiful melodic line
> Middle register (your most beautiful tone)
> Moderate tempo
> Dynamic contrasts
> Subtle rhythmic accompaniment

Dedicate the piece to the one you love, whether this is your true love, your mom, your cat or dog, Fettuccine Alfredo, etc.

Build a Band

Two to four players. One player invents one part of a march (melody, oom-pah, rhythm, counter-melody, etc). Each player enters, adding a different part to the march.

March Madness

Two to four players. Play a march as in *Build a Band*, but change it in as many ways as possible.

> *Suggestions:*   Play it in minor.
>
> Play it in minor with extended techniques (*Halloween March*).
>
> Play it using the whole tone scale and augmented triads (*Debussy march?*).
>
> Change the oom pahs to 1–#4. Inflect various scale tones (e.g., change 6 to ♭6, 4 to #4, 7 to ♭7, 2 to ♭2, etc.).
>
> Change the oom pah to 1–4–♭7–♭3 and use the minor pentatonic scale in the melody (1–♭3–4–5–♭7) or emphasize the interval of the perfect fourth.
>
> Outline some outrageous shifts of key every eight (or four or two) measures (e.g., C major to E♭ minor to A major to F# major to F major to B minor).

Here Comes the Bride

Two to four players. Everyone knows the familiar Mendelssohn *Wedding March* and the "Bridal Chorus" from Wagner's *Lohengrin*. Now it's your turn. Invent new ways to musically accompany a bride down the aisle to the altar.

> *Suggestions:*   Jazz
> Celtic
> Reggae
> John Philip Sousa

Medieval, fanfare
Blues
Brahms
J.S. Bach
Rock 'n' roll
Folk song

One player begins; all other players join in as soon as possible and match the style.

Join the Party

Four players. Players One and Two improvise using long tones in a chorale style. The key may be preset or random. Player Three enters in a contrasting style; the other players must change to the new style. As soon as the new style is established, Player Four enters in another contrasting style. Player One then drops out as Player Two and Player Three adapt to the new style. At some point, Player One signals the end of the game and all return to a brief chorale passage, concluding with a long, held note.

Variation City

One player. Play any familiar tune (see Resources) by heart in the key most unfamiliar to you. Play successive repetitions in different styles.

Examples:	March	Waltz
	Lullaby	Fanfare
	Tango	Blues
	Polka	Elegy
	Jig	Boogie
	Zydeco	Sarabande

See Resources for a list of styles. If you need to do a little listening or research to learn more about the style ("What is the characteristic rhythm of a sarabande?"), go right ahead.

Hallway Recitative

Two players/singers. A pair of singers (or anyone with a singing voice and some familiarity with opera) resolve that, whenever they pass each other in the hallway, they will greet each other in simple recitative (half-spoken, half-sung dialogue), using familiar greetings and answers, but doing so in recitative style.

Examples:	How are you this morning?
	Very well, thank you.
	My dog was ill in the night, but he seems much better now.

| *Tip 1:* | Don't worry whether or not your recitative is Great Art; just do it, and have fun. |

| *Tip 2:* | As with opera, the words don't have to be true—maybe you don't even have a dog. Just sing something interesting in the style. Like opera, it is more important that it be interesting than true or even believable. |

Holiday Time

One-plus players. Invent music to illustrate a holiday. For example, musically recreate the Fourth of July, or turn out the lights and play some spooky Halloween music. Make up music that captures the feeling of Christmas time, or compose a musical Valentine.

Another idea is to improvise music that depicts Thanksgiving from both the Pilgrims' and the turkey's point of view.

Variation: Pick lesser-known holidays to celebrate:

> Festival of Sleep Day (January 3)
> National Candied Orange Peel Day (May 4)
> National Accordion Awareness Month (June)
> National Talk Like a Pirate Day (September 19)
> National Cashew Day (November 23)

See http://library.thinkquest.org/2886/ for more ideas, or invent your own holidays (e.g., The Day My Car Died [April 7], or Musk Ox Appreciation Day [July 31]).

Guess the Style

Two to four players. Improvise in an undeclared style.

Examples:

Country and Western	Rock 'n' roll
Gregorian chant	Fanfare
Klezmer	Bebop
Ragtime	Hip-hop
Waltz	Swing
March	Celtic
Baroque	

See the Style List in Resources for more ideas. Afterwards, listeners must guess what the style of the piece was.

• • •

I was a product of my training, and truly believed that to play piano you first had to learn to read. Read first, play later. How absurd.

—Rena Upitis[85]

---

[85] *This Too Is Music* (Heinemann, 1990): 50.

Chapter 30

Text Games

A good way to begin improvising, or to warm up to the idea of generating material and working with something you know, is to play improv games that deal with something that we are all good at: speaking, or better yet, conversation.

While the language [of improvised speech] itself may lack the precision of an edited reply, the value lies in its freshness and authenticity. We all know what a canned lecture sounds like. Real speech (improvised speech) will always be more interesting, attention getting, and persuasive than its scripted sister.

—Patricia Ryan Madson[86]

Conversations

Four-plus players in even numbers. Pair off. Each pair has a thirty second conversation. A facilitator signals when time is up. Repeat the conversation, word for word. Was it faster? Repeat again Was it yet faster? Repeat. Faster still?

Repeat, but this time change speeds: Sometimes faster, sometimes slower, once with a pause somewhere. Repeat, now varying the volume, sometimes very loud, sometimes very soft. Repeat, varying dynamics and changing the speed at the same time, and include a pause.

Now: Two pairs stand shoulder to shoulder in a line, all facing forward. All carry on conversation at the same time, varying volume, speed, leaving space. Next, feel free to start anywhere in the conversation and repeat any of it.

Now as you recite, feel free to steal bits of other's conversation.

Finally, as you are free-forming bits of original and stolen conversation, see if the group can do a "charge," in which the group synchronizes a loud chant on one word or short phrase and increases in volume and tempo until it can go no more (which might be a good time to stop!).

(From Jennifer Kayle, Professor of Dance at the University of Iowa, an expert in improvised dance.)

---

86   *Improv Wisdom* (Bell Tower, 2005).

Ensemble Telepathy

Eight-plus players. Someone in the group counts aloud: "One, two, three," etc. Anyone may say the next highest number at any time, but if two people say the next number at the same time, the group must start over. This is best played with eyes closed to avoid visual cues. Groups often bomb out at very low numbers at first, but with practice, they find that they can attain ever-higher numbers, even as high as seventy or eighty.

Why is that? What does the group learn? Why does it improve at this game with time when the counting is theoretically random? And why will this help us play better improvisations?

(From creativity expert Kat Koppett, in her book *Training to Imagine*.[87])

Dramatic Names

Six-plus players. Players stand in a circle, alternating male/female. For the purposes of this exercise, all men are named John and all women are named Mary. Each man turns to the woman on his right and says "Mary" to her with some kind of expression; that woman then turns to the man on her right and says "John" to him with another kind of expression. Try to discover as many ways as possible to say the names. Make it different each time.

Variation: Use the actual names of players. Make the way you say the name so interesting that someone else in the room will turn around. Overact! Exaggerate!

(Source: Charles Young.)

Name Game

Six-plus players. The group forms a circle. One person begins, saying her name in rhythm eight times. After the first two repetitions, the person on the right begins with his name, sharing a common pulse and overlapping with the first person (watch out for names whose accents begin on a pickup). When it has gone full circle, the first person begins again using a percussion instrument or clapping.

(Inspired by Doug Goodkin's Name Rhythms game in *Sound Ideas*.[88])

As I Was Saying

Two-plus players in even numbers. Pair off. Converse with the person next to you about a common subject. At a signal from the instructor, continue the conversation in unintelligible gibberish (but use normal vocal inflections) until you receive the signal to resume speaking normally. Continue alternating between gibberish and normal talking with each signal.

Repeat with instruments, this time alternating between something you can play by memory (e.g., scales, patterns, warm-ups, familiar tunes, etc.) and improvisation. Alternate with the signal.

(Source: Charles Young.)

---

87   Stylus, 2001: 141.
88   Warner Bros. Publications, 2002: 34.

My Day so Far

Two players. This game is best done with the accompaniment of a keyboard player who is comfortable with improvising accompaniments, but in a pinch, a guitar player or a mallet percussionist would work as well.

Player One jots down a few words about his day. These may be completely ordinary things, like eating breakfast, brushing teeth, getting dressed, or walking to class. Specific comments are better than general comments.

The accompanist plays a simple chord progression in a moderate tempo (e.g., I–vi–IV–V, I–IV–I–V, I–ii–V⁷, etc.). Player One, perhaps with the help of a word list, then invents a song about "My Day so Far." Rhyming is laudable but not essential. The main thing is simply to keep going. It is better to say any word that comes to mind than to stop. Keep going at all costs. This is challenging at first, but with practice and deliberate abandonment of any attempt at perfection (have fun!), the process gets easier and is great fun for everyone.

Oh Yes, He...

Eight-plus players. Player One recycles the list about everyday occurrences compiled while playing *My Day So Far* by turning it into a gospel chorus-like call-and-response event.

Player One shouts or sings a one-measure phrase in 4/4. The rest of the group immediately shouts (in the next measure, without a break, always beginning with "Oh, yes" or "Oh, no"). Player One, without missing a beat, comes in in the next measure with some new intelligence, followed by the chorus.

Example:	Player One:	I couldn't find my undershirt!
	Others:	Oh, no, he couldn't find his [under]shirt!
	Player One:	But then I saw it on the floor!
	Others:	Oh, yes, he saw it on the floor!

The game continues as long as Player One can keep coming up with new lines.

Suggestions:	It had been there a really long time!
	It smelled like old fish on the line!
	I took it downstairs, don't cha know.
	And put it in the soup! Oh, ho!

When Player One runs out of ideas—when he misses his entrance—his turn is over, and another player takes over. The trick is not necessarily to turn out brilliant literature, but to *keep going and inventing new lines at all costs*. The soloist may even make nonsense noises to fill the space (echoed of course by the group), but no more than three times.

The challenge for the other players (the chorus) will be to keep from laughing, and because they have to fit "Oh, yes" or "Oh, no" into the response, they may have to make some adjustments to the solo line. This creates a certain amount of chaos, which is perfectly fine, and part of the game, as long as it is done with gusto and amplitude.

All efforts should be *forte* to *fortissimo*. This is not a soft or subtle game. Be loud, be convincing, have a ball. It is probably a good idea for someone from the chorus to give Player One his first line just before beginning so that he can't plan anything in advance. Keep the subject ordinary, about everyday events; this makes it easier to come up with material.

Hallway Recitative

Two players/singers. A pair of singers (or anyone with a singing voice and some familiarity with opera) resolve that, whenever they pass each other in the hallway, they will greet each other in simple recitative (half-spoken, half-sung dialogue), using familiar greetings and answers, but doing so in recitative style.

Examples: How are you this morning?
Very well, thank you.
My dog was ill in the night, but he seems much better now.

Tip 1: Don't worry whether or not your recitative is Great Art; just do it, and have fun.

Tip 2: As with opera, the words don't have to be true—maybe you don't even have a dog. Just sing something interesting in the style. Like opera, it is more important that it be interesting than true or even believable.

Talking Groove

Two players. This is similar to *Move With the Groove* (Melody Games). Player One rhythmically speaks a word or two or a short phrase that fits into a 4/4 measure. Player Two does the same with a new word or phrase that is different in some way from the original. The second time around, Player One switches to his instrument, playing the rhythm of his word or phrase in a previously selected key or mode.

Words into Music

One-plus players. Turn parts of speech into scale degrees. Use the resulting melodic line to create an improvised piece. Use the following chart:

SCALE DEGREE	PART OF SPEECH
1	Noun
2	Article
3	Adjective
4	Object (or noun)
5	Verb
6	Adverb
7	Preposition

Write a sentence and turn it into an improv starter (a theme or motive).

Example:　　　　　The quick brown fox jumped over the lazy dog's back.

This becomes scale degrees 2–3–3–1–5–7–2–3–3–1.

In C major: D–E–E–C–G–B–D–E–E–C.

(Source: Charles Young.)

B·A·C·H

One-plus players. J. S. Bach used the letters of his name as a theme for a composition (H is B♮ in German, and B is B♭; so Bach's theme was B♭–A–C–B♮). You can do the same, even if the letters of your name fall outside the A-to-G musical alphabet. Simply assign appropriate pitches to H through Z. There are many ways to do this, and you are free to invent your own system.

Suggestions:

H, I, J	=	A
K, L, M	=	B
N, O	=	C
P, Q, R	=	D
S, T	=	E
U, V, W	=	F
X, Y Z	=	G

Using this system, John Doe would be A–C–A–C–D–C–E, and Jeffrey Agrell would be A–E–F–F–E–D–G–A–G–D–E–B–B.

The following system adds chromatic notes to the mix.

H, I, J, K	=	G♯/A♭
L, M, N	=	B♭
O, P, Q, R	=	C♯/D♭
S, T, U, V	=	E♭
W, X, Y, Z	=	F♯/G♭

Using this chromatic system, John Doe would be A♭–D♭–A♭–B♭–D–D♭–E, and Jeffrey Agrell would be A♭–E–F–F–D♭–E–G♭–A–G–C♯–E–B♭–B♭.

(Suggested by Myrlon Pressly.)

• • •

What is maddening in America is most people have been separated from their culture. They have been told there's a special privileged class of artists who have a special insight. A normal person doesn't have this insight. That is a monstrous lie, and it is hideous because it is taught to us early on. We are taught we're not artists. Every single day we're reminded. The special students are isolated in a class and told, 'You're special, you go on. The rest of you, please become middle-class and boring.'

—Peter Sellars[89]

---

[89]　Quoted in Bill Moyers, *A World of Ideas II: Public Opinions from Private Citizens* (Doubleday, 1990): 24.

Chapter 31

Storytelling Games

Telling stories—the social sharing of a narrative description of events, either fictional or factual, through words and gestures—is as old as humankind, perhaps even predating the use of spoken language. (The earliest stories may have been told through gesture, sounds, and facial expression.) Storytelling has been augmented through the years with drawings and other artwork, and more recently, music, which includes everything from a simple folk song to a Strauss tone poem. Storytelling is as natural to our species as breathing, and, in spite of the distance between modern society and earlier aural traditions, storytelling holds our attention just as much today as in years past, be it through bedtime stories, audio books, television series, or cinematic epics.

Storytelling can be a powerful and effective way to improvise an overarching means that incorporates and integrates all other elements that we study in the course of learning contemporary classical improvisation detailed in this book, including form, melody, rhythm, extended techniques, harmony, texture, and in many other ways. The author and pianist Evan Mazunik frequently use storytelling pieces in their concerts (some descriptions are given below as examples).

The reader is encouraged to construct storytelling pieces from myth, legend, poetry, literature (especially children's literature), and history (world, national, local, and personal). Concerts can be personalized on short notice to include a piece about a story that is meaningful to local residents. In short, storytelling in music is an extremely valuable and engaging way to organize improvisation.

Note:	Various composers, animators, and moviemakers have already set a number of the more famous tales to music, but their versions are not the only possibilities. Do your best to ignore them and create your own, or pick lesser-known tales—there are still plenty of those to tell.
Tip:	Telling stories in music is a great opportunity to use and discover many kinds of extended techniques that are highly useful in creating atmosphere and mood. Extended techniques are difficult to notate and read, but are easy to perform with just a text description as a cue.
Exercise:	Create extended techniques that might work to portray dragon's breath, ogres growling, a witch's cackle, knocking at the door, the wind whistling in the trees, snoring, a train on the tracks, or a galloping horse.

Do not get too fussy about how every part of the thing sounds. Go ahead. All processes are at first awkward and clumsy and "funny."

—Carl Whitmer, *The Art of Improvisation*[90]

Program Notes

One-plus players. Write program notes for a short piece that uses the instruments available in the ensemble. Be vivid! Be dramatic, even melodramatic, whenever possible. Use emotions and senses whenever possible.

First approach:	Write about a scene, or write descriptions of what the instruments do.
Second approach:	Give everyone a copy of the program, then illustrate the program notes with spontaneous music!
Sample scene:	The whales begin their evening song as the blood-red sun touches the horizon. High, wispy cirrus clouds frame the concert in calm seas. Suddenly the far-away buzz of boat motors adds the sound of a drone. Elke Thorsdottir knows that she has only a minute to act to convince the whales to cut short their songs and swim deep and far away to safety. She aims the flare gun just above the pod and fires…

Sample instrumental/musical description:

High muted strings sizzle on a stratospheric C–G drone *sul ponticello*. A single flute plays a mournful Celtic Lydian tune in triple meter. A complex rumble of drums begins *pianissimo*, crescendoing very slowly, with sporadic sharp accents threatening the flute. Clarinet and oboe join the flute; then English horn and bassoon enter, repeating intervals of a minor seventh. A large skin drum starts a steady accented pulse underneath. Cellos creating piercing energy with a steady pulse of accented sixteenth notes join high strings. Muted offstage trumpets play interlocking bi-tonal fanfare figures. The flute switches to a higher octave and adds flutter-tongue. All strings play a *sul tasto tremolo* on the lowest string while singing a low "ah" in unison. A cymbal crash signals the end, with all instruments performing a slow, fall-off *a niente*.

Grimm Tales

Two-plus players. With or without a narrator, depict the following fairy tales by the Brothers Grimm in music. (Reread the originals to refresh your memory of the details if necessary.)

The Three Little Pigs
Sleeping Beauty
Hansel and Gretel
Goldilocks and the Three Bears
Cinderella

---

90   *The Improvisor* [online journal], www.the-improvisor.com/muquotes.html

Little Red Riding Hood
Beauty and the Beast
Robin Hood
Rapunzel
The Bremen Town Musicians
Rumplestiltskin

Hans Christian Andersen

Two-plus players. With or without a narrator, depict the following fairy tales by H. C. A. in music. (Reread the originals to refresh your memory of the details if necessary.)

The Princess and the Pea
The Ugly Duckling
Thumbelina
The Little Mermaid
The Emperor's New Clothes

Various Tales

Two-plus players. With or without a narrator, depict these stories in whole are part in music:

TITLE	AUTHOR
Pinocchio	Carlo Collodi
Heidi	Johanna Spyri
The Wizard of Oz	L. Frank Baum
Treasure Island	Robert Louis Stevenson
Peter Pan	James Barrie
Black Beauty	Anna Sewell
Charlotte's Web	E.B. White
Call of the Wild	Jack London
Winne-the-Pooh	A.A. Milne
Peter and the Wolf	anonymous
Paul Bunyan	anonymous
Brer Rabbit	anonymous
Casey Jones	anonymous
John Henry	anonymous
Robin Hood	anonymous

Note: This is only a tiny selection of the countless possibilities available in children's literature, myths, legends, tall tales, fairy tales, etc. It will pay big dividends to explore and discover and make up stories on your own.

FX

Two players. Player One reads aloud or invents a story, fairy tale, or poem on the spot. Player Two improvises music to go along with it. The music may depict a character (heroic, confused, fearful, etc.), an atmosphere (spooky, mysterious, etc.), or a location (countryside, palace, dragon's lair, etc.) and should use lots of special effects (extended techniques), such as *glissandi*, growling low notes, big *crescendi*, *sforzandi*, accents, trills, etc., depending on the instrument. Anything goes in the service of the drama!

A Little Something about Mary

Two players/singers. Player One sings, accompanied by Player Two on piano. Do a song telling a sad story about the real Mary of "Mary Had a Little Lamb."

And Another Thing...

Two singers. Singers One and Two are an old married couple, and sing a duet in a minor key about all the things each does that drives the other crazy.

Dad/Daughter Scene

Two players. Player One is the stern father of Player Two, his teenage daughter. Daughter has been grounded for coming home after curfew and must cajole papa into letting her go to a party on Saturday night. She tries pleading, crying, charming, aggression, hysteria, etc. He remains gruff and adamant, but finally relents. She rejoices.

Lost

Two players. Players One and Two play or sing a plaintive duet in D minor in 4/4 entitled "Lost on a Desert Island with no Deodorant or Other Comforts of Home."

Lovesick Porcupines

Two players. Players One and Two play piano four hands, depicting the fateful meeting of two lovesick porcupines. Use extended techniques and sharp *staccati* liberally.

Love Talk

Two players. Players One and Two depict a conversation between two lovers. The conversation begins one way; at a certain point, it changes mood and style, ending quite differently than it began.

Tip: Use silence as an integral part of this piece.

The King's Challenge

Three players. The King has advertised far and wide: his daughter, the princess (Player One), has never laughed. The person or persons who can make her laugh will get ten million gold ducats and half his kingdom, but those who fail will be hanged. Who (Player Two or Three) will accept the challenge?

Movie Soundtrack

Four-plus players. The group has one minute to prepare film music for a new movie, "A Tale of Cleveland," a documentary narrated by Players One and Two.

Possibilities: The reintroduction of wolves into suburban Cleveland.
     The new light rail system.
     The sewers.
     Make up your own scenario.

King Kong Soundtrack

Four-plus players. Everyone joins in to create a film soundtrack about a film in which King Kong runs amok in New York, then sees Fay Wray and falls in love. Be excessively dramatic and sentimental. Use extreme contrasts and many extended techniques.

Teddy's Funeral

Five players. Player One plays a one-handed ostinato on piano in A minor for the funeral of a teddy bear. A mournful solo reminiscing about poor Teddy is sung by Player Two. Back humming is provided by Players Three, Four, and Five.

Dragon Tale

Five players. Players One and Two alternate telling a fairy tale with a beginning, middle, and end (the speaking part). The story ends differently than one might expect.

Player Three: Handsome prince.
Player Four: Fair maiden.
Player Five: Ferocious dragon.

All players add necessary sound effects along the way. This is a great chance to try out some extended techniques!

Storyboards

In movie making, filmmakers use graphic representations of scenes as an aid in constructing the cinematic narrative. You can make your own version of such storyboards to help remember the order of your musical story.

While graphics may be all you need, chances are that text descriptions will be the most helpful. Use letters or numbers (or both) to label sections in order. Then add some brief comments to help you remember what and when you want to play in a general sense. The piece will still be improvised, but you can keep the mood changes and techniques in order. Use as few or as many sections as you need, but as a rule of thumb, try to limit the entire instructions to a page or less. Feel free to amend or add to them at any time, including during a performance.

The author and pianist/composer Evan Mazunik have put together several pieces for horn and piano that tell a story. Below are two examples of the storyboards used. There are many ways to construct such storyboards using text, graphics, standard notation, or a mix of all three. It is important that the notes make sense to the performers and that, when performed, the piece as a whole makes sense to the audience.

Note:	Both of these example pieces take about ten minutes to play; in the second one, there is less written detail; more was discovered in concert.
Example 1:	L'Homme Armé (The Armed Man)

The medieval tune "L'Homme Armé" was used in various guises to build a piece that depicted "a day in the life" of a medieval village. After much experimentation, the following (semi-cryptic) map to the improvised version of the song was constructed:

A—Intro—Piano "[morning] Bells" to ostinato. 16m (measures). Add shaker. Stop bells after 16m.

B—Tune.

B2—Dufay chorus [like early counterpoint].

Transition—Piano cues four bars of tune from section B.

C—"Fair." Piano [i.e., pianist] to shaker plus ostinato. Hn.—long legato. A♭ Lyd./Dom. Trail off. Hold F.

D—Horn—declamatory cadenza. End on F (fermata).

E—Piano chord (hn. *tacet*). Whistle chorus. Horn adds low tune at half tempo.

F—Rumble chorus. Hn.—improv fanfare (with mute) in E♭ minor pentatonic. Piano low rumble.

F2—Cue horn melody at pitch in tempo. Pno. retro mel. at half tempo; RH interjections. Tag: Last three (of four) 3X. $\boldsymbol{p}$ cresc. to $\boldsymbol{f}$.

G—Ostinato out. See sheet. 4X. Horn holds first time. Rit. last time.

H—Epilogue. Whistle plus hn. wind sound.

Note:	A version very close to this one adding cello was recorded by Duende (Agrell, Mazunik & Selinger) on the CD *Mosaic* (MSR Classics—www.msrcd.com).

Example Two: The Dragons of Pilatus

Taken from a legend from Lucerne, Switzerland. People in the Middle Ages believed that there were dragons that lived high up on the local mountain, Mt. Pilatus (this took place at a horn festival near Pilatus). A rough outline (below) was constructed; it was performed the next day.

That program also included a new story piece based on Alice in Wonderland that used even less text than "The Dragons of Pilatus." There is no prescribed amount or length or type of notes; whatever works to help performers find their way through a long or complex sectional piece is fair game.

A   Hn.: air sounds; low, X-Tech (i.e., extended techniques);
          multiphonics on F.
      Piano: X-Tech.
      Vamp: D Phrygian and D Dorian.
      Atmosphere: air (short).

B   Piano: boogie.
      Horn: contrast.
      Fourths.
      Leave space.
      Soar.
      Tip-toe: don't wake up the dragon!
      Meet the dragon: give DB (i.e., downbeat): C–F♯–B–F–B–E half
          valve wiggle.

C   Vamp.
      Slow (Brahmsian).
      Vamp.
      Atmosphere.
      Air sounds.
      Out.
      Hold low D.

• • •

Perhaps the cause [of disinterest in school music] is simply that…many students find that "music education" is irrelevant. In this uniquely expressive art form, the student is denied the experience of creation and is limited to a functional role in the re-creation of, at best, historical monuments. He seldom has the opportunity to use music for his own expressive needs, while he is expected to appreciate the expressive works of others. He is refused the role of evaluator or critic because educational attitudes, geared to traditional and fixed positions, do not allow for student judgments. He is usually denied experience in a living art because this too often violates limited concepts of historical doctrines and idiomatic systems upon which educational methods are based. The student may deem the subject matter to be irrelevant, because it appears "completed" and foreign to the realities of life and society as he knows them to be.

—Ronald B. Thomas[91]

Education should concern itself with the freeing of the mind for creativity. That makes a whole person. That's why the idea of a debate as to whether the humanities are any good to a society is appalling.

—Hugh Downs

---

[91] *NMCP Synthesis: a Structure for Music Education* (Media Materials, Inc., 1970).

Chapter 32

Miscellaneous Games

This section is a potpourri of games that don't fit into other categories. As with all games in this book, feel free to alter, extend, or otherwise adapt them to your situation.

Also: Remember that you can add (more) percussion to almost anything.

I never practice. I always play.

—Wanda Landowska[92]

The most important thing is just to play. Practice creating tonal and atonal melodies. Get into a regular routine of just playing—creating when you pick up your instrument. Let go. Watch what happens.

—Ed Sarath[93]

House Music

One player. This is a game to be done at home, but may in fact be done anywhere outside of class (that is, where there are few people around, or with other classmates who will join in, or with tolerant, sympathetic people who don't mind your music-making).

The idea is to make as much music with whatever you have around you in any way that you can, including "multi-tasking."

Example: You are in the kitchen. You have the radio on, tuned to a music station (of any kind)—or not. Shift your weight on your feet, keeping a pulse, perhaps adding an accent now and then. Do this as you move about the kitchen. Do all these movements in time to the rhythm—push down the toaster, put away the silverware, slice the carrots, scrub the dishes. Sway your body with the pulse, swing your arms and head, perhaps, add pirouettes now and then, etc. Make percussive mouth noises to go along with the music, or sing along, singing the melody, a harmony part, a countermelody, or interjections.

         Make up your own words about what you are doing in the moment, e.g., "I knead the bread, the bread, bread, bread, I need to knead the bread, the

---

92   Quoted in Cahn: 33.

93   From an improv workshop at the University of Iowa, October 26, 2005.

bread. I go to bed with all the bread I need to knead, knead to need, need to need, just fold it, push it, smush it, hold it, turn it around and start again."

Plunge ahead fearlessly; keep going no matter what. If you can't think of a word, say anything, or make a noise or say a scat syllable. You can also do only scat, such as: Oh bop do la be dah snap a lap oh bah do bah snip a lop a doona do.

You can also add more sounds using your hands or feet: clap or snap your fingers, stomp on the floor, step in place in time.

Rap or tap any of the objects you find in the room or that you are using in your tasks. For an imaginative (if slickly produced) example of House Music, watch and listen to "Music for One Apartment and Six Drummers" on YouTube: www.youtube.com/watch?v=f2bcPIXl8kc

Be excessive and dramatic: show those potatoes some emotion! Make your gestures extravagant (caveat: be more subtle when you are holding anything sharp or breakable).

If there is another improviser in the room, make it all a grand inter-locking, rocking, socking duet. Lunch need never be the same after this, and we haven't even talked about laundry possibilities. Or bath time. Or yard work. Etc: Improvise! Make music all the time!

Idea: Plan a day in which you make music from the time you wake up until the time you go to bed. Perhaps enlist your entire fraternity or sorority, line up sponsors and a suitable charity, and alert the media and make it an event. Some schools have dance marathons for charity—why not have a Make Music Marathon for charity? Remember the old saying: "If it's worth doing, it's worth overdoing."

Car Music

One to four players. This is done while traveling in a vehicle. If you are the driver, remember your first responsibility is to be alert and to drive safely. This game might help keep you alert on long drives but is not recommended for city or stop-and-go driving. The radio or a CD may be very helpful here.

As with *House Music*, sing along with the music you hear. Feel free to make up words about anything you see, think, or feel. They don't have to make sense, but it's fun to try. They don't have to rhyme, but rhyming is an engaging challenge. You can also make rhythms by tapping fingers on the wheel or using mouth noises.

Do not—repeat—do not tap your feet (it does not go well with a gas or brake pedal). Do hum. Be operatic. Sing of sights passed.

Try extended techniques: imitate the Doppler sounds of semi engines or the hissing of air brakes.

This game is of course easier and more suitable for passengers, who don't have to concentrate on the road. Get something going, somehow, something new or a twist on something old (such as making up new verses to old songs). Follow it wherever it goes, even all the way to Poughkeepsie.

Shower Music

One player (usually). Alluded to in *House Music*.

The daily shower is a chance to sing your heart out and sound terrific. Feel free to sing the oldies, but use the aural enhancement to create new music as well. Sing about the day, about dirt, about soap, about the feeling of hot water and being clean. Sing about a broken heart, about new love, about the sun coming up today. Make it raw, real, and raucous. Do it every day!

Desk Music

One player. This is a great one to do when you are tired, bored, or you need a break.

Look around your desk at all the things that can produce sound.

Ideas: Flip a day calendar.
Whack a stapler.
Shake a box of staples.
Close drawers.
Crumple sheets of paper.
Rip a Kleenex out of its box.
Turn on a printer.
Tap on a desk with pencils and pens.
Rap on a desk with knuckles.
Tap out an ostinato with a coffee mug.

Construct a percussion piece using what you have. If really inspired, make mouth noises or sing lyrics (scat or poetical) along with *Desk Music.*

(Idea from Stephanie Holmes.)

Stadium Music

Eight-plus players. Consider how people make noise at, say, a football game: clapping, cheering, whistling, stomping, jingling car keys, etc. With or without a conductor, make stadium noises, quite loud and as varied as possible, but completely chaotically. Gradually establish a pulse and coalesce into a definite groove. End with one big chaotic explosion of noise (touchdown!).

(Idea from Bethany Eriksen.)

Who Was that Masked Man?

Two-plus players. Players bring distinctive hats and/or masks (animals, monsters, people, etc.) and improvise in the style suggested by their mask's face.

(Idea from Evan Mazunik.)

Scatversations

Two-plus singers, ideally three or four. Adapted from Conversations (Text Games).

The group stands shoulder to shoulder in a line. Each singer invents melodies/rhythms using short scat syllables made up of a consonant and a vowel.

Examples:	Bah	Do	Lee
	So	Ka	No
	Fu	La	Ma
	To	Zee	Wa

A leader signals the start and finish. Pieces should last about ten to fifteen seconds. Each time the game is repeated with a different emphasis.

1. Repeat, playing exactly what you just played, or as much as you remember.

2. Repeat—same again.

3. Repeat. This time very slowly.

4. Repeat, this time, as quickly as possible.

5. Repeat, changing speeds: sometimes faster, sometimes slower, once with a pause somewhere.

6. Repeat, now varying the volume—sometimes very loud, sometimes very soft.

7. Repeat, varying dynamics and changing the speed at the same time, including a pause.

8. Repeat, stealing bits of what others are singing.

9. Repeat all, complete with theft of material. At some point, attempt a "charge": Everyone picks up on the same syllable or two, repeating it over and over, building volume and perhaps tempo, until the piece can go no faster or louder. End on one big whoop/stomp noise.

(Source: Jennifer Kayle, Professor of Dance at the University of Iowa).

Toy Music

Two players (one adult, one child). Give a child any toy or object that easily makes noise (a plastic aspirin bottle half filled with dry rice works nicely as a shaker), and then echo the child's sounds or alternate with him to create a piece.

(Suggested by Stephanie Holmes.)

Playground Music

One-plus players. Find a stick or two and use playground equipment as percussion (don't hit it too hard).

(Suggested by Stephanie Holmes.)

Ritual

Eight-plus players. Each player creates an ostinato using either mouth noises, body percussion, vocal sounds, any combination of the preceding, or an instrument.

Start very softly. The ostinato doesn't have to be continuous; leave some silences. Every so often (but not too often) each player may have an "outburst": a brief, loud, frantic episode of chaos and noise before returning to the ritual ostinato. Make the outburst extreme in contrast to the group sound and avoid making an outburst at the same time as another player. Very gradually increase the dynamic level.

Take time with this; there's no hurry. Outbursts gradually begin to overlap and become longer. At some point, the noise level will be very loud, and the outbursts will become almost continuous. At this point the leader signals the group to find a common pulse and synchronize the sounds. When this is accomplished, the group maintains the synchronized sound as the dynamic level very slowly fades to nothing. When the group reaches silence, everyone should freeze for a few moments to let the mood slowly fade away.

Cave Celebrations

Eight-plus singers. Singer One embodies a cave man who has just returned from a hunt and starts boasting of his exploits in a guttural, rhythmic song-chant in a made-up language. One by one other singers join the chant. Volume, energy, and motion gradually increase until a frenzy is reached at top volume.

At a signal from Singer One all suddenly go silent. The piece ends with Singer One singing a low tone on a scat syllable. All join in and hold for the length of one breath.

Rhubarb, Rhubarb

Eight-plus singers. Everyone begins by muttering "Rhubarb, rhubarb" very quietly, at different speeds, and not in synch with each other. Each player may gradually increase and decrease her volume at will, as well as the speed of pronunciation. Singers may also choose to get in synch with another singer for any period of time.

The leader may indicate *crescendi* and *decrescendi* with a hand signal, but singers are required to obey them only half the time. Each decides when to obey and when to ignore the signals. Signals from a drum circle or the *Soundpainting Volume Fader* gesture work nicely here, but feel free to invent your own simple hand signal, such as up/down to indicate volume.

When the leader finally gives the *Synchronize* signal (interlocking fingers), all players must listen and arrive at a unified chant of Rhubarb at the same tempo.

When the word is synchronized among the singers, the leader indicates a *crescendo*. When volume can go no higher, the leader gives a clear cut-off to end the piece.

Concerto!

Three-plus players. Player One is the soloist, the rest make up the orchestra. The soloist should enter the "stage," walking confidently, even arrogantly, hamming it up as much as possible. Player Two may be the designated "conductor" of the orchestra. Orchestra membes may overact by shaking hands, bowing to each other and the audience, etc.

Player One finally begins (key and/or style may be chosen ahead of time or not), with Player Two (the conductor) waving his arms in random fashion. Orchestra members may follow the conductor or completely ignore him and make up their own accompaniment. Player Two should be at least vaguely responsive to what the soloist is doing (e.g., the soloist may suddenly decide it is time for a cadenza, and the orchestra should be silent—no instruments playing, but they may eat sandwiches, text message on their cell phones, do crossword puzzles, read magazines, open cans of soda, gossip, etc. during the cadenza).

Player One winds up to a grand finish and takes exaggerated bows, throws kisses to the (invisible) audience, retrieves (imaginary) roses thrown at her feet, acknowledges the orchestra (but only very briefly), etc.

Variation: After a completely over-the-top performance as above, play it straight once. Player One should invent an interesting solo line; the orchestra should craft a tasteful accompaniment.

Location, Location

Two players; Player Two must not have perfect pitch.

Player One plays a chord at the piano or on the guitar, harp, etc. Start with major or minor without revealing the key to Player Two. Player Two plays a loud, ringing, accented whole tone of her choice and attempts to discern as quickly as possible (instantly, if possible) the scale degree (altered or not) of her note in the key of the random chord played by Player One, and then resolve it diatonically by step or half step to the nearest chord tone by diatonic step or by *arpeggio* to the tonic.

Example: If Player One's chord is C and Player Two plays an A♭, Player Two hopefully hears that she is playing the ♭6 of the chord and should drop a half step to G, continuing by step or arpeggio to the tonic C.

Repeat many times and switch roles after a bit.

Variation: Player Two may elect to take some time arriving at the tonic, perhaps repeating the first note and its resolution to a chord tone and then continuing the melody in a satisfying manner until the final resolution on the tonic.

Conversations in Motion

Eight-plus players. Each player strolls around the room. When encountering another player, engage in conversation, but with instruments. Embody a mood, personality characteristic, or character type (e.g., sad, paranoid, itchy, nervous, exuberant, jealous, sleepy, evil, starving, puzzled, etc.). Conversations end after a short time, and players make contact with new partners.

(Inspired by Charles Young.)

Simon Says

Two players. This game comes from the extraordinarily creative mind of Dani Reynolds, whose name for this was "Independent Constraints." Each player assigns his partner a limitation for an improvised duet.

Examples: (Note: Dani and Betsy are horn players).

Dani: Play only in F♯ harmonic minor.
Betsy: Play in C, but you have to sing at the same time.

Dani: You can only use your third valve.
Betsy: No mouthpiece.

Dani: You can only make percussive sounds on your horn.
Betsy: You have to remove two valve slides.

Variation: Choose your own restriction.

Make 'Em Laugh!

Four players. In chairs facing each other, each player has fifteen seconds to play something—anything—that will make one of the others laugh. Continue until a giggle escapes someone.

Tip 1: Surprise is your best weapon. Play something completely unexpected, or juxtapose something serious and something ridiculous.

Tip 2: Use acting in addition to music.

Laughter banishes fear! Try this game just before a concert to relax. Games such as these give performers a chance to get "out of their heads."

Play the Room

Two to four players. Select objects or shapes in the room, and "play the room" by depicting those objects or shapes in music. Form: ABA (A = object one; B = object two). Try to find common musical ground for the sake of unity amidst all of the variety.

Play the Room, Really

Four-plus players. All players pick out something in the room and use it to make music (rap/tap on chairs, desks, floor, walls, blackboard; scrape chalk, slide curtains, etc.).

Suggestion: Don't break anything.

The Incredible Mouth Band

Three to six players. Assign instruments to players according to band style: rock (guitar, bass, drums), pop (vocals, turntable), ska (including trumpet, sax), etc. Players may only use the name of their instrument (or parts of their instrument, such as a drum set using just the snare, cymbal, or bass drum) in a melodic or chanting manner, imitating the instrument. Extend to every kind of group (e.g., Dixieland, bluegrass, string quartet, brass or woodwind quintet, marching band, jazz combo, etc.).

(Suggested by Genessa Mak, who took the idea from a video called "The Incredible Mouth Band" seen on YouTube.)

Single-Minded

One-plus player. Devote attention to one musical element or parameter. This may be almost anything: dynamics (play only *ff* or *pp*), articulation (play everything *staccato* or *legato*), register (explore only the lower or upper register), etc.

Variation: Elements may be chosen independently. Each player chooses separately or each pair or trio selects for itself.

Who Started It?

Three to four players plus one. Player One leaves the room. Another player is designated as leader. Others must imitate what the leader does. When Player One returns, she must guess which of the players is the leader.

Clockwork

Six-plus players. Player One stands in front of the group with one arm and hand pointing straight up (twelve o'clock). He makes one slow circle around the minutes of the imaginary clock. The rest of the group may only play one long tone and two short tones. Each decides when she wishes to play. The piece is finished when the clock hand points to twelve once again.

Variation: Go around the clock two or three times, deciding on different rules for subsequent rounds, (e.g., more notes, different timbres, a rhythmic motive, extended techniques, etc.).

Inner Space

Six-plus players. Each player chooses (or is randomly assigned) three numbers from one to twenty. The numbers represent the approximate time in seconds between each player's single-note entrances. When a leader gives a downbeat, all play at once to end the piece.

Variation 1: Change the amount and range of the numbers (e.g., two numbers chosen from between one and twelve).

Variation 2: Instead of a single note, player improvise for a longer period, say five to thirty seconds, with numbers representing the time between entrances.

(Inspired by Brian Dennis.)

Duet for One

One player. Piano is highly suggested for this game, but guitar, strings, or mallet percussion may be used.

Improvise while singing the exact same line in unison. Experiment with leaps, syncopations, repetition of motifs, and other challenges.

(Source: Charles Young.)

Soundpainting Duets

Two-plus players. Players experienced in Soundpainting take turns signing to each other with various Soundpainting gestures.

To obtain a copy of the illustrated manual of basic Soundpainting gestures plus a DVD, see www.soundpainting.com.

Soundpainting: Roll Your Own

Two-plus players. Players who are not yet familiar with Walter Thompson's gestural system of Soundpainting may make up their own gestures and sign to each other.

Opposites

Two players. Player One begins; Player Two plays the opposite of Player One.

Examples: High/low, loud/soft, *legato/staccato*, etc.

Instant Chamber Music

Twelve-plus players. A leader writes the name of each player on a separate 3X5 card. Cards are dealt face down to create duets, trios, and quartets in random fashion. After all cards are dealt, the leader announces who is in each group. Each group creates a piece without discussion based primarily on one of the following: extended techniques, ostinato, long tones. Or not.

Idea: One player in each group must play percussion.

Dubbing

Two players. Player One stands and moves as if performing a virtuosic/soulful solo for the audience. Player Two—not necessarily on the same instrument—stands slightly to the side, facing Player One. Player Two must invent music that reflects the physical image presented by Player One.

Redub

Two players. Reverse the roles in *Dubbing*: Player Two improvises on his instrument while Player One (the actor) must mime what she hears.

Sound Effects

Three-plus players. Player One makes up a story. A row of instrumentalists adds short bits of stylized music or weird sound effects (extended techniques) that the improvising storyteller must incorporate into his story.

(From *The Mind's Ear*, by Bruce Adolphe, who adapted it from a theatrical improvisation game.)

Fun House Mirror

Three-plus players. Take an idea and put it through the fun house mirror, i.e., distort and exaggerate it. One good way to play this game is in a circle: Player One invents a simple phrase; the next player exaggerates or distorts part of it. Move around the circle.

Variation: Use a familiar tune as source material.

(Source: Joel Saltzman via Charles Young.)

Go Wild (a. k. a. Extreme Improv)

Two to four players. Choose an affect (i.e., physical, emotional, intellectual, or spiritual quality). Be extreme—high/low, slow/fast, soft/loud. Nothing halfway! Don't dip your toe in the water—cannonball! Don't be hungry—be starving! Don't light a match—use a flamethrower! Exaggerate to get your point across, being absolutely clear about your intention.

(Source: Charles Young.)

Nothing Succeeds Like Excess

Two to four players. Similar to *Go Wild*. Players may play anything they like—but nothing may be in the middle ground: dynamics, tempo, range, density, etc. Players should listen closely to the others and choose to do the same or the complete opposite.

Construction Cards

Two-plus players. Prepare a series of 3X5 note cards with basic directions and arrange them in these piles (categories):

What (long tones; pointillism; minimalism; three notes).

How ($\boldsymbol{ff}$, $\boldsymbol{pp}$, hairpin dynamics, legato, staccato).

Key (any major or minor key or atonal).

Style (march, lullaby, rock, elegy, love song, scherzo, children's song, gospel, calypso).

Meter (duple, triple, odd meter).

Tempo (fast, slow).

Variation 1: Deal a card from each pile face up. All players improvise from these six cards.

Variation 2: Each player receives a different set of six cards.

Vignettes: Affect Pieces

One to four players. Make a list of four affects. Even better is to get 3X5 cards in four different colors and write an affect on each. Select one affect from each category:

Emotional (happy, sad, elated, eager, enthusiastic, etc).

Mental (states of mind, e.g., confused, focused, clear, muddled, centered).

Physical (movements, e.g., leaping, running, skipping, walking, juggling).

Spiritual (attitudes, e.g., loving, fearful, optimistic, content).

Invent a situation encompassing all four categories.

    Example: Emotional: sad.
                          Mental: focused.
                          Physical: weary.
                          Spiritual: loving.

                          A vignette about a pallbearer at a funeral might use all of these.

Portray the scene in a musical improvisation.

(Source: Charles Young, inspired by "On Affect" by Keith Hill at www.musicalratio.com.)

News Story

Two-plus players. Players scan the newspaper for an interesting news story, and then capture the mood or message of the article in music.

Trading Fours

Two players. It is a common procedure in jazz to trade off improv solos every two, four, or eight bars. Trade fours with a partner against an spontaneously invented rhythmic accompaniment. Keep the rhythmic flow going without any gaps or glitches.

    Variation: Trade twos or eights.

(Source: Charles Young.)

Blind Improv

One player plus a multi-track recorder or computer sequencer program. Record an improvisation on one track, and then—without listening to the first one—record another track to go with the first. Do a third track the same way. Listen to the result!

(Source: Charles Young.)

Wildcard

Three to four players. Player One is the Wildcard. All others create an improvised piece that is synchronized in tempo, style, dynamics, etc. The Wildcard plays unpredictable and wildly contrasting material with spaces between outbursts.

Snowball Fight

Four-plus players. Each player writes down several ideas or parameters for improvisation, one idea per sheet of paper.

> *Examples:* Loud
> Like a roller coaster
> Mysterious
> Bouncy
> Use the rhythm of the name of your home town
> Three notes only

Crumple the sheets and throw them at each other for a while. Then each player picks up one or more sheets and uses the instructions to improvise a piece.

(Source: Elizabeth Barkley.)

Size Matters

Four-plus players. The ensemble begins and ends without any planning; rules are made on the way. The only requirement is length: make this a *long* piece.

> *Options:* Seven to eight minutes.
> Fifteen minutes.
> Thirty minutes.
> Forty-five minutes (!).

Tell a story! Strive for contrasts! Listen! Imitate! Spend time *not* playing to vary the texture. Develop motifs! Be dramatic! Consider unity (be the same) and variety (be different). Enjoy the journey, and find a satisfying ending.

Timing Is Everything

Two-plus players. With one person as timer, play a series of short improvisations for a specified number of seconds (e.g., ten, fifteen, twenty, thirty, forty-five, etc.) Each improvisation may have a pre-planned title (e.g., Adjective/Noun) or be completely unplanned (figure out the rules as you go). Every piece, however short, should have a beginning, middle, and end.

Immortal Improv Sonata No. 47

Four players, any instruments. Choose a leader by rock, paper, scissors. Sit in string quartet formation. All hold a long tone on a cue from a leader, then crescendo. The leader cues next section. Starting with the leader, play the following in order; whoever is soloing cues the movement to the next number.

1. Solo
2. Ostinato
3. Long tones plus silence (50/50)
4. Percussion

Soloists must at some point incorporate extremes of loud/soft and density/sparseness. After all have played each of the four, a free improvisation section begins. The leader signals a gradual slowdown of energy, culminating in a long, held note for the ending.

> *Idea:*   Play the same note as the beginning.

Danceline

Two-plus players. One or more players improvise together. The remaining players are assigned to one of the improvisers and must move or dance according to what their assigned partner plays. Silence means the dancer freezes. Dancers should also attempt to emulate any instrumental interaction (e.g., if two instruments take up the same rhythm, the corresponding dancers should take up the same movement).

Number Off

Six-plus players. Sit in a circle and number off. When a leader calls out a number (no higher than the number of players), that person starts playing. The leader adds random numbers *ad libitum*. The second time a player's number comes up, she stops playing. The leader may also point and give a signal that means *Finish Your Idea*.

> *Variation:*   The leader may roll dice to determine the number.

Silent Partners

Two to six players. All players commence improvising at once, but only in the mind: sing the part silently while fingering the instrument. When a leader points at a player, he plays aloud. When the leader drops her hand, the player stops. The leader may use both hands at once.

Trigger

Four-plus players in even numbers. Players each pick a partner (who is not necessarily sitting next to them). Player Two is assigned a type of playing, such as long tones. Player One improvises freely. Player Two may only play when Player One plays long tones.

> *Variation 1:*   Assign more than one player to be triggered by Player One. Players Three, Four, or more may play something different (such as an ostinato) when Player One plays (say) long tones, or may also play long tones along with Player Two.
>
> *Variation 2:*   Here Player Three is triggered not by Player One, but by Player Two, and may play something different, such as extended techniques.
>
> *Variation 3:*   Use as many players as desired. Each player may decide independently which player and activity to select as a trigger and what kind of musical activity she will play when triggered.

(Idea from Evan Mazunik.)

Free Play Game No. 1

Two players. Improvise a piece that is one minute long. Have a clear beginning, middle, and end. Player One uses long-short-short rhythms. Player Two uses short-short-long rhythms. Vary register and rest occasionally.

Ideas: Agree on a key.

Don't discuss the key, but find a common key while playing.

Don't discuss the key, but pick a key independently and stick to it.

Avoid key centers, or visit them only briefly, playing mostly atonally.

Decide on a style or mood ahead of time (march, love song, etc.).

Decide on a style or mood after the piece begins.

Repeat the process with three or four players.

Add other players on percussion, playing mostly *ostinati*. Percussion is like garlic; it adds a terrific spice to the mix, and there is seldom an upper limit.

Free Play Game No. 2

Two-plus players. Just play! Listen! Respond!

Tips: The larger the group, the more silence each player should use. This requires extreme discipline. Listen for what the piece needs. There should be equal amounts of unity and variety.

• • •

Once a student has begun improvising, and once the barriers of self-doubt and self-consciousness have been broken down, the gap between the level of improvising and that of already acquired playing skills is easily bridged, regardless of the student's age or degree of experience.

—Mildred Portney Chase[94]

Creativity involves breaking out of established patterns in order to look at things in a different way.

—Edward de Bono[95]

---

[94] *Improvisation: Music from the Inside Out* (Creative Arts Book Co., 1988): 4.
[95] http://thinkexist.com/quotes/edward_de_bono

Chapter 33

Improv Set-Ups

These are similar to improv games but usually more specific in detail. Players should get in the habit of inventing their own improv games and set-ups regularly.

> *Free improvisation, in addition to being a highly skilled musical craft, is open to use by almost anyone—beginners, children, and non-musicians. The skill and intellect required is whatever is available. Its accessibility to the performer is, in fact, something which appears to offend both its supporters and detractors... And as regards to method, the improviser employs the oldest in music-making... Mankind's first musical performance couldn't have been anything other than a free improvisation.*
>
> —Derek Bailey[96]

Quick Variations

One player. Player One is given a folk or children's song title by the audience. She plays five variations on it on the piano, beginning simply and ending grandiosely.

Atonal Jazz

Two players. Players use swing eighths and jazz-flavored articulations and inflections while completely avoiding any tonal sounds.

Children's Song

Two players. Player One makes up a children's song in Fs that goes along merrily until a freight train (Player Two) suddenly goes through the playground.

Cowboys & Cooking

Two singers. Singers One and Two use body percussion, and include single non sequitur words now and then to accent the beat. Singer One chooses words from the topic "Cowboys/Wild West," while Singer Two chooses words from the general topic of "Food and Cooking."

---

[96] *Bailey: 83.*

Debate

Two players. This duet takes the form of a debate in which the players musically debate some topic upon which they violently disagree. The players must reach a harmonious musical agreement by the end of the piece.

Diminished Fanfares

Two players. Players One and Two play three brilliant fanfares: one in D major, another in F♯ minor, and a third in C diminished.

Variation: Players pick different keys and play together.

Discussion

Two players. Players One and Two have a musical discussion about some topic of keen importance to one or both without discussion of the parameters.

Fancy Twinkle

Two players. Player One plays "Twinkle, Twinkle, Little Star" as a cantus firmus in the key most unfamiliar to him; Player Two improvises an elaborate countermelody against it.

> *Variation:*   *Repeat in a minor key.*

Lion/Mouse

Two players. Players One and Two depict a conversation in music between a lion and a mouse.

Lyrical Piece

Two players. Players One and Two improvise a lyrical piece, each player silently choosing a major key. At a signal from Player One they move to a contrasting section by changing into a minor key up or down a half step from the original. Player Two signals a return to the original key. End on a long tone in that key.

Negotiations

Two players. Players One and Two are in a Persian market. Player One is selling; Player Two is buying. They depict in music their fierce bargaining negotiations, which are amiably concluded in the end.

Sea Chanty

Two players. Create a lilting sea chantey using harmonies associated with G major. The form is verse and chorus. Play five times or more, trying to remember the first melody you invented and use it as much as possible, and introduce ornamentations and variations to that melody as you go. Vocalists who enjoy a challenge may try this one, inventing verses as they go, perhaps from a topic suggestion by the rest of the group.

Turtles in Love

Two players. Players One and Two are 200-year-old sea turtles who meet and fall in love at first sight. They set a rendezvous in music.

Unfamiliar Arpeggios

Two players. Player One plays an arpeggio figure in her least familiar key, major or minor. Player Two plays in the same key, but using longer or shorter note values and plenty of rests. Player One switches articulation between *legato* and *staccato* at will; Player Two does the opposite articulation as Player One. At a nod from Player One, players switch roles.

Lullaby for the King

Two-plus players. The king cannot sleep, and has advertised for someone to find a way to help him sleep. The spoken word keeps him awake; therefore someone must play music that lulls him gently into slumber. The one who succeeds gets a million gold Kroner. Failures will be thrown into a dungeon with disco music piped in until they go mad. What group of players will accept the challenge?

> *Tip 1:*   Do something using a major pentatonic scale.

> *Tip 2:*   Players with any level of piano skill (including almost none) can play this one on the black keys (only) of the piano.

Long Tone Tune

Three players. Players make up a piece with long tones only. May be done vocally as well.

Name that Pentatonic Tune

Three players. Players make something up using only C major pentatonic (C–D–E–G–A) and an invented title. May be done vocally, or on piano black keys only instead of in C.

America, the Beautiful

Three players. Players play America the Beautiful in an agreed upon key without rehearsal. After the first time through, they improvise a new piece based on motives from America.

> *Variation:*   Each player picks the key independently.

Askew March

Three players. All invent a march in B♭ for a marching band of people who might have celebrated the big game a bit too much the night before. Extra players may join in on percussion, using especially whatever percussion-like objects can be found in the room.

Major Event

Three players. Without discussion, all make something up in a major key, occasionally inflecting (raising or lowering) scale tones.

Secret Emotion

Three players. Without discussion, all make something up that is guided by a secret emotion each has chosen. The emotions are likely to be different, but the players must find a way to relate to each other as well as alternating solo and accompaniment roles.

Salieri's Test

Three players. Salieri has told the Emperor that your application as court composer should be rejected because you cannot improvise interesting variations on a given series of notes. You must prove him wrong Your notes are C–E–F♯–G–A–B♭. The Emperor grants your request for two backup players of your choice. Go!

ABAC

Three singers. The form is ABAC. Section A consists of long tones. A signal given by Singer One leads to section B, which is sparse and uses extended techniques only. Singer Two signals a return to section A. Singer Three signals the shift to C, which is the coda. There is free choice of style or sounds by all players, but they must relate in some way.

Individual Stories

Three players: Player One plays only in major, Player Two in minor, and Player Three chromatically. Keys are individual. As in all pieces, there should be a beginning, middle, and end. There should be a switching of solo/accompaniment roles as well as some kind of motivic development. Listen to each other for strong ideas and use them in your improvisations.

Eighteen Seconds

Three players. Player One is the timer, Players and Three play a piece that is exactly eighteen seconds long. Player One indicates with hand gestures how much time remains. Switch roles until all have been the timer.

Contrasts

Three players. Player One plays rapid notes; Player Two plays long tones; Player Three plays occasional interjections. Switch roles every fifteen seconds, as indicated by a timer (Player One, if no one else is available). After all have switched, find an end to the piece.

This New Old Man

Three players. Player One plays a very slow version of "This Old Man" in B major. Player Two plays a rhythmic ostinato accompaniment figure that occasionally changes in small ways. Player Three solos over this occasionally, inflecting scale tones.

Duel Duet

Three players. Player One is the timer. Players Two and Three have a duel at three paces using any musical material of their choice as weapons. It is important that they end precisely together after exactly thirty-three seconds, as indicated by Player One, who shows by gestures near the end how much time is left.

Name Rhythms Trio

Three players. Players use the rhythms of their names and the D♭ pentatonic major scale to create a piece.

Suggestion: Use augmentation, diminution, and extended techniques.

Happy Birthday

Three-plus players. All players play "Happy Birthday" by ear with C as the starting note. For the second pass, those who didn't find all the notes play the tune again. Those who did should play the roots of the appropriate I–IV–V chords as accompaniment. Those who missed some of the roots should try again on the next pass. Those who found them all should play harmony notes. Those who need another try at the harmony notes should do so on the next pass. Those who had no trouble should play the melody again, this time decorating and ornamenting it. Continue until all players have experienced all levels. Then repeat in another, preferably beastly, key. Repeat the whole game with a new tune. Do this every day for a number of years.

Veggie Blues

Four players/singers. Singers One and Two trade dramatically performed verses in song about the delights or woes of eating spinach, kohlrabi, Brussel sprouts, rutabaga, and other vegetables with a lot of personality. Players Three and Four accompany, Player Three playing a simple bluesy bass line, and Player Four rapping on some part of the piano for percussion.

Tip: Consider throwing in some recitative.

Scheherazade?

Four players. The sultan, having given Scheherazade her freedom, is bored and lonely. Player One must play a melody to calm and bewitch the Sultan or lose his head. He will be accompanied by Players Two, Three, and Four, who play a lilting 6/8 D-major pentatonic background. Additional players may contribute various percussion.

Minor 6/8

Four players. Players make something up in a minor key in 6/8.

Variation: Play in 5/8 or 7/8.

Ode to the Potato

Four players. Players do a slow call-and-response number about their passionate feelings about the many ways to enjoy a potato:

Mashed	French fried	Chips
Scalloped	Hash browns	Roasted
Ripple chips	Boiled	Baked

Circus Divertimento

Four players. All are circus performers. They perform the following brief but intense movements of a Circus Divertimento:

1. The Big Cat Cage
2. Trick Riders
3. The High Wire Act
4. Clowns!

May be done as an eight-hand piano piece. Don't forget to include extended techniques, such as rapping the piano, plucking the inside strings, etc.

Scale Solo

Four players. Player One plays a major scale slowly up and down the octave. Player Two improvises freely over it. Players Three and Four may join in on percussion at any point.

Days of Old

Four players/singers. Using mixed vocal and instrumental or all vocal textures, set a medieval and mysterious mood. May be performed by candlelight.

Beware

Four-plus players/singers. Player One plays chords on piano, guitar, or harp. Singer Two must sing a song about things in life of which to beware. The rest of the group must shout out a topic just before she sings each verse.

Timbre!

Five players. String Player One uses only *pizzicato*. Players Two, Three, and Four make mouth noises and occasional body percussion. Together the four create a mechanical ostinato over which Player Five takes an angular atonal solo.

Elegy

Seven players/singers. Brass Players One and Two play with mutes, making up an interlocking ostinato. Player Three plays an introduction in A♭ minor to a plaintive song about the death of a beloved goldfish. Singer Four sings, about this topic, freely inventing lyrics. Sings Five and Six are directed by Player Seven to sing a long tone or drone background.

• • •

Keep in mind two suggestions...1) less is more; and 2) the purpose of improvisation is to intensify the expressive force and character of the music, not to provide an opportunity to show finger skills.

—Daniel N. Leeson, *Spontaneous Improvisation*
in Mozart Performance

Chapter 34

Extended Combination Games

The games in this book are assigned to various categories to aid access, understanding, and organization. The disadvantage of this is that it may hinder the wider and more imaginative use made possible by combining games from different categories or with newly invented material (i.e., not printed in this book). Players (and especially leaders and facilitators) should constantly encourage the use and invention of combination games. Simple suggestions for combining games appear at the end of some chapters. In this chapter, this is taken to the next level of complexity by combining a number of games.

Note: These are only examples. Players should not hesitate to tweak these games and/or invent their own extended combination games using various games from this book—or entirely new ones.

A college cannot control the attitudes, standards, and acquired knowledge of those already active in the profession, but it can seek to produce graduates with minds receptive to experimental and innovative concepts and techniques.

—David Willoughby[97]

Combination No. 1

Accents, drone, long tones, and group point-to-point.
    Twelve-plus players. Form: ABA'C (coda)

Section A: Group One (six-plus players) plays steady eighth notes at a moderate tempo on a variety of drums or drum-like instruments, which may include body percussion and found percussion (noisemakers from the kitchen, shop, bathroom, office). Those with the deepest drums may beat half notes.

After a while, players may decide on a repeating accent pattern. This may be one accented hit every so often (e.g., every ten, six, five, four, three, or two beats. Just try not to accent every beat!

Other possibilities include combining accent patterns such as 2+3, 3+2, or 2+2+3. These patterns may continue or may be isolated by stretches of steady unaccented eighths. It is also possible to accent two notes in a row, followed by a stretch of unaccented notes.
Any instrument may rest for a stretch.

---

97   *Comprehensive Musicianship and Undergraduate Curricula* (Contemporary Music Project, 1971): 3.

Group Two plays a low drone. The group may synchronize (i.e., group members find a common pitch) or not.

Group Three sings long tones in the middle register. Group members may have a common key and a conductor who uses hand gestures to indicate relative pitch level (high-middle-low).

Group Four is optional. Group members use any instrument or the voice to issue sharp hits or stabs of very short, loud notes that are cued by a conductor (or a group member acting as one). Make this a very long section.

Section B: This section is completely free, except that only one or two groups may play at a time. A leader or conductor indicates these groups. They play as long as the leader is pointing at them and are silent otherwise.

Section A':   Repeat Section A. At a signal from the leader, go to the coda.

Section C (Coda):   A brief section. Everyone plays a trill-like, bumble-bee sound in their lowest register. The leader signals by hand gesture for all to progress quickly to their highest range. In Soundpainting, this is known as the *Level Fader*). All *crescendo* until the leader gives a cutoff.

Combination No. 2

Ostinato, extended techniques, floating duet, and crossover.
    Eight-plus players.

Group One: Four players. This group plays short, soft, sparse *ostinati* using extended techniques. Players may change at will to a new ostinato pattern.

Group Two: Everyone else. All play freely as soloists, but never more than two at a time (*Floating Duet*). Players may be polite and wait their turn or may be bold and jump in any time, forcing out other players. At a signal from the leader, both groups switch roles. This is the *Crossover* Soundpainting gesture.

Combination No. 3

Bass line, melody, long tone, ostinato, and accompaniment roles.
    Four-plus players. Player One plays a bass line or outlines the chords to a simple familiar tune (the title is a secret!) using arpeggios. He cycles through the tune continually. Player Two makes up a melody to play over the chords. Player Three plays long tones the first time through, then animates the piece with an ostinato rhythm. Player Four plays little answers to Player Two's melody at the end of phrases. A leader signals role changes for all players.

Combination No. 4

Dynamics, energy, silence, scale, mirror, and ostinato.

Four players. Player One plays as fast and as soft/loud (alternately) as she can, but frequently punctuates the outbursts with complete silences of irregular length. Player Two is only allowed to play when Player One is silent, and improvises something completely different each time, stopping instantly when Player One starts up again. Player Three plays a long, sinuous melody in D harmonic minor. Player Four shadows Player Three, trying to mirror as closely as possible what he plays. If possible Player Three should play a high-register instrument; Player Four a low-register instrument. Player Three also stops occasionally. When this happens, Player Four plays a wide-ranging but sparse ostinato figure until Player Three returns.

Combination No. 5

Fanfare, Que Será Será, ostinato, room percussion, accent, body percussion, mouth noise, long tones, foot music, call-and-response, and dynamics.

Four players. The form is ABA'.

Section A:

Player One plays a fanfare sotto voce (and/or with a mute, if applicable) in the major key least familiar to him, adding occasional rests and trying out figures in various registers (high, middle, low).

Player Two plays from any sheet of printed music, but invents note values on the fly (as in the description in *Que Será Será* (Technique Games), adding appropriate silences between phrases.

Player Three finds something in the room (*Room Percussion* [Technique]) to use to create an ostinato figure as accompaniment, using accents to create the feeling of 4/4 and may switch to a new "instrument" and ostinato figure at will.

Player Four joins the accompaniment, creating ostinato figures with various body percussion and mouth noise sounds. Player Four is also encouraged to sing sporadic long tones using random syllables.

Section B:

After a while, someone in the group signals a new section. Now everyone stomps a steady quarter note beat on the floor while each player takes an eight-beat (more or less) solo. The first part of each solo should steal a bit from the preceding player, then add something new. This continues for a little while, then all players join together to improvise a ten-second ensemble solo, *fortissimo*, followed by a *decrescendo* down to almost nothing.

Section A':

Section A is repeated, this time beginning with Player Four, then adding Players Three, Two, and finally Player One. There is a five-second delay between each entrance. The piece ends with a signal from Player One for all to should "Hey!" loudly in unison. The word, "Hey" may be freely substituted by group consensus before beginning; it may have meaning or just be fun to say: "Wow!" "Tuxedo!" "Carpe Noctem!" "Shhhhh!" "Chrysanthemum!" "Razzmatazz!"

Combination No. 6

Mixed meters, accents, chant, pointillism, free, and sparse texture.
   Lots of players (sixteen-plus). The form is ABA'.

Section A:	Group One. Player One plays straight quarter notes at about ♩ = 72 on any large drum or drum-like object, accenting every fourth beat. Player Two does the same (a drum is recommended, but the exact instrument is negotiable), but accents every three beats. Player Three does the same with a smaller drum, accenting every five beats. Additional players (if available) accent every two, seven, eleven, or thirteen quarter notes respectively.
	Group Two. Player One plays steady eighth notes on a smaller percussion instrument of some sort, accenting every fourth note. Player Two does the same, accenting every third note. Player Three accents every fifth note. As in Group One, more players may be added.
	Group Three includes a large group of players who either sing or play instruments capable of holding a sustained note (no pianos, marimbas, cymbals, or guitars). This group floats freely in D minor Dorian. A soloist chooses which long note in the scale to play and when; all others must pay attention to this and follow the leader by changing to the new note. There will be a delay as all find the leader's pitch. This is okay.
	Group Four is composed mainly of instruments that play short notes well (piano, marimba, clave, guitar, wood block, kalimba, etc.). One player is designated as leader (perhaps at random) and chooses to make brief, intense, but widely spaced flurries of short random hits.
	The groups enter one by one, and all groups play for a considerable period.
Section B:	At a signal from the leader of Group Four, the entire group abandons the roles described here and plays freely, the one restriction being that each player must rest for approximately five times as long as he plays. Continue in this way for a while.
Section A':	At some point the leader of Group Four signals the return of section A. After all have joined and play has gone on for some time, the leader of Group Four gives one more signal to indicate that all players should wind down and stop within the next three minutes. The choice of when is up to the individual. Players who have stopped should simply sit quietly and listen, eyes closed. When all players have stopped, everyone should sit motionless for thirty seconds, and then open their eyes, breathe deeply, smile, stand up, stretch, and go on to the next thing.

In much current practice, the development of musical techniques is often completely divorced from actual experience with music as sound; technique is often taught as "gymnastic skill."

            —David Willoughby[98]

---

[98] *Comprehensive Musicianship.*

Chapter 35

Improvisation Principles

Risk. Trust. Listen. Reflect. Respond.

Be affected by what you hear.

Imitate. Copy what you hear (either from yourself or others). Say it once. Say it again. Then say it again, but change something.

Keep repeating an idea—but play it differently every time.

Don't be afraid to repeat something. Over and over and over.

Do the opposite. Contrast! Vividly! Don't hold back! Stay away from the "middle."

Mean what you say, say what you mean (not what you think someone wants to hear, or what someone else would say).

Practice inventing motifs of three to four notes. Be able to fluently transpose to all keys and to play these motifs in sequence, both diatonically and chromatically.

Learn to transform short motifs in a variety of ways.

Use short and memorable thematic material or motifs.

Lower your expectations. Go for quantity.

When you hear a good idea (either your own or someone else's), support it or relate to it in some way.

Music is not about playing the right notes—it's about using your imagination.

Silence is a very important part of interesting music. Don't forget to rest at times.

Practice improvising with a partner as often as possible. A partner can challenge and inspire you, be an "ear," give you creative energy and ideas, and help you "show up."

Jam with a group as often as possible. Improvisation is about a social as well as a musical connection.

The more people in the group, the less each one plays.

Record your improvisations as often as possible. Listen carefully to learn from your choices and glean ideas for future improvisations and practice.

Rhythmic ostinati are powerful foundations for compositions.

You can add some type of percussion to any improvisation.

Almost anything can be used as a percussion instrument: kitchen utensils, shop tools, office supplies, etc.

Sometimes it is good to do the opposite, or play in a way that contrasts to what the others are doing.

Listen to everything all the time. Improvise continually with the world around you. As you walk, sing low scat, tap/snap your fingers, whistle, move and sway. Improvise all the time, everywhere!

Use everything available to create music: instruments, voice, mouth noises, claps, slaps, stomps, stamps, whistling, words, air sounds, finger snaps, humming, etc.

You can build an entire piece using only rhythms.

Don't forget to explore shades and variations of *timbre*.

Continually expand your repertoire of extended techniques on your instrument.

Limitations make it easier to create improvised pieces.

Listen to anything and everything—music, noises, nature sounds, machine sounds—to learn and enhance the palette of sounds you have available for music making.

When you have created a wonderful improvisation, let go of it and do something completely different the next time.

Experiment with different densities, from very sparse to very dense.

Be extreme: loud/soft; sparse/dense; high/low; wild and mixed timbres. Beware of the middle!

Be expressive. Put your heart into everything you play!

Occasionally play as loud as you can.

Look for times when you can play extremely softly.

As you improvise, shamelessly steal everything you can from other players: dynamics, shapes, motifs, moods, rhythms, etc.

Become fluent in adding ornaments or embellishments to melodies or motifs.

Play familiar tunes by ear every day.

Practice often (including playing familiar tunes) in keys least familiar to you.

Always practice with a rhythm source (a metronome, play-along device, etc.).

Make the continual acquisition of new patterns (short scale "shapes," learned diatonically and chromatically) a lifelong goal.

Start learning other types of scales: all the minors, all the modes (Dorian, etc). whole tone, diminished, Klezmer, blues, etc.

After every improvisation, ask: What happened? What worked well? What might have improved the piece?

Chapter 36

Improvisation Books, Articles, and Links

(The order is roughly in order of recommendation.)

The Mother of All Improvisation Books

Stephen Nachmanovitch, *Free Play*

Highly Recommended

Jeffrey Agrell, *Improvisation Games for Classical Musicians*

William L. Cahn, *Creative Music Making*

James Oshinsky & David Darling, *Return to Child: Music for People's Guide to Improvising Music and Authentic Group Leadership* (see www.musicforpeople.org/store.html)

William Westney, *The Perfect Wrong Note: Learning to Trust Your Musical Self*

Tony Wigram, *Improvisation: Methods and Techniques for Music Therapy Clinicians, Educators, and Students*

Walter Thompson – *Soundpainting: The Art of Live Composition*. Workbook [with DVD; see www.soundpainting.com]

Alan Dworsky and Betsy Sansby, *A Rhythmic Vocabulary*

Doug Goodkin, *Sound Ideas: Activities for the Percussion Circle*

Bert Ligon, *Comprehensive Technique for Jazz Musicians*

Mike Steinel, *Building a Jazz Vocabulary*

Recommended

Julie Lyonn Lieberman, *The Creative Band and Orchestra Director*

Mildred Portney Chase, *Improvisation: Music from the Inside Out*

Edwin Gordon, *Improvisation in the Music Classroom*

Mikael Elsila, *Morphs: Etudes for Improvisation* [with CD]

Rod Paton, *Living Music: Improvisation Guidelines for Teachers and Community Musicians*

Arthur Hull, *Drum Spirit Circle*

Christine Stevens, *The Heart and Art of Drum Circles* [with CD]

Kalani, *Together in Rhythm* (drum circles)

Kalani, *The Amazing Jamnasium* [with CD] (drum games; a companion to *Together in Rhythm*)

Julie Lyonn Lieberman, *Planet Musician: World Music Sourcebook*

Chalo Eduardo & Frank Kumor, *Drum Circle: A Guide to World Percussion*

Pauline Oliveros, *The Roots of the Moment*

Pauline Oliveros, *Deep Listening: A Composer's Sound Practice*

Alice Kay Kanack, *Musical Improvisation for Children*

Alice Kay Kanack, *Fun Improvisation for Piano* (incl. CD)

Edward S. Lisk, *Intangibles of Musical Performance*

Derek Bailey, *Improvisation: its nature and practice in music*

Gerre Hancock, *Improvising: How to Master the Art* [organ]

Jan Overduin, *Improvisation for Organists*

Kenneth Bruscia, *Improvisational Models of Music Therapy*

Christopher Azzara, Richard Grunow, Edwin Gordon, *Creativity in Improvisation* Vol. 1 & 2 [with CD]

Christopher Azzara and Richard Grunow, *Developing Musicianship Through Improvisation*

George Wolfe, *Motivic Improvisation: A New Approach to Improvising in the Classical Style*

Bruce Adolphe, *The Mind's Ear*

Michiko Yuko, *Music Mind Games*

Michiko Yuko, *Music Theory for Children*

Bert Ligon, *Jazz Theory Resources Vol. I & II*

Jerry Coker, et al, *Patterns for Jazz*

Mark Levine, *The Jazz Theory Book*

Jamey Aebersold Playalong Series

Kenny Werner, *Free Play* (Vol. 104 of the Aebersold Playalong Series) [with CD]

Ed Tomasi, *Motivic Development* (DVD)

Bob Stoloff, *Scat!: Vocal Improvisation Techniques*

John Marshall, *Hand Drums for Beginners*

Hal Crook, *How to Improvise*

Hal Crook, *Beyond Time and Changes: A Musician's Guide to Free Jazz Improvisation*

Scott Reeves, *Creative Jazz Improvisation*

Paul Berliner, *Thinking in Jazz: the infinite art of improvisation*

Dan Haerle, *Scales for Improvisation*

Mark Levine, *The Jazz Piano Book*

Rena Upitis, *The Compositions and Invented Notations of Children*

Rena Upitis, *This Too is Music*

Polly Carder, ed., *The Eclectic Curriculum in American Music Education* [Dalcroze, Kod_ly, Orff]

Robert Starer, *Rhythmic Training*

Anne Carothers Hall, *Studying Rhythm*

Ronan Guilfoyle, *Creative Rhythmic Concepts for Jazz Improvisation*

Viola Spolin, *Theater Games for the Classroom*

Malcolm Goldstein, *Sounding the Full Circle*

Bruno Nettl, ed., *In the Course of Performance: Studies in the World of Musical Improvisation*

Walter J. Ong, *Orality & Literacy*

Kenny Werner, *Effortless Mastery*

For String Players:

Julie Lyonn Lieberman, *Alternative Strings: The New Curriculum*

Julie Lyonn Lieberman, *Improvising Violin*

Sarah Stiles, *Improv: Free Improvisation in String Playing for Teachers and Pupils, for Violin, viola, cello, double bass*, publ. Stainer & Bell

Sarah Stiles, *Dual Band* – violin duos with improvisations, Stainer & Bell

Alice Kay Kanack, *Fun Improvisation for Violin* (incl. CD)

Phyllis Young, *The String Play*

Links

Music for People (www.musicforpeople.org) has offered workshops in music improvisation for almost two decades. Directed by cellist David Darling.

Village Music Circles (www.drumcircle.com). Workshops in rhythm and teamwork by Arthur Hull.

Rhythmic Connections (www.rhythmicconnections.com). Music programs and rhythm workshops by Mary Knysh.

Julie Lyonn Lieberman (http://julielyonn.com), author of many improv books, also gives workshops.

Jeffrey Agrell and Evan Mazunik - improvisation workshops, lectures, concerts: see www.creativehorn.com

Articles

Keith Hill, "Improvise Intentionally "
Available online at: www.musicalratio.com/gpage1.html13.html

Keith Hill, "Improvise Intentionally Part 2"
Available at: www.musicalratio.com/gpage1.html14.html

Keith Hill and Marianne Ploger, "On Affect"
Available online at: www.musicalratio.com/gpage.html1.html

Charles Young, "Is Music a Dead Language?"
Available at: www.uwsp.edu/music/people/faculty/cyoung/resources/deadlanguage.htm

David Rosenboom, "Improvisation and Composition – Synthesis and Integration into the Music Curriculum" Available as a pdf file online at
http://music.calarts.edu/~david/writings/articles_docs/NASM.improv.composite.pdf

Bill Dobbins, "Improvisation: An Essential Element of Musical Proficiency," Music Educators Journal, January 1980, p. 36-41.

Harold M. Best, "Music Curricula in the Future"
Available online at www.leaderu.com/offices/haroldbest/curricula.html

LaDonna Smith, "Improvisation in Childhood Music Training and Techniques for Creative Music Making." Available at:
www.the-improvisor.com/web%20ARTICLES/Improvisation%20&%20Education.html

Christopher Azzara, "An Aural Approach to Improvisation," Music Educators Journal, 86:3 (November 1999), p. 21-25.

Peter R. Webster, Annotated Bibliography: Music Education and Creative Thinking in Music. Available on line at: http://pubweb.northwestern.edu/~webster/createbib.html

William Harris, Improvising as a Lost Art: The Art of Realtime Composition. Available online at http://community.middlebury.edu/~harris/MusicPapers/MusicAlive.html

Books on Creative Thinking

Joel Saltzman, *If You Can Talk, You Can Write*
Joel Saltzman, *Shake That Brain!*
Roger Van Oech, *A Whack on the Side of the Head*
Roger Van Oech, *A Kick in the Seat of the Pants*
Tom Wujec, *Five Star Mind*
Tom Wujec, *Pumping Ions*
Edward de Bono, *Lateral Thinking*
Edward de Bono, *Six Thinking Hats*
Edward de Bono, *Serious Creativity*
Patricia Ryan Madson, *Improv Wisdom*

Chapter 37

Constructing Improvisation Compositions

The author is going to go out on a limb and construct a loose definition of contemporary classical improvisation: it is improvisation that attempts to create a satisfying artistic experience for both performers and audience through a balance of unity and variety, that retains the edgy pizzazz and sparkle of improvisation while being alloyed with the sense and order of classical music. While extended techniques are often used, they are a spice and not the entrée, and, like much classical music, classical improvisations often employ melodies, harmonies, themes and motivic development, and have a strong rhythmic element. The pieces are often tonal, but may have atonal elements as well.

Unlike "free improvisation" in jazz, which consciously avoids styles or idioms, contemporary classical improvisation may use or combine all kinds of styles—or not. The contemporary classical improviser plays to and for the audience, which is an indispensable part of the process. The audience should be able to predict what is going to happen about fifty percent of the time; too much unpredictable variety leads to frustration; too much unity leads to boredom. Contemporary classical improvisation requires performers to transform their heretofore-theoretical knowledge of harmony, form, and technique into practical knowledge of music and of the instrument and thus know how to use all the elements of music in an aesthetic, dramatic, and musical way to produce a convincing extemporaneous performance.

Contemporary classical improvisers must be their own composers, constructing vehicles for their new/old kind of improvisation. Although "improvisation composition" may be somewhat of an oxymoron, and, although it is perfectly acceptable to invent the entire performance on the spot, it is very useful for the contemporary classical improviser to be familiar with constructing compositions that include improvisation or act as "frameworks" for improvisation. One might well ask, why compose at all, when most of the piece is going to be improvised? One reason is to enable that which is almost impossible in ensemble improvisation: unison playing. The tightly controlled and intricately detailed playing possible in written sections gives the audience something to grab on to at the beginning and balance the looser, if livelier, improvised sections that follow.

Another reason is that audiences are accustomed to having printed programs, and titled works are an expected staple in classical concert halls. Along these lines, there is still the unavoidable matter of status: written materials in this culture simply have higher status than improvisations, and framework compositions cover both sides. The author often performs improvised concerts with pianist and composer Evan Mazunik, and most often two-thirds to three-fourths of the concert consists of compositions that "frame" the improvised sections (the other one-third to one-fourth of the concert is invented on the spot from audience suggestions). Some of the ideas we use to construct pieces are given below. It is not an exhaustive list; use it as a resource and a place to begin in learning to invent your own improvisation compositions. (Note: "we" refers to Evan Mazunik and the author in their performing duo).

Basics

Every composition—even an improvised composition—needs some basic elements: a title, an orchestration, and a tempo. Musical sages Keith Hill and Marianne Ploger might also say that a composition or improvisation should arise from a mental, physical, spiritual, or emotional affect (see www.musicalratio.com for further discussion). An affect might be reflected in the title, an expressive marking (*doloroso*, *con fuoco*, etc.), or even in the program notes.

Written Material?

Don't get rid of that music stand yet. We play entirely invented pieces with no ink, but we use also paper and ink for improvisation compositions whose themes, chord progressions, or structures (see *Storytelling* below) are long or complex enough that it is not (yet) memorized. Playing from graphic or other nontraditional scores (see below) is another reason to hang on to the music stand.

Form

Form is an important part of unity for both performer and the audience. Every piece has structure—even if it is only determined after the piece is under way. We often use ABA, with section A being a written out melody or melody plus accompaniment and section B being an improvised section. Like jazz musicians, we usually return to the initial melody after the improvisations are done. Also, we often add a short introduction at the beginning and a coda for a flourish at the end. We also use Rondo form (ABACA) sometimes, such as in *Repercussions*. The written-out A part may be very short; four to sixteen measures is usually enough to establish a style, mood, motif, etc. that prepares the way for an improvisation.

It is also important to use form—repetition of themes and contrasting material—in completely improvised sections. It is a challenge for a player to remember what he has invented, develop it, and then bring it back later. To help memory, keep it simple—if you, the inventor, can't remember what you played, how will the audience?

Improvising over Chords

The composer may require players to improvise over one or more chords, just as jazz musicians commonly improvise over a set chord progression. We occasionally use a set sequence of chords in our improvisation compositions, although we seldom use many of the ii–V^7 or ii–V^7–I progression typical of most jazz standards. An improvisation may be over one, two, or more chords, and the chord types may be simpler types such as major, various types of minor (natural, harmonic, melodic, Dorian, Phrygian, etc.), or more complex chords (jazz descriptions are practical) such as C+, C°, C7($\sharp$11), C7($\sharp$9), CADD2, C7ALT, C6/9, CMAJ7, and so on (See *Scale and Chord Chart* [Resources]). A vocabulary of exotic chords can be gradually developed over time, but there is no rush. Wonderful improvisations are possible using the simplest of materials. It is more important for the classical musician to first learn to spice up improvisations using rhythm and timbre than to try and master many scale and chord types right away. In one of our most popular pieces, "Two Winters," we improvise over exactly two chords: two bars of Cm–Fm repeated four times. In "Mad Hatter's Tea Party" (from *Looking Glass*

Suite), we used a different approach: We labeled concert E♭ major as a home key from which we took spontaneous excursions to other keys. Improvising over chords is an important part of improvisation, but the easiest way to learn and to enjoy playing that way is to start very simply.

Improvising over a Scale

Although similar, this is not quite the same as improvising over a chord. A common scale (any scale) allows the players to roam freely over all diatonic chords in the scale, guided by what they hear from the other player and where the line seems to be going. For instance, we recorded one piece (*Diminished Intelligence* by Evan Mazunik) that uses only a single diminished scale. "Cheshire Cat" from *Looking Glass Suite* uses the interesting scale of C–D♯–E–G–A♭–B. But there is nothing wrong with simply using a major or minor scale. The composer can set up such a piece by using only one scale in the theme and then inviting players to invent freely using that scale until returning to the theme at the end.

Motivic Development

When we invent a piece from minimal material, such as a form ("Sonata Libera") or a title that the audience gives us (e.g., "The Eccentric Clown"), or if we just take a breath and begin, we will usually invent a (simple!) thematic motif immediately and build much of the piece around it. After that, much of what happens is simply development of that motive using such devices as repetition, transposition, sequence, mode change, fragmentation, adding or subtracting notes, augmentation, diminution, embellishment, etc. A composer would do well to remember that, when constructing the written part of an improvisation composition, *simple* motifs are the most practical and effective; it is very difficult to develop a line of music that is already complex. On the other hand, a very simple theme offers almost unlimited possibilities (e.g., examine the themes from Beethoven's Fifth Symphony or Bach's "Art of the Fugue" for good examples).

Improvising from Written Music

Printed music can serve as an effective basis for improvisation. We have used this in such compositions as *Only in Winter* by Evan Mazunik and "O Euchari" by Hildegard von Bingen. Here the player selects and improvises with sequences of notes at will, using various motivic development devices while integrating them with what the other is playing. A composer may simply compose a short melody and instruct players to use it as source material for improvisation. We did this in *Only in Winter* and played the tune in unison only at the very end. We once gave a recital where we played pieces from the standard literature and then repeated them, this time using them as sources for improvisation. We used the Romantic chord progressions from one piece as a basis; another piece was contemporary, without much in the way of recognizable chords, so we used rhythmic and melodic motifs as sources for improvisation. Motifs can serve as both solo and accompaniment material.

Improvising over the Mood of the Piece

This is probably the best description of how we do most of our contemporary classical improvisation. While using all of the techniques described above, improvising over the mood of the piece is somewhat freer. We combine the above techniques at will and the mix is always different. *Night Sonata* (recorded on the CD *Repercussions*) is one example of this. *September Elegy* (also on *Repercussions*) has four sections, three of which are completely improvised on the mood of the piece with few other instructions.

Storytelling

Sometimes we construct a story and then tell the different parts of the story using various kinds of improvisation. With Duende (horn, cello, piano), we used the medieval tune "L'Homme Armé" as the basis for a story that told "a day in the life" of a medieval village, with scenes that featured the sunrise, a church service, a marketplace, armies clashing, and the aftermath. The one-page "map" that we used for the ten-minute piece might not have much meaning to someone else, but it worked for us. See Storytelling Games for more information.

Soundpainting

Soundpainting is real-time composition as the conductor and performers interact and shape the piece on the fly. A composer might construct a piece that uses some Soundpainting gestures or approximates the way Soundpainting works (with or without a conductor), taking such gestures as *Minimalism* (*ostinati*), *Synchronize*, *Crossover*, *Long Tones*, *Pointillism*, *Extended Techniques*, *Shapeline*, etc.

Nontraditional Scores

Soundpainting's *Shapeline* gesture is one kind of nontraditional score, in which performers interpret the physical movements of the conductor in music. There are many other possibilities. Any piece of graphic art, from a crayon squiggle to the Mona Lisa may be used to inspire improvisation. Audiences may be prevailed upon to contribute doodles or drawings that may be instantly set to music. A composer may do the drawing himself or select any source of graphic material that suits the composition. Once a player is empowered to improvise, anything can serve as a "score," including the room itself or the objects within. Strings of text may likewise serve to generate improvised music. The composer's imagination is the only limit if he has a willing and able group of contemporary classical improvisers at his disposal.

Combinations

The composer need not be limited to using any single method described above (or elsewhere)—the composer is free to use any combination or succession of these new compositional techniques in the construction of an improvisation composition. One caveat: don't write too much. It is easy to be lulled by the siren song of the ink and write too much or music that is too complex. Write simply and concisely, and then let the performer do the rest. Trust the performer to finish the creation. Insist that they pay minimal attention to any ideas that you, the composer, might have. Ask them to experiment, explore, and develop their own vision and version of the piece. Insist that they play the piece differently every time. Remind them that anything may be changed for the benefit of the piece. It is just ink, not holy writ. If they find better ways to play it, alleluia. Go for it. You want a living, breathing, and growing piece, not a museum exhibit, not an unchanging plastic-laminated event. Record it if you want to remember that particular performance, but rejoice that your piece will be always fresh and new, different for every performer and performance.

Chapter 38

Comprehensive Musicianship Chart

Comprehensive Musicianship = Literate + Aural	
Literate Tradition	**Aural Tradition**
Fundamental Characteristics	
• Interpretation of written notation • "Consumer" of music	• Spontaneous creation of melody • Playing a familiar tune by ear • Producer of music
Value (What's important)	
• Accuracy of re-creation; deviations from the printed notation to be avoided at all costs • Product • Working as a member of a team	• Invention, imagination, originality of the musical creation; "mistakes" are seen as opportunities, essential to the process of experimentation and discovery. • Process • Individuality
Pluses	
• Good technique and musical literacy opens the door to a huge body of written literature • Suitable for playing in traditional groups: band, orchestra, chamber ensembles • Wealth of pedagogical material • Pedagogical tradition establishes correct and efficient habits on instrument • Relatively easy to assess/judge/criticize • Preservation of tradition • Groups and literature familiar to audiences	• Fosters versatility, flexibility, ability to respond to the moment, deal with many styles • Highly motivating • Self-expression • Fun, enjoyable, confidence-building • Develops advanced musicianship skills • Create music suited to individual abilities, needs, and tastes, not dependent on existing literature • Renewal of tradition • Technical material includes that required for "classical" literature and more

Minuses	
• Limited self-expression	• Scary to a novice (excepting children)
• Without written music, no playing	• Like languages, training is best when started early
• Primacy of the group	• Sessions can seem chaotic
• Boredom can set in	• Assessment requires rethinking from traditional model
• Pressure to achieve; stress in performance	• Inexperienced teachers will have to learn along with the students
• Lack of practical understanding of theory behind the music	• Scarcity of non-jazz pedagogical material
• Lack of ability to play by ear, compose, or improvise	• Exclusive aural training neglects ability to interpret written notation
• Relative narrowness of stylistic ability	

Technique/practice	
• Major, minor, and chromatic scales and arpeggios; played up and down in one, two, or three octaves	• Many kinds of scales, modes, patterns, arpeggios, including major, minor (natural, melodic, harmonic, Dorian, etc), dominant seventh, altered dominant, diminished, augmented, and more
• Considered a boring if necessary evil; avoided when possible	• Practiced creatively with many variations
	• Lifelong learning, development, interest

Music Theory	
• Theoretical understanding may be limited, since it is not required to interpret notation	• Practical understanding of melodic and harmonic material, form, and motivic development is an essential part of the process
• Advanced players may learn traditional 19th century theory	• Much theory is personally discovered and assimilated by trial and error
• Separate from performance	
• More historical than practical	

Tone/timbre	
• Conformity encouraged; timbre changes (e.g. mutes, effects) dictated in the notation	• Individual; regular and integrated use of extended techniques such as flutter-tongue, trills, mutes, glissando, etc.

Rhythm	
• Relatively rudimentary rhythmic abilities, both in "feel" and reading	• Advanced rhythmic feel from exposure to and practice of many kinds of music, including jazz, Latin, African, percussion, use of electronic/CD/computer accompaniment.
• Highly complex notation requires considerable study to re-create	• Rhythmic development especially due to process of keeping a pulse while spontaneously inventing rhythms
	• Highly complex rhythmic variation and embellishment are a basic feature of individual phrasing.

Style	
• Traditional "classical" orchestral and band literature	• Jazz, pop, rock, folk/world, plus personal style
	• Classical styles can be emulated for study purposes and deeper learning

Aural ability	
• Pitch discrimination required for tuning, matching dynamics in performance. • Classroom work may require solfege, dictation and other aural training	• Ability to hear a pitch and remember and reproduce it (via transcription or call and response) • Ability to respond to improvisation collaborator instantaneously • Listener can learn from all sound sources
Process	
• Re-creation of printed notation	• Experimentation, exploration, creative thinking, free play, creation of music, spontaneous interplay
Motivation	
• Camaraderie	• Love of the process
Composition	
• Separation of performer and composer • Players do not normally compose	• Composition is an essential part of the aural tradition • Integration of performer and composer
Role of Player in Group	
• Replaceable "cog"	• Individual voice and personality of player is an essential feature of improvised music

Chapter 39

Soundpainting Gestures: the Basics

Soundpainting is a compositional sign language developed over the past two decades by New York composer Walter Thompson for musicians, dancers, actors, poets, and visual artists working in the medium of structured improvisation. At present the language comprises over one thousand gestures that the composer/conductor signs to indicate the type of improvisation desired of the performers. Soundpainting was developed as a method of communicating with the musicians during a performance without having to shout above the music. In its early days, the technique was primarily used as a tool for keeping windows of improvisation close to the style of the notated music. When using the Soundpainting language, an entire concert, dance or theatre work, film score, or educational presentation can be realized spontaneously. Soundpainting is live or real-time composition.

Following is a list of some of the most basic gestures. A practiced Soundpainting ensemble will be fluent in 100–200 gestures, but complete novices of any age, instrument, or level can begin Soundpainting in just minutes using a few basic gestures. Players also have two signs that they can use to communicate back to the conductor: *Player does not understand [the gesture]* and *Player cannot continue*.

See www.soundpainting.com for more information. A DVD and manual of forty basic gestures is available.

Soundpainting uses a specific syntax to deliver the signs:

–Who is going to play?
–What are they going to play?
–How to play.
–When to start.
–When to stop.

Who

        Whole Group
        Rest of Group
        Group One, Two, Three…
        Woodwinds, brass, strings, percussion, actor, dancer, visual artist

When

        Play (enter)
        Cut off (exit)
        Enter/exit slowly

What
  Air sounds
  Anaphora
  Cell
  Crossover
  Cycle
  Drone
  Long tone [high, middle, low]; pointed long
    tone
  Finish your idea (soloist)
  End the piece (groups)
  Going on/back to
  Key (flat, sharp)
  Hit
  Palette
  Pointillism
  Minimalism
  Memory (One, Two, Three)
  Continue
  This
  Pitch up/down
  Extended techniques
  Laughter
  Measure
  Memory (One, Two, Three)
  Note
  Only
  Open
  Repeat
  Silence
  Sit/stand
  Stab Freeze
  Shapeline
  Major/minor; key
  Relate to
  Palette
  Play/can't play
  Sing (open/closed)
  Speak
  Swarm
  Synchronize
  Tear up (end)
  This
  Quotes
  Watch me

Whistle
With/Without

How
  Badly; good
    Organically develop
  Over the top

Modes
  Scan
  On/off scan
  Point-to-point
  Launch mode
  Note mode

Intent
  Murderous
  Peaceful
  Loving
  Anchorman (passionless)
  Cell phone (ignore)
  Continuous intent

Faders
  Volume
  Tempo
  Density
  Level

Feedback
  Performer doesn't understand
  Performer can't continue

Feel (style)
  March, rock, Latin, country western, techno,
    Irish, funk, swing, machine, French café,
    reggae, Klezmer, classical

Other
  And
  Or
  If

Chapter 40

Chord Symbols Reference List

Below is a listing of common chord designations used in jazz and commercial music. Any harmonic structure can be named through this shorthand system.

A chord is comprised of basic triads plus extensions, if any.

Triads

NAME	SCALE DEGREES	EXAMPLES
Major	1–3–5	C
Minor	1–♭3–5	Cm
Augmented	1–3–♯5	Caug
Diminished	1–♭3–♭5	Cdim

Extensions

NAME	SCALE DEGREES	EXAMPLES
Major sixth	1–3–5–6	C^6
Minor sixth	1–♭3–5–6	Cm^6
Dominant seventh	1–3–5–♭7	C^7
Major seventh	1–3–5–7	C$_{MAJ}$^{7}
Minor seventh	1–♭3–5–♭7	Cm^7
Half-diminished seventh	1–♭3–♭5–♭7	C$^{7(♭5)}$
Diminished seventh	1–♭3–♭5–♭♭7	Cdim^7
Dominant ninth	1–3–5–♭7–9	C^9
Minor ninth	1–♭3–5–♭7–9	Cm^9
Altered Dominants		
Flat ninth	1–3–5–♭7–♭9	C$^{7(♭9)}$
Sharp ninth	1–3–5–♭7–♯9	C$^{7(♯9)}$
Sharp fifth, sharp ninth	1–3–♯5–♭7–♯9	C$^{7(♯5♯9)}$
Elevenths		
Dominant eleventh	1–3–5–♭7–9–11	C^{11}
Minor eleventh	1–♭3–5–♭7–9–11	Cm^{11}
Sharp eleventh	1–3–5–7–9–♯11	C$_{MAJ}$$^{7(♯11)}$
Suspended	1–4–5–♭7	C$^{7(SUS)}$

Chapter 41

Scales Types: Study Groups

Scales are arranged roughly in the order of importance. Always practice with a metronome or other rhythm/tempo source. Work on scales, both diatonically and cycling through the circle of fifths. Vary the tempo, accent groupings, articulation, register, dynamics, etc. In each practice session play a familiar tune using the scale you are studying and spend some time on free improvisation as well. Practice frequently with a partner.

Group 1

NAME	SCALE DEGREES
Major	1–2–3–4–5–6–7

Group 2

NAME	SCALE DEGREES
Minor "root" scale (common for many minor scale types)	1–2–♭3–4–5
Melodic minor	1–2–♭3–4–5–6–7
Harmonic minor	1–2–♭3–4–5–♭6–7
Natural minor	1–2–♭3–4–5–♭6–♭7

Group 3

NAME	SCALE DEGREES
Dorian	1–2–♭3–4–5–6–♭7
Dominant seventh (Mixolydian mode)	1–2–3–4–5–6–♭7
Pentatonic major	1–2–3–5–6
Pentatonic minor	1–♭3–4–5–♭7
Lydian	1–2–3–♯4–5–6–7

Group 4

NAME	SCALE DEGREES
Whole tone	1–2–3–#4–#5–#6
Aeolian	1–2–♭3–4–5–♭6–♭7
Phrygian	1–♭2–♭3–4–5–♭6–♭7
Spanish Phrygian	1–♭2–3–4–5–♭6–♭7
Lydian Dominant	1–2–3–#4–5–6–♭7
Blues	1–♭3–4–#4–5–♭7

Group 5

NAME	SCALE DEGREES
Diminished (Octotonic) scale	
Whole-half	1–2–♭3–4–♭5–♭6–6–7
Half-whole	1–♭2–♭3–3–#4–5–6–♭7
Locrian	1–♭2–♭3–4–♭5–♭6–♭7
Altered [dominant]	1–♭2–♭3–♭4–♭5–♭6–♭7
Harmonic major	1–2–3–4–5–♭6–7
Klezmer	1–♭2–3–4–5–♭6–7
Hungarian	1–2–♭3–#4–5–♭6–7

Chapter 42

Scale and Chord Chart

SCALES

NAME	SCALE DEGREES
Chromatic	1–#1–2–#2–3–4–#4–5–#5–6–#6–7

Major

Major (Ionian)	1–2–3–4–5–6–7
Pentatonic major	1–2–3–5–6
Lydian	1–2–3–#4–5–6–7
Klezmer (Ahava Raba)	
(fifth mode of harmonic minor)	1–♭2–3–4–5–♭6–♭7
Middle Eastern	1–♭2–3–4–5–♭6–7
Bebop major	1–2–3–4–5–♭6–6–7
Harmonic major	1–2–3–4–5–♭6–7
Spanish Phrygian	1–♭2–3–4–5–♭6–♭7
Hungarian	1–#2–3–#4–5–♭6–7
Javanese	1–♭2–♭3–4–5–6–♭7

Minor

Melodic (jazz) minor	
(ascending/descending)	1–2–♭3–4–5–6–7
Melodic minor (traditional)	
ascending	1–2–♭3–4–5–6–7
Melodic minor (traditional)	
descending	♭7 ♭6–5–4–♭3–2–1
Natural minor	1–2–♭3–4–5–♭6–♭7
Harmonic minor	1–2–♭3–4–5–♭6–7
Dorian	1–2–♭3–4–5–6–♭7
Pentatonic minor	1–♭3–4–5–♭7
Blues	1–♭3–4–#4–5–♭7
Aeolian	1–2–♭3–4–5–♭6–♭7
Phrygian	1–♭2–♭3–4–5–♭6–♭7
Balinese	1–♭2–♭3–4–5–♭6–7
Klezmer minor (Misheberekh)	
(fourth mode of harmonic minor)	1–2–♭3–#4–4–5–♭7

Dominant
    Dominant seventh (Mixolydian)   1–2–3–4–5–6–♭7
    Lydian dominant   1–2–3–#4–5–6–♭7
    Bebop dominant   1–2–3–4–5–6–♭7 7

Altered dominant
    Superlocrian
        (seventh mode of melodic minor;
        see Diminished below)   1–♭2–♭3–♭4–♭5–♭6–♭7

Half-diminished
    Locrian   1–♭2–♭3–4–♭5–♭6–♭7
    Jazz Locrian   1–2–♭3–4–♭5–♭6–♭7

Diminished
    Whole-half   1–2–♭3–4–#4–#5–6–7
    Half-whole   1–♭2–♭3–3–#4–5–6–♭7

Whole tone   1–2–3–#4–#5–♭7

CHORDS

NAME	SCALE DEGREES	EXAMPLE	LETTER NAMES
Major	1–3–5	C	C–E–G
Major sixth	1–3–5–6	C6	C–E–G–A
Major six-nine	1–3–6–9	C6(9)	C–E–A–D
Major seventh	1–3–5–7	CMAJ7	C–E–G–B
Major ninth	1–3–5–7–9	CMAJ9	C–E–G–B–D
Minor	1–♭3–5	Cm	C–E♭–G
Minor sixth	1–♭3–5–6	Cm6	C–E♭–G–A
Minor seventh	1–♭3–5–♭7	Cm7	C–E♭–G–B♭
Minor ninth	1–♭3–(5)–♭7–9	Cm9	C–E♭–(G)–B♭–D
Minor (major seventh)	1–♭3–5–7	Cm(MAJ7)	C–E♭–G–B
Augmented	1–3–#5	Caug	C–E–G♯
Augmented seventh	1–3–#5–♭7	C7(#5)	C–E–G♯–B♭
Dominant seventh	1–3–5–♭7	C7	C–E–G–B♭
Dominant ninth	1–3–(5)–♭7–9	C9	C–E–(G)–B♭–D
Dominant thirteenth	1–3–♭7–9–13	C13	C–E–B♭–D–A
Dominant seventh/ sharp eleventh	1–3–♭7–9–#11	C7(#11)	C–E–B♭–D–F♯

Altered Dominants

Dominant seventh/ flat ninth	1–3–♭7–♭9	C7(♭9)	C–E–B♭–D♭
Dominant seventh/ sharp ninth	1–3–♭7–♯9	C7(♯9)	C–E–B♭–D♯
C altered	1–3–♯5–♯9	C7alt	C–E–G♯–D♯
Diminished	1–♭3–♭5	Cdim	C–E♭–G♭
Half-diminished seventh	1–♭3–♭5–♭7	Cm7(♭5)	C–E♭–G♭–B♭
Diminished seventh	1–♭3–♭5–♭♭7 (C–E♭–F♯–A)	Cdim7	C–E♭–G♭–B♭♭
Suspended	1–4–5–♭7	C7(SUS)	C–F–G–B♭

Note:　　Chord spellings given here are often not the voicings used by chordal instruments, which may use rootless voicings and/or omit certain tones, such as the fifth.

Chapter 43

Variants

Improvisation requires maximum flexibility, which comes from experiencing many different kinds of musical and technical situations. To obtain this requisite variety, vary as many elements as possible during practice.

VARIANT	NOTE
Tempo	from very slow to very fast
Articulation	slurred, tongued, various combinations, double and triple tonguing for winds
Rhythm	uneven values and syncopation are possible
Dynamics	*crescendo/decrescendo*
Keycycle through all keys	
Meter	2/4, 3/4, 4/4, 5/4, 5/8, 7/8, 9/8, unevenly divided 4/4 (e.g., 3+3+2), etc.
Accents	regular and irregular
Extended techniques	
Vibrato/non-vibrato	
Style	swing, Latin, rock, boogie, New Age, etc. See *Style List* (Resources)
Tuplets	triplets, quintuplets, etc.
Groups of three in duple meter	
Rests	
Limited number of notes in a pattern or scale	
Loop	
Register	range
Mode changes	major to minor, etc.

Scale Practice Variants

Limit the number of notes (e.g., two to four notes), creating patterns or cells.

Learn short, basic diatonic patterns, altering scale degree relationships while ascending.

Cycle patterns through the circle of fifths, keeping scale degree relationships the same.

Chromatic patterns.

Practice scales in all lengths from two to nine notes.

Start on every scale degree.

Practice descending as well as ascending scales, and in alternation.

Start before and after the downbeat.

Loops make practice more effective. Varying rhythms add fun and pizzazz.

Practice all types of scales:

> Major
> Mixolydian
> Pentatonic major
> Lydian
> Dominant seventh
> Lydian dominant
> Dorian
> Melodic minor (raised sixth and seventh both ascending and descending)
> Harmonic minor
> Pentatonic minor
> Blues
> Whole tone
> Diminished
> Phrygian
> Aeolian
> Locrian
> Superlocrian
> Klezmer
> Chromatic

Practice the corresponding arpeggios/chords of the above.

> *Tip:*   *Always* practice with a timekeeper. Metronomes, play-along CDs, and computer accompaniment programs are all good, but a friend with a percussion instrument is best. Then trade off.

And finally, forget all the drills, and jump in and improvise. Put all that practice of variants to work.

Chapter **44**

Patterns and Scales

Compact List for Technical Practice

*All scales and patterns can be practiced descending as well as ascending, and can
be practiced ascending/descending in alternation in cycles or diatonic progression.
Patterns may also be combined (e.g., 1–2–3–4 5–3–2–1).*

Cycles

C–F–B♭–E♭–A♭–D♭–G♭/F♯–B–E–A–D–G

C–G–D–A–E–B–F♯/G♭–D♭–A♭–E♭–B♭–F

C–F–G–B♭–D–E♭–A–A♭–E–D♭–B–G♭

C–D♭–D–E♭–E–F–F♯/G♭–G–A♭–A–B♭–B

C–B–B♭–A–A♭–G–G♭/F♯–F–E–E♭–D–D♭

C–D–E–F♯–A♭–B♭–D♭–E♭–F–G–A–B

C–B♭–A♭–G♭–E–D–D♭–B–A–G–F–E♭

C–B–A–G–F–E♭–D♭–B♭–A♭–G♭/F♯–E–D

C–F♯–D♭–G–D–A♭–E♭–A–E–B♭–F–B

C–G♭–B–F–B♭–E–A–E♭–A♭–D–G–D♭

C–D♭–B–D–B♭–E♭–A–E–A♭–F–G–F♯

C–E♭–F♯–A–B–D–F–A♭–B♭–D♭–E–G

C–A–F♯–E♭–B–A♭–F–D–B♭–G–E–C♯

C–E–G–B♭–A♭–F–B–D–E♭–F♯–A–D♭

C–A–F–E–B♭–A–G–E♭–B–D♭–D–G♭

B♭–A–C–B–A♭–D–F–G–E–D♭–E♭–F♯

Major

    Basic scale: 1–2–3–4–5–6–7

      Patterns: 1–7–1

               1–2–3

               1–2–3–4

               1–2–3–4–5

               1–2–3–5

               1–2–3–5–6 (pentatonic major; may be varied with ♭6)

               1–2–3–5–7

               1–2–3–5–7–9

1–3–4–5
1–3–5–(8)
1–3–5–6
1–3–5–7
1–3–5–7–9
1–2–4–5

Dominant Seventh
Basic scale: 1–2–3–4–5–6–♭7
Patterns: 1–3–5–♭7
1–2–3–5–♭7
1–3–5–♭7–9
1–3–5–♭7–♯9–♭9– (8)

Whole Tone
Basic scale: 1–2–3–♯4–♯5–♭7
Patterns: 1–2–3–♯4–♯5
1–2–3–♯5
1–3–♯5
1–3–♯5–♭7

Minor
Patterns: 1–2–♭3
1–2–♭3–4–5
1–2–♭3–4–5–6 (or ♭6)
1–2–♭3–5
1–2–♭3–5–♭7
1–2–♭3–5–♭7–9
1–♭3–4–5
1–♭3–4–5–♭7 (minor pentatonic)
1–♭3–5
1–♭3–5–6
1–♭3–5–♭7 (or ♮7)
1–♭3–5–♭7–9

Diminished
Basic scale: 1–2–♭3–4–♭5–♭6–♭♭7–7 (whole-half)
1–♭2–♭3–3–♯4–5–6–♭7 (half-whole)
Patterns: 1–♭3–♭5
1–♭3–♭5–6 (♭♭7)
1–2–♭3–♭5
1–2–♭3–4–♭5

Additional Scales From Which to Extract Patterns

Dorian:	1–2–♭3–4–5–6–♭7
Phrygian:	1–♭2–♭3–4–5–♭6–♭7
Spanish Phrygian:	1–♭2–3–4–5–♭6–♭7
Lydian:	1–2–3–♯4–5–6–7
Mixolydian:	1–2–3–4–5–6–♭7
Aeolian:	1–2–♭3–4–5–♭6–♭7
Locrian:	1–♭2–♭3–4–♭5–♭6–♭7
Superlocrian:	1–♭2–♭3–♭4–♭5–♭6–♭7
Lydian Dominant:	1–2–3–♯4–5–6–♭7
Chromatic:	(i.e., fluency from any note to any note)
Blues:	1–♭3–4–♯4–5–♭7
Klezmer No. 1:	1–♭2–3–4–5–♭6–♭7 (Ahava Raba)
Klezmer No. 2:	1–2–♭3–♯4–5–6–♭7 (Misheberekh)
Jazz (melodic) minor:	1–2–♭3–4–5–6–7 (both ascending and descending)
Harmonic minor:	[♭6–♮7]

Intervals

   Scales in thirds

   Scales in fourths

   Variations/extensions: 1–4–♭7

                             1–4–5–(1)

                             1–4–5–♭7–1

   Leap from the tonic to all other notes, both diatonically and chromatically, ascending and descending.

   Any interval through all keys, ascending and descending.

Approaching Patterns

   Add chromatic or diatonic approaches to arpeggios and patterns.

Chord Progression

ii⁷	–	V⁷	–	I
Dm⁷	–	G⁷	–	C
Gm⁷	–	C⁷	–	F
Cm⁷	–	F⁷	–	B♭
Fm⁷	–	B♭⁷	–	E♭
B♭m⁷	–	E♭⁷	–	A♭
E♭m⁷	–	A♭⁷	–	D♭
A♭m⁷	–	D♭⁷	–	G♭
C♯m⁷	–	F♯⁷	–	B
F♯m⁷	–	B⁷	–	E
Bm⁷	–	E⁷	–	A
Em⁷	–	A⁷	–	D
Am⁷	–	D⁷	–	G

Chapter 45

Cycles

These are simply lists of keys in various orders, some logical, some surprising. Use these to run through patterns and scales in different keys. They are only suggestions; make up your own!

1. C–F–B♭–E♭–A♭–D♭–F♯–B–E–A–D–G

2. C–D♭–D–E♭–E–F–G♭–G–A♭–A–B♭–B

3. C–B–B♭–A–A♭–G–F♯–F–E–E♭–D–D♭

4. C–D–E–F♯–A♭–B♭–D♭–E♭–F–G–A–B

5. C–B♭–A♭–G♭–E–D–D♭–B–A–G–F–E♭

6. C–G–D–A–E–B–G♭–D♭–A♭–E♭–B♭–F

7. F♯–D♭–B–A♭–E–A–D–G–E♭–B♭–F–C

8. C–B–A–G–F–E♭–D♭–B♭–A♭–F♯–E–D

9. C–F♯–D♭–G–D–A♭–E♭–A–E–B♭–F–B

10. C–G♭–B–F–B♭–E–A–E♭–A♭–D–G–D♭

11. C–D♭–B–D–B♭–E♭–A–E–A♭–F–G–F♯

12. C–E♭–F♯–A–B–D–F–A♭–B♭–D♭–E–G

13. C–E♭–F♯–A–C♯–E–G–A–D–F–A♭–B

14. C–E–G–B♭–A♭–F–B–D–E♭–F♯–A–D♭

15. C–A–F–E–B♭–A–G–E♭–B–D♭–D–G♭

16. B♭–A–C–B–A♭–D–F–G–E–D♭–E♭–F♯

17. C–E–A♭–D♭–F–A–D–F♯–B♭–E♭–G–B

Chapter 46

Familiar Tunes

This list is not at all comprehensive. Add your own!

The Beatles
All My Loving

Hey Jude

In My Life

Maxwell's Silver Hammer

Norwegian Wood

She Loves You

When I'm 64

Yesterday

Bossa Nova
The Girl From Ipanema

Meditation

Broadway and Movie
76 Trombones

Do, Re, Mi
Don't Cry For Me,
Argentina

Edelweiss

Give My Regards to
Broadway

Hey, Look Me Over

I Feel Pretty
If I Were a Rich Man
Impossible Dream

Maria
Master of the House
Moon River

My Favorite Things

Over the Rainbow

Send in the Clowns
Sunrise, Sunset

Classical themes
The Anvil Chorus

Barcarolle
Brahm's Lullaby
Bridal Chorus from
Lohengrin

The Can-Can
The Carnival of Venice

The Fledermaus Waltz
Für Elise

Habañera
Hallelujah Chorus
The Hunter's Chorus
(Freischütz)

It Was a Lover and His Lass

La Che Darem La Mano
La Donna é Mobile
The Light Cavalry
Overture

The New World Symphony

Ode to Joy

The Peer Gynt Suite
Pilgrim's Chorus
Polovetsian Dances
Pomp and Circumstance

Sumer Is Icumen In
Surprise Symphony

Tales from the Vienna
Woods

Una Voce Poco Fa

Wedding March from
Lohengrin
Wedding March
(Mendelssohn)
The William Tell Overture

Foreign Language
Alouette
Au Clair de la Lune

Frère Jacques
Funiculi Funicula

Gaudeamus Igitur

Hava Nagila

La Cucaracha
La Marseillaise

Santa Lucia

General
Abide With Me
America, The Beautiful
Annie Laurie
Arkansas Traveler
Auld Lang Syne
Aunt Rhody
Aura Lee
Ave Maria

Barbara Allen
The Bear Went Over the
 Mountain
Beautiful Dreamer
Bicycle Built for Two
Big Rock Candy Mountain
Billy Boy
Blow the Man Down
Blue Bells of Scotland
Blue Tail Fly
Buffalo Gals

Camptown Races
Careless Love
Clementine
Cockles and Mussels

Dixie
Do Your Ears Hang Low?
Down In the Valley
Drunken Sailor

The Entertainer (rag)
Erie Canal
Every Night When the Sun
 Goes In

The Farmer in the Dell
Flow Gently, Sweet Afton
Foggy, Foggy Dew
For He's a Jolly Good
 Fellow
Frankie and Johnny
Froggie Went a-Courtin'

Gladiator March
Go Down, Moses
Go Tell It on the Mountain
Good Night, Ladies
Green Grow the Lilacs
Greensleeves

Hail, Hail the Gang's All
 Here
Heigh Ho
Here We Go Round the
 Mulberry Bush
Home on the Range
Hot Cross Buns

I Gave My Love a Cherry
I Want a Girl (Just Like the
 Girl)

I'm Forever Blowing
 Bubbles
I've Been Working on the
 Railroad
Irish Washerwoman
It's a Long Way to
 Tipperary

Jimmy Crack Corn

Kookaburra

Lightly Row
Little Brown Jug
Loch Lomond
London Bridge
Londonderry Air
Long, Long Ago

The Man on the Flying
 Trapeze
Mary Had a Little Lamb
Michael Row the Boat
 Ashore
Molly Malone
My Bonnie
My Country, 'Tis of Thee
My Love Is Like a Red, Red
 Rose

Oats, Peas, Beans, and
 Barley Grow
Oh, Dear, What Can the
 Matter Be?
Oh, Dem Golden Slippers
Oh, Susanna
Old Chisholm Trail
Old Dan Tucker
Old Folks At Home
Old Gray Mare
Old MacDonald
On Top of Old Smoky

Peg O' My Heart
Polly Wolly Doodle
Pop Goes the Weasel

The Rakes of Mallow
Red River Valley
The Riddle Song
Rock o' My Soul
Rock-a-Bye Baby
Rule, Brittania

Scarborough Fair
Sentimental Journey
She'll Be Comin' 'Round
 the Mountain
Shenandoah
Shoo Fly, Don't Bother Me
Shortnin' Bread
Sidewalks of New York
Skip to my Lou
The St. James Infirmary
The Star Spangled Banner
The Stars and Stripes
 Forever
The Streets of Laredo
The Streets of New York
Sweet Betsy from Pike

Ta Ra Ra Boom Di Ay
There is a Tavern in the
 Town
There'll Be a Hot Time in
 the Old Town Tonight
This Old Man
Turkey in the Straw
Twinkle Twinkle

Wait for the Wagon
Waltzing Matilda
Washington Post March
When Irish Eyes Are
 Smiling
When Johnny Comes
 Marching Home

Yankee Doodle
Yellow Rose of Texas
You Are My Sunshine

Zum Gali Gali

Holiday
Angels We Have Heard On
 High
Auld Lang Syne
Ave Maria

Bring a Torch, Jeanette
 Isabella

Deck the Halls
Dreidel, Dreidel

The First Noel

God Rest Ye Merry
Gentlemen
Good King Wenceslas

Hark the Herald Angels
Sing
Here We Come A-
Wassailing

I Saw Three Ships
It Came Upon a Midnight
Clear

Jingle Bells
Joy to the World

O Come, O Come
Emmanuel
O Du Fröhliche
O Holy Night
O Little Town of
Bethlehem
O Tannenbaum
O Come, All Ye Faithful

Rudolph, the Red-Nosed
Reindeer

Silent Night

The Twelve Days of
Christmas

We Three Kings of Orient
Are
We Wish You a Merry
Christmas
What Child Is This?
White Christmas

Jazz Standards
All of Me
All the Things You Are
Angel Eyes
Autumn Leaves

Bewitched
Blue Bossa
Blue Monk
Body and Soul

Caravan
Cherokee

The Days of Wine and
Roses

Green Dolphin Street

How High the Moon

In the Mood

Misty
Mood Indigo

Night and Day

Out of Nowhere

Satin Doll
The Shadow of Your Smile
Stella by Starlight

Take Five
Take the A Train

Love Songs
Careless Love
Clementine

Down in the Valley

On Top of Old Smoky

Scarborough Fair
Sittin' on Top of the World

Miscellaneous
Happy Birthday

Simple Gifts

Oldies but Goodies
Alexander's Ragtime Band

Beer Barrel Polka
Bill Bailey

Camptown Races

Long, Long Ago

Oh, Susanna!

Sentimental Journey

Rock n Roll
Hit the Road, Jack

Johnny B. Good

Love Potion Number Nine
Rock Around the Clock

Rounds
Dona Nobis Pacem

Frere Jacques

Heigh Ho

Kookaburra

Row, Row, Row Your Boat

Scotland's Burning

Three Blind Mice

Spirituals, Gospel, Hymns
Amazing Grace

Do, Lord
Down by the Riverside

Go Down, Moses
Go Tell it on the Mountain

Joshua Fit the Battle of
Jericho

Kum Ba Yah

Michael, Row the Boat
Ashore
A Mighty Fortress
Motherless Child

Oh Mary, Don't You Weep

Swing Low Sweet Chariot

Wayfaring Stranger
When the Saints Go
Marching In

Waltzes
The Anniversary Waltz

The Blue Danube Waltz

The Merry Widow Waltz

Tales of the Vienna Woods
The Tennessee Waltz

Wiener Blut (Vienna
Blood)

Chapter 47

Musical Styles and Forms

Adagio	Can-can	Early music	Habanera
Air	Canon	Easy listening	Hard rock
Aleatoric	Cantata	Electronic	Hillbilly
Anthem	Canzona	Elegy	Hiphop
Antiphonal	Caprice	English madrigal	Hoedown
Arabesque	Carol	Etude	Honky tonk
Aria	Chaconne	Europop	Horror music
Asian Music	Chance music		Hunting music
Atonal	Chanson	Fandango	Hymn
Avant-garde	Children's song	Fanfare	
	Chinese music	Film score	Impressionist
Bagatelle	Choral Prelude	Flamenco	Impromptu
Ballad	Chorale	Folk music	Isorhythm
Barcarolle	Circus music	Foxtrot	
Baroque	Comic opera	Fugue	Japanese
Bebop	Concerto	Funeral music	Jazz
Beguine	Concerto Grosso	Funk	Jig
Bel Canto	Conductus	Fusion	Jingle (advertising)
Berceuse	Cool jazz		Jive
Bluegrass	Counterpoint	Gamelan	Jug band
Blues	Country rock	Gansta rap	
Boogie-Woogie	Country Western	Gavotte	Ländler
Bossa Nova	Cowboy song	Girl group	Lied/Lieder
Brazilian jazz	Csardas	Gospel	Line dance
British folk music		Graduation music	Lounge music
Broadway	Dance music	Greek	Love song
	Dirge	Gregorian chant	Lullaby
Cajun	Discant	Grunge	
Cakewalk	Dodecaphony	Gypsy	Madrigal
Calypso	Drone		Mambo

March

Masque

Mass

Mazurka

Medieval music

Meditation music

Merengue

Mexican

Microtonal

Minimalist

Minnesang

Minuet

Motet

Motown

Musette

Music hall

Musical

Muzak

Nashville sound

Neoclassical

New Age

New Orleans jazz

Nocturne

Odd meter

Ode

Opera

Operetta

Oratorio

Ostinato

Overture

Partita

Passacaglia

Pastorale

Pavane

Pentatonic

Polka

Polonaise

Pop

Program music

Psychedelic

Punk rock

Quadrille

Raga

Ragtime

Rap

Recitative

Reel

Reggae

Renaissance

Requiem

Rhapsody

Rhumba

Rhythm & Blues

Rock

Rock 'n' Roll

Rockabilly

Romance

Rondo

Salsa

Saltarello

Samba

Sarabande

Scherzo

Schottisch

Sea Chanty

Serenade

Serial

Singspiel

Ska

Skiffle

Soft rock

Son montuno

Sonata

Song

Soul

Spiritual

Spoken Word

Square dance

Stabat Mater

Stile Antico

Stride

Striptease

Surf music

Swing

Symphonic

Tango

Tap dance

Tarantella

Te Deum

Techno

Tejano

Theme and variations

Toccata

Tone poem

Trio Sonata

Troubadours and trouveres

Tuvan throat-singing

Vamp

Variation

Vaudeville

Virelais

Waltz

Wedding music

Western swing

Work song

World music

Yodeling

Zydeco

Chapter 48

Improvisation Starter Generator

Combine one or more adjectives with a noun from the lists below and depict in music.

Optional: Add a musical style or form from the list below.

These are just starters; feel free to add to the lists.

Remember to follow your inspiration wherever it goes, even if you end up in a very different place than where you started.

Adjective

Acrimonious	Cadaverous	Fastidious	High-pressure
Adorable	Chartreuse	Festering	Highly illegal
Agitated	Clipped	Flamboyant	
Agricultural	Comatose	Flexible	Icy
Alcoholic	Congealed	Flirtatious	Incomprehensible
Ambiguous	Crabby	Fluffy	Inside out
Ambitious	Creepy	Foolish	Intellectual
Amorous		Fossilized	Introspective
Argumentative	Delightful	Frantic	Irregular
Asinine	Diamond-studded	French fried	Irritated
Astonished	Disappointed	Frolicking	Itchy
Astronomical	Disgusting	Frosty	
	Dismal	Furious	Jealous
	Distraught	Fuzzy	Jovial
Baby blue	Dolly Parton's		
Bar-coded	Dolorous		Laughing
Barrel-sized	Drunken	Gargantuan	Lonely
Befuddled	Dysfunctional	Giddy	Lovely
Bewildered	Dyspeptic	Giggling	Love-starved
Blackened free-range		Glamorous	Low budget
Blatant	Egocentric	Grandiose	Lugubrious
Blimp-sized	Egregious	Greasy	Lumpy
Blinking	Electrifying	Greedy	Luscious
Bloated	Elusive	Grumpy	
Blue	Enormous		Maniacal
Bouncing	Exhausted	Hairy	Melancholy
Bright red	Extreme	Harvard-educated	Moldy
Buff		Heart-pounding	
		Hideous	

Naughty
Nauseous
Nervous

Odiferous
Oily
Old-fashioned

Paleolithic
Paranoid
Passionate
Pink polka-dotted
Plaid
Pompous
Pulsating
Purple
Putrid

Queasy

Rancid
Rasping
Romantic

Sardonic
Sassy
Savage
Seasick
Seductive
Seething
Shimmering
Shy
Silly
Sleepy
Slimy
Slippery
Sloppy
Slothful
Smeared
Smooth
Snobbish
Somber
Sophisticated
Sorrowful
Southern fried

Spooky
Squeamish
Squishy
Starving
Sticky
Stubborn
Supercilious
Suspicious

Tasty
Tempestuous
Ten-ton
Thorny
Thoughtful
Totally cool
Toxic
Turgid
Twitching
Two-headed

Underwater
Undulating

Vicious

Wacky
Warlike
Weevil-infested
Whimsical
Whining
Whipped
Whirling
Whispering
Whistling
Wistful

X-rated

Zany

Noun
Acorn
Alligator
Anchovy
Ankles

Appetite

Baboon
Baby
Bacteria
Banana
Banana boat
Barbecue
Belly button
Belly button lint
Biceps
Big toe
Blubber
Booger
Boyfriend
Breakfast
Bric-a-brac
Bubble gum
Bugaboo
Bungee Cord
Burp

Carburetor
Carp
Casserole
Caterpillar
Chainsaw
Checking account
Cheerleader
Cheese
Cheesecake
Chipmunk
Cigar
Clam
Clouds
Corn Flakes
Cow

Dart
Diamond
Diaper
Diplomat
Disc jockey
Donkey
Doormat

Dragon
Duck breath
Dump truck

Ear wax
Earlobe
Eggbeater
Elbow
Elephant
Eyebrows

Feast
Ferris wheel
Fish bait
Fish oil
Flamingo
Foghorn
Football
Frog
Fruit bat
Fruit salad
Fungus

Girlfriend
Glacier
Glass slipper
Goat

Haberdasher
Hair
Hairball
Haircut
Head coach
High heels
Hippopotamus
Horse
Hummingbird

Iceberg
Icicle
Iguana
Italy

Kangaroo
Kayak

Kiss
Kittens
Kleenex

Large intestine
Lasagna
Laundry
Lightning
Linebacker
Lottery ticket
Lunch

Makeover
Marshmallow
Matriculation
Meatball
Microscope
Molasses
Monkey
Moonshine
Moose
Motorcycle
Mushroom
Muskrat

Nincompoop
Nose
Nostril

Octopus
Onion
Oyster

Panda
Peanut butter
Penguin
Petticoat
Philosopher
Pillow
Pimple
Pirate
Pizza
Platypus
Poison ivy
Poodle

Pot pie
Potato
Princess
Pudding
Pumpkin
Python

Rainbow
Rollerblades
Roommate
Rutabaga

Saber-toothed tiger
Sailor
Sandwich
Sardine
Scissors
Scrambled eggs
Sea urchin
Sewer
Sheep dip
Socks
Squid
Squirrel
Stiletto
Submarine
Sweet potato

Tadpole
Tank
Tapeworm
Tattoo
Taxi
Teddy bear
Teeth
Thermos jug
Toad
Toboggan
Toe fungus
Toilet
Tonsils
Toupee
Tourist
T. rex
Turkey

Underarm deodorant
Underwear
Unicorn

Vulture

Walrus
Warthog
Wink
Woodpecker

Yak

Musical Styles and Forms

6/8 hunting music

AABA
Adagio
Advertising jingle
Allegro
Allegro con brio
Anthem
Aria
Atonal
Augmented
Avant-garde

Ballad
Baroque
Bebop
Beethovenesque
Beguine
Belly dance
Bluegrass
Blues
Boogie woogie
Broadway show tune
Bulgarian wedding

Cajun
Cakewalk
Calypso
Cancan
Canon

Cha cha
Chant
Charleston
Children's song
Chorale
Chromatic
Circus music
Computer music
Concerto
Concerto Grosso
Country Western
Cowboy song
Csardas

Debussyesque
Diminished
Dirge
Doloroso
Drone

Easy listening
Elegy
Elvis style
English drinking
  song
English music hall
Etude

Fanfare
Fantasia
Fifths
Fight song
Fourths
Foxtrot
Funeral music
Funk

Gavotte
Girl group
Glissando
Gospel
Graduation music
Grand Ol' Opry
Ground bass

HabaZera
Halftime music
Halloween music
Hip hop
Hoedown
Hornpipe
Horror music
Hymn

Intermezzo

Jazz-rock
Jig
Jive
John Cage music
Johnny Cash style

Ländler
Legato
Love song
Low register
Lullaby
Lyrical

Madrigal
Major
Mambo
March
Mazurka
Medieval music
Mexican
Minimalism
Minor
Musette
Muzak

National anthem-
   type
New Age

Odd meter
Ostinato
Overture

Passacaglia
Pastorale
Pavane
Pentatonic
Percussive
Perpetual motion
Pizzicato
Pointillistic
Polka
Pulsating

Raga
Ragtime
Rain dance
Rap
Reel
Renaissance dance
Rhapsody
Riff
Rite of Spring
   Music
Rock n roll
Rockabilly
Romance
Romantic movie
   theme
Rondo
Rossini-esque
Round
Rumba

Salsa
Sarabande
Scherzo
Sci-fi/alien music
Sea Chanty
Sea Monster music
Serenade
Shimmy
Shuffle
Ska
Skiffle
Slow dance
Slow march

Son montuno
Sonata
Song
Sousa March
Spanish
Staccato
Stephen Foster tune
Stride
Striptease
Surfin' music
Swing

Tango
Tap dance
Tarantella
Techno
Tejano

Theme and Variations
Threnody
Tone poem
Tuvan throat singing
Twelve-tone

Vamp
Verdi opera chorus

Waltz
Wedding music
Weird sounds
World music

Yodeling

Zorba the Greek dance
Zydeco

Chapter 49

Creative Percussion Instruments

Every traditionally trained musician interested in the improvisation process would do well to spend extra time emphasizing that which is most deficient in our training: rhythm. This can be done on the player's primary instrument, of course, but rhythm should also be pursued on various types of percussion instruments as well. Percussion helps us move away from our traditional pitch fixation and enables us to focus purely on rhythm. Nothing animates an improvisation more than lively rhythms.

It is very useful to have an array of "personal" percussion: small, inexpensive (even toy) percussion instruments for rhythm practice or for use in an improvisation class, jam sessions, or concerts. There are many, many kinds of personal percussion instruments of this sort. Here is a small selection of examples:

Bell tree
Berimbau
Bodhran
Cabasa
Claves
Drums (e.g., tom-tom, snare, bongos, congas, djembe, cuica, slit drum, dombek)
Finger cymbals
Flexatone
Gong
Guiro
Log drum
Maracas
Marimba
Rattle (many kinds)
Singing bowls
Tambourine
Triangle
Vibraslap
Whistles
Wood block

Whether or not these percussion instruments are available, be aware that the possibilities of creating your own percussion are endless. On one hand, you can make percussive sounds using whatever is around you (see *World=Percussion* and *Bricolage*). On the other hand, you can make percussion instruments out of simple materials. As with many aspects of creativity, the educational system encourages small children to do this, but for some unknown reason, it stops even mentioning the possibility of such creation for older children and adults. Don't let the limits of the current education system prevent your imagination and creativity from blossoming. Take charge and do it yourself!

Examples of Homemade Percussion

Let's Make Music! By Jessica Baron Turner and Ronny Susan Schiff (1995, Hal Leonard Corp.) provides ideas and know-how in making your own percussion instruments. The book shows how to make simple homemade percussion instruments from around the world, such as maracas (from plastic bottles), rainsticks, clappers, pien chung (temple bells), wood scrapers, castanets, buzz disks, *shekeres*, frame drums, and more.

The Internet offers immediate access to information on constructing homemade percussion as well. Rhythmweb (www.rhythmweb.com/homemade/index.html) and Drum Journey (www.drumjourney.com/world/make/index.htm) are two of the better sources.

Rhythmweb has extensive resources on "Homemade Percussion and Junk," with information on many kinds of instruments, including shakers, sticks and beaters, water bottles, can drum orchestra, coffee can drums, metal bowls, wooden boxes, and more, plus a list of books on instrument building. Rhythmweb also offers homemade percussion workshops in the Dallas/Ft. Worth area.

Drum Journey has a rich set of offerings, including "Intro to Homemade Drums and Percussion Instruments," which has instructions for building both "real" and homemade drums, such as coffee can drums, moon drums, water bottle *shekeres*, poster tube rainsticks, shakers, and more.

A Step Beyond: Odd Musical Instruments

If your interest in creating unusual instruments has been piqued, look at any of the following websites for further inspiration:

The Oddmusic Gallery (www.oddmusic.com) has a vast list of an amazing array of unusual instruments, complete with photos and audio samples, some of which are folk instruments, and many of which are invented.

Examples:

Aeolian wind harp	Gravikord
Amazing pencilina	Hang drum
Aquaggaswack	Optivideotone
Bamboo saxophones	Rumitone
Bikelophone	Shruti stick
Bowafridgeaphone	Skatar
Clackamore	Surba-half
Daxophone	Tamburitza
Fluba	Uberorgan
Glass armonica	Vienna vegetable orchestra

Experimental Musical Instruments (http://windworld.com/index.htm) sells books, CDs, instrument-making and electronic hardware, plus back issues of the Experimental Musical Instruments Quarterly Journal, and also has a good set of links to other sites.

Index A

Games in Alphabetical Order

Games by Chapter

Improvisation Game Techniques

Melody Games

Motivic Development Techniques

Nontraditional Score Games

Rhythm Games

Index C

Games by Number of Players

Index D

Games by Chapter and Number of Players

In this Index, the term, "plus," as in "Two-plus," indicates that a game may be played by that number of players or more.

For example, "One-plus" indicates games that may be played by one player alone, or two, three, four, or more, up to a reasonable number. A quartet, therefore, should consider games listed as One-plus, Two to Four, One to Twelve, Two-plus, Three-plus, Three to Six, and so on, not just those listed as Four or Four-plus.

Some of the games listed as One-plus, Two, or Two-plus may be played by a Facilitator plus a group member, one at a time in turn, or by pairs in the group in turn, as a "serial duet." Imagination is the key to the use and adaptation of all games here, which are, in the end, just starters for your own creativity.

Nothing here is holy writ; all games may and should be changed at any time to suit individual circumstances, needs, and desires.

Finally, many games come with suggested variations, some of which may be done with different numbers of players. Take note of these as well.

Note: The assignment of numbers is somewhat arbitrary. The number of players a game can accommodate is also a function of the instrumentation. Some games work well with twenty players, whereas more than four trombones might strain the limits of mutual audibility. Thus many games are given a generic, middling number. Many games can be slightly tweaked and played by different numbers than indicated, so use the number of players given as only a rough guide.

Remember that percussion of some kind can be added to almost every game, so that even games for one or two players can easily add another player or two or three on percussion. Trading off is another way to increase the number of players participating in any game.